T0357513

"Duane Garrett's book is appropriately titled ⟨...⟩ seeking to understand the person and mess ⟨...⟩ armed to interpret the significance of this c ⟨...⟩ ⟨...⟩. Yet, Garrett is equally effective to challenge today's Christian readers to take up the message of the book's proclamation into their own spiritual journey. Garrett brings forward the life story of the prophet which illuminates his theology and message. Garrett is not shy regarding the troublesome aspects of the book, such as its date and composition of the book and the textual history of Septuagint Jeremiah and Hebrew Jeremiah. Scholars, pastors, teachers, and students will greatly benefit from this excellent introduction."

—Kenneth Mathews,
Professor of Divinity Emeritus,
Beeson Divinity School

"Duane Garrett and Calvin Pearson wisely focused on the text and its meaning in their commentary, *Jeremiah and Lamentations: A Commentary for Biblical Preaching and Teaching* (Kregel, 2022). In the present volume, Garrett deals in greater depth with significant and sometimes thorny issues in the book of Jeremiah such as its historical context, structure, chronology, text, theology, and use in the church today. As we have come to expect from Garrett's previous work, the volume is insightful, creative (in the best way), clearly written, and accessible. I was challenged academically and edified in my faith. This outstanding volume will be an invaluable resource for those preaching and teaching the book of Jeremiah."

—Eric J. Tully,
Professor of Old Testament and Semitic Languages,
Trinity Evangelical Divinity School

"Dr. Duane Garrett has demonstrated mastery of his craft in this impressive volume. This book provides a detailed, insightful, and careful treatment of the compositional, historical, literary, and theological matters of the book of Jeremiah, complementing his separate commentary on *Jeremiah and Lamentations* (with Calvin Pearson). In my view, the key value of this volume is Dr. Garrett's proposition on the palindromic structure of Jeremiah and how he argued for the compositional development of Jeremiah. Robustly researched, deft, and comprehensive, this work is an excellent contribution. I heartily recommend this volume!"

—Peter C. W. Ho,
Academic Dean of the School of Theology,
Singapore Bible College

"Out of the abundance of Duane Garrett's work on Jeremiah this volume speaks! As a complement to his Kerux commentary, this volume brings out many of the historical, literary, and theological treasures that were almost left on the cutting room floor. Yet Garrett's insights, from his distinctive proposal for the structure of Jeremiah to his presentation of the life and message of the prophet, work together to help readers make sense out of this puzzling prophetic book. Garrett's unyielding high view of Scripture and pastoral heart both shine through at every turn. This book will serve students and pastors alike."

–Andrew M. King,
Assistant Professor of Biblical Studies,
Midwestern Baptist Theological Seminary & Spurgeon College

"Writing a short, accessible, and useful book on Jeremiah is a difficult task, but Duane Garrett has risen to the challenge! *Understanding Jeremiah* is an excellent tool for pastors and students who want to read the message of Jeremiah in its historical context for the sake of hearing God speak in our contemporary world. Garrett helps readers navigate the complex compositional and historical issues in Jeremiah. He shows us that the goal of a journey through Jeremiah is to see the enduring hope of God's redemption at the center of the prophet's message."

—Cory Barnes,
Dean of Graduate Studies and Associate Professor of Old Testament,
New Orleans Baptist Theological Seminary

UNDERSTANDING JEREMIAH

Its Setting,
Composition,
and Message

Duane A. Garrett

Library of Congress Cataloging-in-Publication Data

Names: Garrett, Duane A., author.
Title: Understanding Jeremiah : its setting, composition, and message / Duane A. Garrett.
Description: First edition. | Grand Rapids, Michigan : Kregel Academic, [2025] | Includes bibliographical references.
Identifiers: LCCN 2024039831
Subjects: LCSH: Bible. Jeremiah—Commentaries.
Classification: LCC BS1525.53 .G38 2025 | DDC 224/.207—dc23/eng/20240913
LC record available at https://lccn.loc.gov/2024039831

ISBN 978-0-8254-4808-9

For Hershael W. York,
Dean of the School of Theology
of the Southern Baptist Theological Seminary,
with deep appreciation for his leadership and friendship

CONTENTS

PREFACE

The desire to write this book grew out of my work on a commentary I wrote in collaboration with my lifelong friend Calvin Pearson. Together we produced *Jeremiah and Lamentations: A Commentary for Biblical Preaching and Teaching* for the Kerux series published by Kregel Publications.[1] As its full title implies, it was meant to give guidance to those engaged in the expository preaching of the Bible. As we worked through each passage of the two biblical books, I wrote the exegetical sections and Calvin wrote the homiletical sections. It was an intriguing and engaging exercise.

The book of Jeremiah especially fascinated me, not in spite of but because of all the problems it has. It appears to have no structure whatsoever. Episodes are often undated, and even when they are dated they are frequently out of chronological order. The book often refers to kings and incidents from the last days of Judah, but it does so in an unsystematic way and with little narrative context, requiring the reader to work through the history of the period and then try to tie the various episodes of Jeremiah to their historical backgrounds. In addition, the book is filled with bits and pieces of information about the life of Jeremiah, but because of the seemingly randomized and incomplete way the biographical data are relayed we are frustrated, having only fleeting glimpses of the man rather than a coherent and complete narrative.

And then there is the matter of the Septuagint, the ancient Greek translation of the book, which is considerably shorter than the Hebrew and presents much of the text in a different sequence. I found myself desiring to answer many questions: Does the book have a coherent structure—and if it does, why does it take this form? Can we reconstruct the story of Jeremiah's life from the text and set it in its context, and how will this help us to better understand the book? Can we postulate a plausible history of the composition of Jeremiah that explains why the Hebrew and Greek versions are so different?

Fortunately, I was able to answer these and similar questions to my own satisfaction prior to writing the commentary. (It was fortunate because

---

1. Duane A. Garrett and Calvin F. Pearson, *Jeremiah and Lamentations,* Kerux (Grand Rapids: Kregel, 2022).

otherwise I would have had to admit defeat and give up on the project!) However, the commentary was not the place to lay out my solutions in detail. Again, the primary mission of the Kerux series is to assist in the preparation of expository sermons, and a lengthy treatment of the above issues would have been a severe distraction. Fortunately, however, the editors at Kregel were sympathetic and allowed me to write this monograph on Jeremiah as a companion to the commentary.

Obviously this book reflects many conclusions I came to in writing the commentary; this is indicated by the footnotes where I refer the reader to the commentary for further explanation. Even so, this is an entirely different book. It explores in detail many issues only touched upon in the commentary. Indeed, much of the material in this book concerns issues that do not appear in the commentary at all. Out of respect for any reader who reads both works, I have endeavored to ensure that this book does not repeat the commentary but makes a distinctive contribution. The commentary was naturally a verse-by-verse exposition; this work pulls back from the individual trees and looks at the layout of the whole forest. It seeks to present in detail how the individual oracles of Jeremiah relate to the life of the prophet and in turn to how his personal experiences elucidate the meaning of the book. One example is how Jeremiah's experience preaching the "temple sermon" served to redirect his thinking toward his fellow countrymen. To give another example, this book examines the historical setting of the Jews in Egypt in a manner that was not practical in the commentary. In so doing, it explains in a fresh way the significance of the oracles of Jeremiah 44.

In three parts, this book examines the historical setting and life of Jeremiah, the structure and composition of the book, and the message of the book. Naturally, there is some overlap in these areas. Sometimes a text that is important for understanding Jeremiah's life and career is also important for understanding the book's structure or message. Again, however, I have tried to show respect for the reader by avoiding repetition; I may briefly mention a passage of Jeremiah in one chapter of this book but look at it in more detail or from a different perspective in another chapter.

Writing this book has given me a new appreciation for the repetition and apparent disorder in the book of Jeremiah. Like the biblical text, this book must strive to give the reader a coherent sense of the background, structure, and message of Jeremiah without getting overly entangled in itself. Although parts of this book, especially chapter 7, may be somewhat demanding, I have tried to make it as accessible as possible for the general reader. Discussions of Hebrew or Greek are found only in footnotes. Throughout the book, I have provided original translations of the passages I discuss. This is partly because sometimes my interpretation will make no sense without seeing how I believe the passage should be translated, but it is also to assist the reader. I prefer that people be able to read this book without constantly having to put it down to go find the Bible passage I am discussing.

I can honestly say that I have come to appreciate Jeremiah the prophet above any person of the Old Testament. This is because his humanity shines so clearly through his book. He was a spokesman for God in a time of moral decay and political turmoil. He went through a most extraordinary spiritual pilgrimage, one in which new disappointments, sorrows, and threats confronted him daily. Although he made prophecies that were in the course of time vindicated, not a single miracle is attributed to him. Other prophets had warned of catastrophic destruction; he lived through it. He anticipated Jesus's experience as a man of sorrows and well acquainted with grief, and he is a model for all believers who live through harrowing times. This book is a true labor of love. It represents my reflections and ruminations, and I hope that through this book the reader will see the beauty of both Jeremiah the book and Jeremiah the man.

I would be remiss if I did not thank the editors at Kregel, especially Catherine DeVries and Shawn Vander Lugt, for allowing me to pursue this project. I am deeply grateful to Russell Meek, Carl Simmons, and James Spinti for their careful review of the manuscript. I also wish to express my gratitude to my commentary coauthor Calvin Pearson, who has continued to be a source of encouragement. I would also like to thank the trustees and president of The Southern Baptist Theological Seminary for granting me a sabbatical, allowing me time to complete this work. Finally, I would like to thank my PhD students who read an early, unpolished version of this work and made many valuable corrections and suggestions. Among these, an especial thanks goes to Mr. John Davis, Ms. Eunhee Hong, and Ms. Wenya Yang.

—Duane A. Garrett

ABBREVIATIONS

AB	Anchor (Yale) Bible
ABD	Freedman, David Noel, ed. *Anchor Bible Dictionary*. 6 vols. New York: Doubleday, 1992.
ABRL	Anchor (Yale) Bible Reference Library
BDAG	Danker, Frederick W., Walter Bauer, William F. Arndt, and F. Wilbur Gingrich. *Greek-English Lexicon of the New Testament and Other Early Christian Literature*. 3rd ed. Chicago: University of Chicago Press, 2000.
BibOr	*Biblica et Orientalia*
BZAW	Beihefte zur Zeitschrift für die alttestamentliche Wissenschaft
CC	Continental Commentaries
DMOA	Documenta et Monumenta Orientis Antiqui
ErIs	*Eretz Israel*
HSM	Harvard Semitic Monographs
IEJ	*Israel Exploration Journal*
Int	*Interpretation*
ISBE	Bromiley, Geoffrey W., ed. *The International Standard Bible Encyclopedia*. Rev. ed. 4 vols. Grand Rapids: Eerdmans, 1979–1988.
JETS	*Journal of the Evangelical Theological Society*
JSOT	*Journal for the Study of the Old Testament*
JSOTSup	Journal for the Study of the Old Testament Supplement
NEAEHL	Stern, Ephraim, ed. *The New Encyclopedia of Archaeological Excavations in the Holy Land*. 4 vols. Jerusalem: Carta, 1993.
NICOT	New International Commentary on the Old Testament
NIDB	Sakenfeld, Katharine Doob, ed. *New Interpreter's Dictionary of the Bible*. 5 vols. Nashville: Abingdon, 2006–2009.
OTL	Old Testament Library
TC	*Textual Criticism: A Journal of Biblical Textual Criticism*
VT	*Vetus Testamentum*
WBC	Word Biblical Commentary

PART 1

THE HISTORICAL SETTING

CHAPTER 1

ASSYRIA, BABYLON, AND EGYPT

J eremiah lived from approximately 640 to 575 BC. He was present at the greatest calamity of Israelite history, the fall of Jerusalem, and his lifespan sits at a historical nexus. This was the era when the stories of the three great empires of Israelite history—Assyria, Egypt, and Babylon—converged. The Assyrian Empire collapsed while Jeremiah was still a young man, but the memory of what it had done had an abiding impact on the world of the prophet. Babylon and Egypt more directly interacted with the Jerusalem of his time. To understand the book, one must know something of these empires.[1]

ASSYRIA

The homeland of the Assyrians was the upper Tigris region of northeastern Mesopotamia. It began as a small city, Ashur, which first emerged to prominence in what is called the Old Assyrian period (approximately 2000–1700 BC). At this time, Ashur had no true empire, but it did have far-flung colonies

---

1.   For a full history of Assyria, see Eckart Frahm, *Assyria: The Rise and Fall of the World's First Empire* (New York: Basic Books, 2023). For a useful and accessible history of Assyria and Babylon, see Arthur Cotterell, *The First Great Powers: Babylon and Assyria* (London: Hurst & Company, 2019). See also J. J. M. Roberts, "Assyria and Babylonia," *NIDB* 1:312–35; and D. J. Wiseman, "Babylon," *ISBE* 1:384–92. Ronald H. Sack, *Images of Nebuchadnezzar: The Emergence of a Legend*, 2nd ed. (Selinsgrove, PA: Susquehanna University Press, 2004), describes the sources used for reconstructing the history of Nebuchadnezzar's reign. It is, however, more concerned with how he was perceived and portrayed through the ages than with providing a systematic account of his life. D. J. Wiseman, *Nebuchadrezzar and Babylon* (Oxford: Oxford University Press, 1983), is an extremely valuable but quite technical resource on Nebuchadnezzar. For a full history of Egypt, see Georg Steindorff and Keith C. Seele, *When Egypt Ruled the East* (Chicago: University of Chicago Press, 1957); and Nicolas Grimal, *A History of Ancient Egypt* (Oxford: Blackwell, 1992). Other useful works include Ian Shaw, *The Oxford History of Ancient Egypt* (Oxford: Oxford University Press, 2000); and Ian Shaw and Paul Nicholson, *The Dictionary of Ancient Egypt* (New York: Abrams, 1995); and David P. Silverman, *Ancient Egypt* (Oxford: Oxford University Press, 1997).

that created a significant trade network. After a period of weakness, Assyria rose again in the fourteenth century to a new age of glory, the Middle Assyrian period. This time, it became a military empire and dominated its environment under kings such as Tukulti-Ninurta I (reigned approximately 1243–1207 BC). However, during the turmoil that swept through the entire ancient Near East at the beginning of the twelfth century,[2] and under pressure from waves of Arameans from the west in the eleventh century, Assyria almost disappeared. Nevertheless, it endured and recovered.

Beginning with the reign of Ashur-dan II (reigned approximately 943–912 BC), Assyria began to recover its lost empire and initiated the period of the Neo-Assyrian Empire. In the eighth century, however, Assyria suffered a number of setbacks on the battlefield and was ravaged by plague. But by the second half of the century, they were once again highly aggressive and expansive, eventually creating an empire that would extend all the way into Egypt. This was the Assyria that would come into conflict with Israel and its neighbors. This phase began under Tiglath-pileser III (reigned approximately 745–727 BC). Ahaz of Judah became his vassal when confronted by a coalition of Damascus and Samaria, as described in Isaiah 7. Assyria crushed Damascus in 732 and, under Shalmaneser V (reigned approximately 726–722 BC), destroyed Samaria in 722. The southern kingdom of Judah was then all that remained of the Israelite nation. Sennacherib (reigned approximately 705–681 BC) is famous in the Bible for having ravaged Judah but also for being forced to withdraw from Jerusalem after suffering catastrophic losses through an act of God (Isa. 36–37).

Although these events all took place long before Jeremiah's lifetime, they had a significant impact on his generation. The Israelites maintained a deep hatred for Assyria (as illustrated by Jonah), but they recalled that God had delivered Jerusalem even though he had not saved Samaria. This created the myth that Jerusalem was impregnable. Its citizens thought it would always enjoy YHWH's protection because it had the temple and the Davidic monarchy. Also, people wondered why, if God brought about a miraculous deliverance for the city under Isaiah's ministry, he did not do the same thing under Jeremiah's. We will explore these issues below.

The homeland of the Assyrian Empire had great cities, including Ashur, Calah (Nimrud), and Nineveh. For readers of the Bible, the latter would become its most famous capital because of its prominence in Jonah and Nahum. All three cities were destroyed by the combined forces of Medes and Babylonians (Nineveh fell in 612 BC). Remnants of the Assyrian forces fled west to Harran in northern Mesopotamia, but that city fell in 610. With their

---

2. Around 1200 BC, civilizations throughout the ancient world went through a period of chaos. Long established centers of power were thrown into disarray. For example, the Hittite Empire of Anatolia broke apart and eventually collapsed, and the city-state Ugarit was obliterated. This period also marked the end of the Bronze Age. Scholars still debate what precipitated this international upheaval.

Egyptian allies, the Assyrians launched a last attempt to regain Harran in 609 but failed. Assyria was then no more.

Neo-Assyrian Empire (911 BC–627 BC)
Asshurnasipal (883–859) Shalmaneser III (858–824) Shamsi-Ada V (823–811) Adad-Nirari III (810–783) Shalmaneser IV (783–773) Ashurdan III (772–755) Ashur-Nirari V (754–745) Tiglath-pileser III (745–727) Shalmaneser V (726–722) Sargon II (722–705) Sennacherib (705–681) Esarhaddon (680–669) Asshurbanipal (668–627)
Neo-Babylonian Empire (626 BC–539 BC)
Nabopolassar I (626–605) Nebuchadnezzar II (604–562) Amel-Marduk (562–560) Neriglissar (560–556) Labashi-Marduk (556) Nabonidus (556–539)
Egyptian Empire (2700 BC–526 BC)
Old Kingdom (2700–2160) Middle Kingdom (2106–1786) New Kingdom (1550–1069) Third Intermediate Period (1069–665) Late Period (664–526) Psammetichus I (664–610) Necho II (610–595) Psammetichus II (595–589) Apries [= Hophra] (589–570) Amasis II (570–526)

BABYLON

Babylon Before the Neo-Babylonian Empire

Babylon appears to have been founded in the late third millennium BC. Befitting its later reputation as a cosmopolitan city, Babylon has been ruled by many different peoples. At its founding, two of the earliest peoples of Mesopotamia, the Sumerians and Akkadians, dominated the region. The earliest written reference to Babylon is in an Akkadian text dated to ca. 2250 BC. The city briefly became an empire, ruling over several subordinate states during the Old Babylonian period. It was at this time governed by Amorites, a northwest Semitic people. The most famous of the Amorite rulers was Hammurabi (ca. 1792–1750), whose code of laws has been preserved. This can be regarded as Babylon's first golden age.

In 1595 BC, Babylon fell to the Hittites of Anatolia (modern Turkey). This began the Middle Babylonian period (1595–1155 BC). Hittite domination of the city did not last long, and for most of this period, Babylon was governed by a people called the Kassites (the origin of this people is unknown, but they may have come from northern Mesopotamia). During this time, Babylon was generally stable and strong. The Elamites, a people to the east (in modern Iran), conquered Babylon in about 1155 BC, and the Kassite dynasty ended. As a supreme indignity, the Elamites carried off the image of Marduk, the patron god of Babylon. Thereafter, local Semitic peoples ruled the city. The most famous Babylonian king of this time was Nebuchadnezzar I (1124–1103 BC). He gained glory by defeating the Elamites and recovering the stolen statue of Marduk. He was unsuccessful, however, in his military incursions against Assyria to the north. Thereafter, the city was in the shadow of the growing power of the Assyrians.

From the ninth through the seventh centuries, Babylon was generally subservient to the Neo-Assyrian Empire. At the same time, there was within Babylonia an ongoing struggle for control between the native Babylonians and a people called the Chaldeans. This was a group who had migrated from the west into Mesopotamia during the tenth century and eventually became an important part of the mix of peoples in the region. One important Chaldean was Marduk-apla-iddina (the Merodach-Baladan of the Bible), who managed to gain control over the city in the years 722–710 and 703–702 BC. He sent envoys to Hezekiah of Judah seeking allies in his struggle against the Assyrians (Isa. 39). Eventually the Assyrian Sennacherib, wanting to be free of the Babylonian problem once and for all, destroyed Babylon in 689.

This was regarded as a great sacrilege, however, and his son Esarhaddon rebuilt the city. Upon Esarhaddon's death in about 669 BC, his elder son Shamash-shuma-ukin was made king over Babylon, and a younger son, Ashurbanipal, became ruler of Assyria and thus the suzerain over his older brother. Eventually, in 652, Shamash-shuma-ukin rebelled against his brother and launched a civil war. After a bloody conflict, Babylon fell in 648, and Shamash-shuma-ukin died. Although Ashurbanipal was victorious, Assyria was left exhausted, and subsequent Assyrian kings had to deal with unrest and rebellion in an empire that was coming apart.

Nabopolassar

In this context, in about 626 BC, the Chaldeans under Nabopolassar gained full control of Babylon. The Chaldean kings overthrew Assyria and established the Neo-Babylonian Empire, and they ruled Babylon during the time of Jeremiah, Daniel, and Ezekiel.

Nabopolassar's origin is somewhat unclear. He may have been from among the leading families of Uruk, at the time a garrison city of the Assyrian Empire. With the empire in decline, he became leader of an anti-Assyrian faction. In about 616, he allied himself with the Median king Cyaxares by marrying his daughter. He drove what remained of Assyrian power out of the lower Mesopotamian cities Uruk and Nippur, and Cyaxares took the Assyrian city Ashur. Their united forces conquered and destroyed Nineveh in 612. The Assyrians under Assur-uballit II retreated to Harran in Syria, but with its fall the Assyrian Empire ceased to exist in 609. With Assyria gone, Nabopolassar was now ruler over all Mesopotamia.

Assur-uballit II had been aided in his resistance to Babylon by Egypt under Pharaoh Necho II of Egypt, who feared that the balance of power would be heavily tilted in Babylon's favor if Assyria were eliminated. Necho's first campaign in the north, where he tried to hold Harran, failed, and he returned south. But he soon returned north and continued his struggle with Nabopolassar for control of Syria. But Nabopolassar fell sick and had to return to Babylon, and he left his son Nebuchadnezzar in charge of campaigns on the Upper Euphrates and in Syria (607–606). As crown prince of Babylon, Nebuchadnezzar met with Necho for the decisive battle at Carchemish in 605 BC. He thoroughly defeated Necho and forced him to abandon plans for a new Egyptian empire stretching to the Euphrates.

Nebuchadnezzar II

The victorious prince, known to us as Nebuchadnezzar II, was the eldest son of Nabopolassar and ruled from 605 to 562 BC. Nebuchadnezzar may have been so named to imply that the former glory under Nebuchadnezzar I was returning to Babylon, although he was not related to Nebuchadnezzar I.

Nebuchadnezzar's victories decisively checked Egyptian power in Syria. Prior to this, many Syrians had sided with the Egyptians. Two events followed soon after the battle of Carchemish. First, Nabopolassar died in Babylon and Nebuchadnezzar rushed back to the city to assume the throne. His enthronement seems to have been uneventful; he became king without a power struggle in August of 605. Second, in several campaigns, he set about consolidating power in the Levant (a region made up of modern Syria, Lebanon, and Israel, and called "Hatti" by the Babylonians). He forced many local kingdoms to submit and swear allegiance to him, including Judah. Jehoiakim gave his new overlord tributary gifts and aristocratic hostages, including Daniel (Dan. 1:1). Nebuchadnezzar sacked at least one significant city of the Levant, probably Ashkelon, ca. 604. The next year included at least one major siege, but the name of the place has not survived. It may have been another Philistine city, Gaza. He again campaigned in the Levant in 602 and 601, but again we do not know precisely where (but he does claim to have brought an enormous amount of plunder back to Babylon).[3] However, the campaign of 601 was to lead to near disaster for Nebuchadnezzar. He attempted to invade Egypt, no doubt intending to eliminate Egyptian involvement in the Levant once and for all and to firmly consolidate his control over the region. The Babylonians were badly mauled, although the Egyptians also appear to have suffered heavy casualties. Nebuchadnezzar had to use the following year rebuilding his forces, and Egypt, although bloodied and wary of facing the Babylonians again, was still standing.

In Jerusalem, many were convinced that the Egyptians could provide protection against Babylon. At some point in this general time frame, Jehoiakim took the fatal step of rebelling against his Babylonian overlord. In January of 597, the Babylonian army invaded Judah and laid siege to Jerusalem. Judah quickly submitted, surrendering on March 15 or 16, 597, according to the Babylonian Chronicle. It is unusual for the Chronicle to date such an event so precisely; the purpose may have been to point out how quickly the enemy capitulated.[4] Jehoiakim died during the siege, and his successor Jehoiachin was taken into exile along with an enormous amount of plunder, some of it from the temple.[5] Jehoiachin's uncle, Zedekiah, assumed the throne in Jerusalem and swore an oath of allegiance to Nebuchadnezzar.

For the next few years, Nebuchadnezzar's military campaigns were less frequent. In about 595 he led a force to the east, possibly against the Elamites. On this occasion, no battle was necessary. Upon hearing that the Babylonians were encamped nearby, the enemy fled.[6] For the most part, the empire was secure. But Zedekiah, probably goaded by Egypt, was busy plotting to lead the west in a rebellion against Babylon. He sought the support of Tyre and Sidon (which had long maintained close diplomatic relations with Egypt), as well as that of Moab, Ammon, and Edom (Jer. 27:3).

Nebuchadnezzar could not leave this challenge unanswered. D. J. Wiseman, citing Jeremiah 39:1, calculates that he began his assault on Jerusalem on January 15, 588 BC.[7] The Babylonians destroyed several fortified towns in Judah, including most notably Lachish. At this outpost, short communications scratched out on ostraca (potsherds used for short letters) were sent to and received from other command centers of Judah. Archaeologists discovered a stash of these communications, now known as the "Lachish letters." In letter 4 of this collection, an unknown person writes to the garrison at Lachish that a garrison at a place called Beth-harapid has been abandoned and that the fire-signals from the garrison at Azekah were no

---

3.   This may have been the occasion for Daniel's deportation to Babylon. See Wiseman, *Nebuchadrezzar and Babylon*, 24.

4.   Wiseman, *Nebuchadrezzar and Babylon*, 32.

5.   The problem of the circumstances of Jehoiakim's death is discussed under "The Last Kings of Judah," below.

6.   Wiseman, *Nebuchadrezzar and Babylon*, 34.

7.   Wiseman, *Nebuchadrezzar and Babylon*, 36.

longer visible. This suggests that the Babylonian process of picking off these outposts was underway.[8] Meanwhile, Jerusalem was under siege. At some point during this process, Pharaoh Hophra tried to relieve the siege, and for a time the Babylonians did pull back from Jerusalem to confront this threat. But the Egyptians were repelled and hurried back to their own land. Babylonian forces finally broke into the starving city of Jerusalem and destroyed it entirely.

Besides Jerusalem, Nebuchadnezzar also carried out a lengthy siege of the island city-state of Tyre. In this, he was only partially successful. He did not militarily take the city (Ezek. 29:18), although Tyre returned to the status of Babylon's vassal and sent royal hostages to Babylon.[9] A fragmentary cuneiform text suggests that Babylonian forces made a sortie against Egypt in 568 BC.[10] In addition, Nebuchadnezzar completed the rebuilding of Babylon and made it the greatest city of the time. Today, when one reads of the great walls, gates, temples, and avenues of ancient Babylon, one is reading about Nebuchadnezzar's city.

After Nebuchadnezzar

Upon Nebuchadnezzar's death in 562, the throne was taken by his son Amel-Marduk (called Awel-Marduk or Evil-Merodach in English translations of the Bible). Although many sources are from a later period and details are uncertain, it appears that Amel-Marduk was often in conflict with his father and that some members of the palace court were not happy with him being on the throne.[11] Other than releasing from prison Jehoiachin, the deposed and captive king of Judah (Jer. 52:31–32), we know little of what he did as king. Amel-Marduk was murdered in a palace coup by his brother-in-law Neriglissar in August of 560.

Neriglissar (Akkadian name: Nergal-šarra-uṣur) is thought to be a man called Nergal-Sharezer (or Nergal-sar-ezer) in Jeremiah 39:3 (the text is perhaps corrupt; it mentions two Babylonian officials called Nergal-Sharezer, and they may both refer to the same person).[12] He is believed to have been a foreign prince who married Nebuchadnezzar's daughter Kashshaya.[13] His one known major accomplishment as king was conducting a successful military

8.   Robert A. Di Vito, "Lachish Letters," *ABD* 4:127–28.

9.   H. J. Katzenstein and Douglas R. Edwards, "Tyre," *ABD* 6:690.

10. Wiseman, *Nebuchadrezzar and Babylon*, 39–40.

11. Ronald H. Sack, "Evil-Merodach (Person)," *ABD* 2:679.

12. As argued by William L. Holladay, *Jeremiah 2: A Commentary on the Book of the Prophet Jeremiah, Chapters 26–52*, Hermeneia (Philadelphia: Fortress, 1989), 268. However, John Goldingay argues that they are two people of the same name. Goldingay, *The Book of Jeremiah*, NICOT (Grand Rapids: Eerdmans, 2021), 764. Complicating the situation is that Sharezer may not be part of a proper name but a title. The Hebrew נֵרְגַל שַׂר־אֶצֶר can be translated as "Nergal, ruler of a land," meaning that he is a high-ranking person of a vassal state.

13. Wiseman, *Nebuchadrezzar and Babylon*, 11–12.

campaign in southeast Anatolia in 557 BC.[14] Neriglissar died in 556 and was succeeded by his son Labashi-Marduk, who ruled only a few months before being slain in a palace coup by Nabonidus and his son Belshazzar. Although these men are important for Daniel, they are not involved in the events of Jeremiah's life. Cyrus II of Persia conquered Babylon in 539/538 BC.

EGYPT

Egypt Prior to the Time of Jeremiah

Ancient Egypt was situated along the Nile Valley. Egypt was the "black land." This was in two parts: the fertile land in the delta region (Lower Egypt); and south of that, the thin strip of soil on either side of the Nile River (Upper Egypt). The arable black land, where agriculture could thrive, was the domain of Egyptian civilization. Beyond the confines of the Nile Valley was the desert or "red land," the region of strange beasts, disorder, and death. Because the black land was in two parts (Upper and Lower Egypt), the pharaoh wore a double crown, symbolizing his rule over both.

Egyptian history is traditionally divided into "dynasties." Originally, their number was reckoned to be thirty, but now historians speak of thirty-three dynasties. Kings are generally located chronologically by their dynasty (for example, all the pharaohs of Jeremiah's time were in the Twenty-sixth Dynasty). Also, Egyptian history is broken up into a series of long eras. There were three eras in which Egypt was unified and powerful: the Old Kingdom (2700–2160), the Middle Kingdom (2106–1786), and the New Kingdom (1550–1069). These were the times of Egypt's legendary magnificence. For example, the pyramids were built during the Old Kingdom, and the famous Ramses II ruled during the New Kingdom. After each of these "kingdom" periods was a period of severe decline, called respectively the First, Second, and Third Intermediate periods. During these times, Egypt was not unified; several competing pharaohs might rule at the same time over different parts of Egypt, or the country might be under foreign domination. It is not necessarily the case that Egypt was entirely prostrate during these times; a pharaoh of the Third Intermediate period, Shoshenq I (reigned 945–924), invaded Judah and plundered the temple. He is the Shishak of 1 Kings 14:25. He was, however, a Libyan and not a native Egyptian, and the Egypt of the Third Intermediate period possessed but a pale image of the glory it had enjoyed during the New Kingdom.

The Twenty-fifth Dynasty (ca. 780–656 BC) is reckoned to have been the last of the Third Intermediate period. This, too, was a foreign dynasty. It was Cushite (or Nubian), and because its rulers were from sub-Saharan Africa, they are sometimes called the "Black Pharaohs." They were able to unify Egypt but could not expand their power into the Near East because this was also

---

14.   Sack, *Images of Nebuchadnezzar*, 115.

the time of the Neo-Assyrian Empire, with whom they clashed on several occasions and generally suffered defeat. For Bible readers, the most famous pharaoh of this dynasty was Taharqa, who briefly aided Hezekiah while Sennacherib of Assyria besieged Jerusalem (2 Kings 19:9, where the pharaoh is called Tirhakah). However, the Egyptians were restive under foreign kings, and the Assyrians used this to their advantage and broke the power of the Cushite dynasty.

Egypt During the Time of Jeremiah

The Assyrian king Esarhaddon invaded Egypt in 671 BC and placed native Egyptians over the cities of the Nile Delta. The ruler of the city of Sais, in the western delta, was Necho I. In 665, the Cushite Tantamini invaded the delta and reasserted Cushite control there. Necho I died in battle and his son, Psammetichus I, fled to Syria. The Assyrians, under Ashurbanipal, invaded Egypt and restored to power Psammetichus who, with Sais as his base of operations, gained control over the whole of Egypt. His reign marks the beginning of the Twenty-sixth or "Saite" Dynasty, the last era in which Egypt would be a significant world power under native rule. Five pharaohs, all from the Twenty-sixth Dynasty, ruled Egypt during and immediately after the lifetime of Jeremiah. Following the chronology of Kenneth Kitchen, these are: [15]

> 664–610: Psammetichus I (fifty-four years)
> 610–595: Necho II (fifteen years)
> 595–589: Psammetichus II (six years)
> 589–570: Apries [= Hophra] (nineteen years)
> 570–526: Amasis II (forty-four years)

Psammetichus I (Also Called Psamtek I)

Although a native Egyptian, Psammetichus I had been trained by the Assyrians and relied heavily on Greek mercenaries for military support. Indeed, the use of foreign mercenaries was a fixture in the Egyptian army throughout the dynasty. He eliminated all his rivals in Lower Egypt, drove the Cushites out of Upper Egypt, and gained firm control of the sacred city of Thebes, where his daughter was given the politically and religiously important title of "God's Wife of Amun." With all Egypt under his authority, he instituted a new era of assertive Egyptian nationalism.[16]

Necho II (Also Called Neco II)

An energetic and aggressive king, Necho came to the throne legitimately, as the son and successor of Psammetichus, but during a time of crisis. With Nineveh already destroyed and the remnants of the Assyrian Empire having

---

15.   Kitchen, "Egypt, History of: Chronology," ABD 2:321–31.
16.   Shaw and Nicholson, Dictionary of Ancient Egypt, 229.

moved west to Harran to put up a last stand, he faced the prospect of Babylon dominating all the Fertile Crescent as an empire without rivals. He thus went north in person to try to prop up the Assyrians as a buffer state. While moving north, he encountered Josiah of Judah in battle at Megiddo and killed him (2 Kings 23:29). Although he had some success in his first Syrian campaign, he failed to save the Assyrians at Harran, and they disappeared from history. His second campaign to Syria also showed that he was a vigorous leader, but he suffered a calamitous defeat against Nebuchadnezzar at Carchemish in 605 and withdrew to Egypt. He was able to regroup and rearm, however, and his repulse of the attempted Babylonian invasion in 601 showed that Egypt was still a power to reckon with. Besides his wars with Babylon, Necho tried to make Egypt into a maritime power. He unsuccessfully attempted to have a canal cut from the Gulf of Suez to the Nile River. He is also reported to have sent an expedition of Phoenician sailors from Egypt south to the Red Sea and all the way around the Cape of Good Hope, which continued north to Gibraltar and the Mediterranean and finally back to the Egyptian delta (Herodotus 4.42).

Psammetichus II (Also Called Psamtek II)

Psammetichus II was the son of Necho II. Although he continued to encourage Jerusalem to rebel against Babylon, most of his attention was focused on the south, where the Cushites were showing signs of reasserting themselves and moving against Egypt. He invaded Nubia and broke the power of the Cushites, so that they were no longer a threat to Egypt. He did, however, lead a military expedition into the Levant in 592, which reinforced the conviction in Jerusalem that Egypt was a major military power and could be depended upon if Judah switched its allegiance from Babylon to Egypt.[17]

Hophra (Also Called Apries)

The son of Psammetichus II, his reign was a troubled time. Jerusalem, now in open rebellion against Nebuchadnezzar, sought his help against the Babylonian force besieging the city. Hophra did dispatch a force toward Judah, and for a brief time the Babylonians lifted their siege of the city to confront the threat at their back. The Egyptians, however, quickly withdrew and did not intervene again as the Babylonians brought down Jerusalem. In addition, during Hophra's reign native Egyptians resented the presence of foreign mercenaries in their territory. Matters came to a head when Dorian Greeks invaded Egypt from Libya. Hophra suffered a humiliating defeat, and the Egyptians rose against him and installed Amasis II, who had been a general under Psammetichus II during the Nubian campaign. The details of what followed are somewhat unclear. Hophra appears to have fled to the

---

17. Moshe Greenberg, *Ezekiel 1–20: A New Translation with Introduction and Commentary*, AB 22 (Garden City, NY: Doubleday, 1983), 8. See the table of dates on pp. 8–11, and especially note 6 on p. 10, for specific historical information on the campaign of Psammetichus into the Levant.

Babylonians, who attempted to invade Egypt in 568 to restore him to power. This was not successful, however, and Hophra either died in battle or was captured and killed soon after.[18]

Amasis II (Also Called Ahmose II)

Although not a lineal descendant of the preceding pharaohs, Amasis II is still considered to be part of the Twenty-sixth Dynasty (to add legitimacy to his claim to the throne, he married a daughter of Hophra). He continued to use foreign mercenaries but did so more discreetly to avoid enraging the native population. However, during his reign Babylon was supplanted by a new great power, Persia. Amasis is said to have tried to assuage the Persians and forestall the threat, but it was to no avail. Upon his death, he was succeeded by his son Psammetichus (Psamtek) III, who reigned only six months before being killed by the Persian king Cambyses, who conquered Egypt and brought the Twenty-sixth Dynasty to an end.[19]

From that time forward, Egypt was perpetually under the rule of outsiders: first the Persians, then the Macedonian Greeks (Alexander the Great and then the Ptolemies), and finally the Romans.

---

18.   Shaw and Nicholson, *Dictionary of Ancient Egypt*, 36–37.
19.   Shaw and Nicholson, *Dictionary of Ancient Egypt*, 229.

CHAPTER 2

THE LAST KINGS OF JUDAH

By the time Jeremiah was born, Samaria (the Northern Kingdom of Israel) no longer existed. Little Judah stood alone. It did, however, enjoy the one moment of great glory when the Assyrians, who had recently obliterated Samaria, came to do the same to Jerusalem in the time of Hezekiah. However, YHWH answered the king's prayer and fulfilled Isaiah's prophecies by intervening to destroy the Assyrian invader (Isa. 36–37). This event is never explicitly mentioned in Jeremiah, but as mentioned above, it must have had an enormous impact on the psyche of the kings and people of Jerusalem. When the Babylonians were outside the gates, they wanted Jeremiah to repeat the miracle of Isaiah's time and obliterate the Mesopotamian enemy. This would not happen, and a burden of the book of Jeremiah is to explain why.

Judah's decline into paganism, as described in Samuel–Kings, was temporarily halted during the reign of Hezekiah. His son Manasseh (reigned ca. 687–642) led Judah back into idolatry and spiritual decline, and this continued in the short reign of Amon (reigned ca. 642–640). In the reign of Josiah, however, there was a final push to purge the land of idols and return Judah to orthodoxy.

JOSIAH

At the age of eight, Josiah was placed on the throne and reigned for thirty-one years (2 Kings 22:1), from 640 to 609. The Chronicler describes Josiah's reform in three stages. First, in the eighth year of his reign (when he was about sixteen), he began to "seek the God of his father David" (2 Chron. 34:3a). Second, in his twelfth year as king, he began to purge Jerusalem, Judah, and even outlying areas in the former Israel, of Asherah poles, shrines to Baal, and other pagan objects of worship (2 Chron. 34:3b–7). Third, in the eighteenth year of his reign, at about age twenty-six, he began to refurbish the temple. In the process of doing this, a copy of the book of the law was found, and when it was read, Josiah was mortified at how deeply apostate Judah had become. The prophetess Huldah affirmed that indeed Judah's sin was so great that YHWH would destroy the nation, but not in Josiah's lifetime. The king led the nation in a covenant renewal ceremony to reaffirm their commitment to YHWH, and he redoubled his efforts to purge the land of paganism. He organized a national celebration of Passover and closed all outlying shrines so that worship would be carried out exclusively at the Jerusalem temple. The religious life of the nation was placed entirely under the eyes of the priests and the royal house so that local, paganized worship could no longer flourish (2 Chron. 34:8–35:19).[1]

Although there was a group of people around Josiah who encouraged and supported the reformation, it is clear from subsequent events that a majority of the people, including members of his own family, did not. Idolatry flourished again under later kings. When Ezekiel in September of 592 saw in a vision what was really happening in and around the temple, he found it to be filled with every kind of object of pagan veneration (Ezek. 8). After Jerusalem was destroyed, many of the people blamed Josiah for it, because he prevented them from worshipping "the Queen of Heaven" (Jer. 44:15–19). Furthermore, his reign ended abruptly and violently. As Pharaoh Necho was moving north to try to save what remained of Assyrian power, Josiah tried to block his movement and was killed in the attempt. This further convinced some people that Josiah's reformation had itself been an act of apostasy and that his death was divine punishment.

It is not clear why Josiah went to Megiddo to confront Necho. He may have done it out of hatred for the Assyrians, who had destroyed the Northern Kingdom of Israel and had badly ravaged Judah. Also, he may have believed that subservience to Assyria was a motivating factor behind the introduction of pagan cults to Judah. If these things were his incentives, then Josiah was trying to block Necho from bringing aid to Assyria to be sure that Israel's nemesis would never rise again. The narrative in Kings does not criticize Josiah, and Jeremiah was fulsome in his praise for Josiah's righteousness (Jer. 22:15–16). The Chronicler, however, indicates that Josiah's move to fight Necho was impetuous and unwise, and curiously enough quotes Necho delivering a rebuke to Josiah in God's name, even affirming that what the pharaoh said was a true word from God (2 Chron. 35:21–22). Josiah "did not listen to what Necho had said at God's command." But Chronicles does affirm that Josiah was a righteous king and that his reformation was a worthy undertaking. Jeremiah was born at the time Josiah became king, and the events of Josiah's life and death profoundly shaped the young prophet.

---

1.   Second Kings 22:3 omits reference to events in Josiah's eighth and twelfth regnal year, beginning its story of the reformation with the work on the temple and the finding of the law in the eighteenth year of his reign.

JEHOAHAZ

Jehoahaz was a throne name; his given name was Shallum (1 Chron. 3:15). He was twenty-three years old when he became king in 609 BC, and he reigned a mere three months (2 Kings 23:31). After Josiah's death, the "people of the land" chose him to be the next king even though he was Josiah's fourth son (2 Kings 23:30). This does not mean that he was democratically elected. "The people of the land" was one of the political factions in Judah at this time, and although it was probably populist in orientation some of its members were almost certainly highly placed members of the aristocracy. Amon, Josiah's father, had been assassinated by a group of his nobles, but the "people of the land" overthrew them and placed the young Josiah on the throne (2 Kings 21:23–24). But why did Josiah's fourth son have enough support to gain the throne? We cannot know with certainty, but considering how rapidly Necho deposed him, it is likely that the "people of the land" were a faction in Judah that favored Josiah's attempt to block Necho at Megiddo. Evidently, Jehoahaz identified with that faction. Soon after he gained the throne, however, Necho summoned him to his field headquarters in Riblah (2 Kings 23:33):

> Pharaoh Necho put [Jehoahaz] in chains at Riblah in the land of Hamath [in Syria] so that he might not reign in Jerusalem, and he imposed on Judah a fine of a hundred talents of silver and a talent of gold.

Necho was obviously not happy with Judah's choice for a king. Jehoahaz spent the rest of his life in exile in Egypt, where he died (2 Kings 23:34; Jer. 22:11).

JEHOIAKIM

After his unsuccessful attempt to preserve the remnants of the Assyrian Empire at Harran, Necho returned to Egypt and along the way deposed Jehoahaz. He installed Jehoahaz's half-brother Eliakim, who took the throne name of Jehoiakim, as king of Judah in late 609 BC. He came to the throne, therefore, as a vassal of Egypt. But when Nebuchadnezzar vanquished Necho at Carchemish, continued loyalty to Egypt was no longer prudent. By plundering at least one significant city in the region, Philistine Ashkelon, Nebuchadnezzar gave the other states a valuable object lesson, and Jehoiakim became his vassal. Nevertheless, Jehoiakim still favored alliance with his original patron, Necho and Egypt, and would soon rebel against Babylon.

Second Kings 24:1–6 recounts the history of conflict between Nebuchadnezzar and Jehoiakim:

> In [Jeohiakim's] days, King Nebuchadnezzar of Babylon approached [Judah]. And Jehoiakim became his servant for three years. And then [Jehoiakim] turned against [Nebuchadnezzar] and rebelled. And YHWH

sent against [Jehoiakim] bands of the Chaldeans, bands of the Arameans, bands of the Moabites, and bands of the Ammonites. [YHWH] sent them against Judah to destroy it, in accordance with the word of YHWH that he spoke by his servants the prophets. Indeed, this happened to Judah at the command of YHWH, so that he could remove them from his sight because of the sins of Manasseh, as a response to all he had done. It was also because of the innocent blood that he had shed; he filled Jerusalem with innocent blood, and YHWH was not willing to forgive. And the rest of the deeds of Jehoiakim, and all that he did, are they not written in the Book of the Annals of the Kings of Judah? And Jehoiakim slept with his fathers, and his son Jehoiachin ruled after him.

Jehoiakim's initial submission to Babylon, when Nebuchadnezzar "approached," implies only that the Babylonians initially made a show of force in the area. It does not imply that there was any combat between Babylon and Jerusalem, and it certainly does not imply that Jerusalem was under siege. It does not even explicitly claim that Nebuchadnezzar's forces got within sight of the city. It only requires that Nebuchadnezzar had troops who made their presence felt in the area and that Jehoiakim, realizing that the Babylonians were now the dominant power, made a show of submission and declared himself to be Babylon's vassal. This suggests that soon after his victory at Carchemish and enthronement, during his "Hatti" campaign, Nebuchadnezzar made sure that all the states of the Levant knew that he had defeated Egypt. They needed to realize that the power of Egypt was now broken and that their survival depended on their submission to Babylon. Jerusalem quickly capitulated.

Jeremiah 46:2 puts the battle of Carchemish (605) in Jehoiakim's fourth year. This indicates that the military action in the north and the subsequent demands upon the states of the southern Levant occurred around this time. However, 2 Kings 24:1 also tells us that after three years (in around 602/601), Jehoiakim rebelled against the Babylonians. Judah then suffered an undefined period of warfare, when Babylonian, Syrian, Moabite, and Ammonite troops conducted raids in the land (2 Kings 24:2). This does not imply that Jerusalem was at any time under siege during this period. It was a period of harassment prior to the full assault on Judah. Thus, Babylon's local vassal states made the incursions into the southern Levant in the years 602–600.

During this critical period, Jehoiakim died and Jehoiachin succeeded him (2 Kings 24:6). At some point within this time frame, Babylon laid siege to Jerusalem, and in the eighth year of Nebuchadnezzar's reign (the seventh by Babylonian reckoning), in 597, he captured the city and removed Jehoiachin in exile to Babylon (2 Kings 24:11–12). The narrative in 2 Kings implies that Jehoiakim died in Jerusalem before or during the Babylonian siege of Jerusalem and that Jehoiachin, a few months after having been crowned, surrendered. This appears to be supported by Jeremiah 22:18–19:

Therefore, thus says YHWH regarding Jehoiakim son of Josiah king of Judah: They will not mourn for him: "Alas, my brother! Alas, my sister!" They will not mourn for him: "Alas, my master! Alas, his majesty!" He will be buried with the burial of a donkey—dragged away and thrown outside the gates of Jerusalem.

Prophetic language should not necessarily be pressed literally, but this passage does make two specific claims. First, Jehoiakim would not have the normal funeral rites for even a common person ("Alas, my brother! Alas, my sister!"), much less receive rites befitting a king ("Alas, my master! Alas, his majesty!"). Second, his body would be "dragged away and thrown outside the gates of Jerusalem" to be buried (or left to rot), implying that he would die in the city. In addition, although it is clear that there was a great deal of consternation in Jerusalem over Jehoiachin's exile to Babylon, and a fervent hope that he would return soon, the book of Jeremiah never implies that anyone was aware that his father Jehoiakim had been removed to Babylon as well.

For these reasons, 2 Chronicles 36:5–6 creates a significant problem for reconstructing events surrounding Jehoiakim's demise. It appears to assert that Jehoiakim was taken captive to Babylon:

Jehoiakim was twenty-five years old when he began to reign, and he reigned in Jerusalem eleven years. He did evil in the eyes of YHWH his God. Nebuchadnezzar king of Babylon came up against him and bound him with bronze chains to take him to Babylon.

Given the very terse nature of the biographical information found in the biblical texts, it is difficult to know precisely what happened. We can, however, construct a hypothesis that reconciles the passages. First, 2 Chronicles 36 does not say that Nebuchadnezzar took Jehoiakim to Babylon; it only says that he bound him in chains with the purpose of taking him to Babylon. Second, Jeremiah does not say who cast out Jehoiakim's body like a donkey carcass. It was presumably not the leaders and people of Jerusalem, whom Jeremiah presents as being strongly in favor of his policies and who at any rate would be loath to treat one of their kings in such a manner. It is far more likely that the Babylonians, who would have been enraged at his treachery and happy to make an example of him, would have subjected his corpse to such abuse. Thus, we can propose the following: Jehoiachin became coregent with his father several months before the city fell. It may be that Jehoiakim became incapacitated in some way and Jehoiachin had full authority to make decisions, and exercised his authority by surrendering to Babylon. Alternatively, it may be that the nobles staged a coup against Jehoiakim, imprisoned him, and put Jehoiachin on the throne. These men held considerable power; King Zedekiah feared them and acted in secret whenever he thought they would disapprove of his actions (Jer. 37:17; 38:5, 24–26).

Either way, the leaders of Jerusalem offered to give Jehoiakim to the Babylonians as part of the terms of surrender. Upon entering the city, the Babylonians seized, bound, and imprisoned Jehoiakim, the agent of the rebellion, intending to carry him away; but he died during his Jerusalem confinement. They then unceremoniously threw his body outside the city and forbade that he be given a burial or funeral rites. And instead of Jehoiakim, they took his son Jehoiachin to Babylon. The language that the Chronicler uses to recount Jehoiakim's demise may be intended to communicate that he fell into the hands of his enemies before he died.

The Bible, especially in Jeremiah, is unsparingly harsh in its condemnation of Jehoiakim. Second Kings 24:3–5 attributes the fall of Jerusalem to the child sacrifice instituted under Manasseh, but by implication this condemns Jehoiakim as well: "It was also because of the innocent blood that [Manasseh] had shed; he filled Jerusalem with innocent blood, and YHWH was not willing to forgive. And the rest of the deeds of Jehoiakim. . . ." Josiah put an end to the child sacrifice at the Ben Hinnom Valley (2 Kings 23:10; also translated as "Valley of the Son of Hinnom"), but this policy was reversed under Jehoiakim and the practice was resumed (Jer. 7:30–31). Jehoiakim had no respect for the word of YHWH, and showed this by mutilating and burning a scroll of Jeremiah's prophecies (Jer. 36:23–24). Had Jeremiah not fled and hidden himself, Jehoiakim would have had him murdered (Jer. 36:19, 26), just as he had murdered the prophet Uriah (Jer. 26:20–23). Interestingly, Matthew's genealogy of Jesus skips over Jehoiakim (Matt. 1:11).

JEHOIACHIN

The son and successor of Jehoiakim had the given name Jeconiah (Jer. 24:1), which was sometimes shortened to Coniah (Jer. 22:24). He only reigned for three months and ten days, and was eighteen years old at the time (2 Chron. 36:9). Thus, with the Babylonians at the gates of the city, Jerusalem was under a boy king. As suggested above, the best way to make sense of the confusing situation in Jerusalem at this time is to assume that he was coregent but had full authority to act. In agreement with Jerusalem's ruling aristocracy (and probably heavily pressured by them), he chose to give up the fight and surrender to Nebuchadnezzar in mid-March of 597 BC.[2] Second Kings 24:12 describes the event:

> And Jehoiachin king of Judah, his mother, his attendants, his nobles, and his eunuchs went out to the king of Babylon [to surrender]. And the king of Babylon, in the eighth year of his reign, took him [into exile].

The people of Jerusalem heavily grieved the loss of their young king and hoped he would speedily return. This was probably because they had affection

---

2.   This date is derived from the Babylonian Chronicle. See Wiseman, *Nebuchadrezzar and Babylon*, 32.

for him on account of his youth, sympathy for how he had been cast onto the throne in the middle of a crisis, and a profound hostility toward the Babylonians. They were receptive to prophets who predicted the fall of Babylon and return of their young king (Jer. 28:1–4; 29:8–9, 15–23). To the contrary, however, he spent the rest of his life in Babylon, and throughout the reign of Nebuchadnezzar, he was in a prison cell. Akkadian administrative texts from the time of Nebuchadnezzar speak of provisions made for him and his fellow prisoners, suggesting that his imprisonment was not extremely harsh.[3] Even so, he was neither free nor recognized as king of Judah. Near the end of life, however, he had a measure of his dignity restored:

> And in the thirty-seventh year of the exile of Jehoiachin king of Judah, on the twenty-fifth day of the twelfth month,[4] Awel-Marduk, king of Babylon, in the year of his accession to kingship, pardoned[5] Jehoiachin king of Judah and released him from prison. He spoke kindly to him and gave him a seat higher than those of the other kings who were with him in Babylon. And Jehoiachin no longer wore his prison clothes but ate regularly with the king for the rest of his life. And his allowance was a perpetual allowance, provided daily for him by the king of Babylon as long as he lived, till the day of his death. (Jer. 52:31–34)

Amel-Marduk (also known as Evil-Merodach or Awel-Marduk) succeeded his father Nebuchadnezzar in October of 562. His reign was short (only two years), and as described above, almost nothing is known of his reign (some later sources suggest he had once tried to usurp his father or that there was opposition to his becoming king among the nobles, but these are late and dubious).[6] We do not know why he released Jehoiachin from prison and honored him above other captive kings. The perpetual confinement Jehoiachin endured may have been because Nebuchadnezzar had felt especially betrayed first by Jehoiakim and then by Zedekiah, and therefore he retaliated against the sole surviving king of Judah. Perhaps Amel-Marduk felt that Jehoiachin's humiliation had been too severe, having been held in prison much longer than other subjected kings.

Also, because Amel-Marduk's reign was so short, it is unclear how long Jehoiachin enjoyed this favorable treatment. It may be that Jehoiachin died before Amel-Marduk, or that Jehoiachin outlived him and was still held in esteem by his successor Neriglissar. On the other hand, since Neriglissar

---

3. James B. Pritchard, *Ancient Near Eastern Texts Relating to the Old Testament*, 3rd ed. (Princeton, NJ: Princeton University Press, 1969), 308.

4. The parallel text in 2 Kings 25:27 says that this was the twenty-seventh day of the month. The LXX of Jeremiah says it was the twenty-fourth day.

5. This is literally, "he lifted the head," an idiom for pardoning, as in Gen. 40:13. See Holladay, *Jeremiah 2*, 443.

6. Sack, "Evil-Merodach (Person)."

overthrew Amel-Marduk, he probably would not have regarded Jehoiachin with the same favor that Amel-Marduk had. But based on the claim that Jehoiachin "ate regularly with the king for the rest of his life," it looks like he died soon after his pardon and before the fall of Amel-Marduk.

Although Jehoiachin reigned only a short time, the Bible presents him as an evil king (2 Kings 24:9). Jeremiah 22:24–26 is especially harsh, declaring that YHWH would throw away Jehoiachin even if he were YHWH's signet ring (the symbol of his authority) on his right hand. This metaphor pertains especially to his role as YHWH's anointed and the heir of the Davidic monarchy, the visible representation of YHWH's kingship. The casting away of the ring implies the end of the Davidic dynasty as an earthly, political institution. This is made more explicit in the verses that follow:

> Is this man Coniah [Jehoiachin] a despised, shattered pot? Is he a vessel that no one cares about? Why are he and his offspring hurled away? Why are they cast away in a land that they do not know? Land, land, land, hear the word of YHWH! Thus says YHWH: Record this man as childless, a man who in his days will not be successful. For none of his offspring will succeed in sitting on the throne of David and continuing to rule in Judah. (Jer. 22:28–30)

The metaphor of pottery is important in the book of Jeremiah. In Jeremiah 18:1–10, it represents YHWH's freedom to deal with a nation however he wishes, just as a potter can make or discard a pot he is forming. In Jeremiah 19:1–13, the smashing of a clay vessel represents YHWH's determination to destroy Jerusalem. The metaphor of divine judgment here, in Jeremiah 22:28, is more narrowly focused on the house of David and on Jehoiachin, a "despised, shattered pot." Jerusalem may be rebuilt, and the Jews may repopulate it, but an earthly Davidic monarchy will never again exist. Jehoiachin is to be recorded "as childless." He in fact had seven sons (1 Chron. 3:17–18), but none ever became king, and in that sense he was no different from a king with no offspring. The claim of Jeremiah 52:32 that Amel-Marduk "spoke kindly to him" may imply that the Babylonian king reached an agreement with him to return him or one of sons to Jerusalem to rebuild the city. In turn, Jehoiachin's descendants would resume serving Babylon as vassal kings.[7] If there ever were such a plan, it was cut short by the overthrow of Amel-Marduk, and no descendant of Jehoiachin was able to claim the throne.

ZEDEKIAH

Zedekiah was another son of Josiah and the uncle of Jehoiachin (2 Chron. 36:10 calls him the "brother" of Jehoiachin, but this should be understood

---

7.   This is suggested by John M. Berridge, "Jehoiachin (Person)," *ABD* 3:663.

in the more general sense of "relative"). His given name was Mattaniah, and Zedekiah was his throne name (2 Kings 24:17). He was put on the throne by Nebuchadnezzar after the surrender of Jehoiachin (Ezek. 17:12–14), and was only twenty-one years old at the time (2 Kings 24:18). He ruled for eleven years (ca. 597–586).

We know little of his reign beyond what is reported about his rebellion against Babylon and subsequent downfall. We do know that he led a delegation to Babylon in the fourth year of his reign (Jer. 51:59), no doubt to assure Nebuchadnezzar of his fealty. In that same year, however, Zedekiah convened a conference of local states with the purpose of forming a coalition, which, with the support of Egypt, could expel the Babylonians from the region. Jeremiah, however, showed up at the meeting and delivered an oracle warning that the plan was doomed to fail:

> In the beginning of the reign of Zedekiah son of Josiah, king of Judah, this word came to Jeremiah from YHWH. Thus said YHWH to me: Make for yourself a yoke of straps and bars and put it on your neck. And send [this oracle] to the king of Edom, the king of Moab, the king of the Ammonites, the king of Tyre, and the king of Sidon by the hand of the envoys who have come to Jerusalem to Zedekiah, king of Judah. And command them [to convey this message] to their masters. Thus says YHWH Sabaoth, the God of Israel, This is what you shall say to your masters: I made the earth, with the people and animals that are on the earth, by my great power and my outstretched arm. And I give it to whomever I wish. And for now, I have given all these lands into the hand of King Nebuchadnezzar of Babylon, my servant, and I have given him even the wild animals of the field to serve him. All nations will serve him and his son and his grandson, until the time [of reckoning] for his own land comes. Then many nations and great kings shall make him their vassal. But I will punish any nation or kingdom with the sword, with famine, and with pestilence that will not serve him, Nebuchadnezzar, king of Babylon, and that will not put its neck under the yoke of the king of Babylon. [I will do this,] says YHWH, until I have completed their destruction by his hand. (Jer. 27:1–8)

The assembled delegates were no doubt stunned by the oracle and the spectacle of Jeremiah walking about wearing a yoke. Zedekiah and his associates were surely angered at how the prophet had thrown their orchestrated attempt to form an anti-Babylonian alliance into disorder. But Zedekiah was attempting rebellion against Babylon despite his oaths of fealty to Nebuchadnezzar and in defiance of YHWH's terrible warnings of how it would turn out.

Beyond that, the book of Jeremiah describes incidents that give us insight into Zedekiah's character. He appears to have been weak, vacillating, and unreliable. He wanted Jeremiah to pray for deliverance from Babylon, and so he understood Jeremiah to be a true prophet, but he did not heed Jeremiah's explicit predictions that Jerusalem would fall and that Zedekiah's only hope for survival was to surrender. He was afraid of the nobility and yielded to them when they wanted to kill Jeremiah, but then he allowed the faithful Ebed-Melech to rescue the prophet. In another episode, members of the upper class made a covenant before YHWH to free their Judahite slaves, but they quickly reversed their decision, rounded up all their recently manumitted slaves, and forced them back into servitude. Zedekiah was to some degree complicit in this; at the very least, he failed to use his authority to prevent this outrage (see Jer. 34:8–22; 37:1–38:28).

A single episode, Jeremiah 38:14–26, tells us a great deal about the politics of Zedekiah's reign and his personality, which we quote in part here:

> And King Zedekiah sent for Jeremiah the prophet and summoned him to the third entrance to the temple of YHWH. And the king said to Jeremiah, "I am going to ask you something. Do not hide anything from me." . . . And Jeremiah said to Zedekiah, "Thus says YHWH God Sabaoth, the God of Israel: If you surrender to the officers of the king of Babylon, your life will continue, and this city will not be burned down in a fire. You and your household will survive. But if you will not surrender to the officers of the king of Babylon, this city will be given into the hands of the Babylonians, and they will burn it down in a fire. And you will not be delivered from them." And King Zedekiah said to Jeremiah, "I am worried about the Jews who have gone over to the Babylonians, for the Babylonians may hand me over to them and they will torture me." And Jeremiah said, "They will not hand you over. Obey YHWH by doing what I tell you, and it will go well with you, and you will survive. But if you refuse to surrender, this is the message YHWH revealed to me: Now listen! All the women remain in the palace of the king of Judah will be brought to the officials of the king of Babylon, and those women will say to you, "The men you trusted misled you and gained control of you. Your feet are sunk in the mud. They were disloyal." . . . And Zedekiah said to Jeremiah, "No one can be allowed to know about this conversation, or you may die. If the officials hear that I talked with you, and they come to you and say to you, 'Tell us what you said to the king. Do not hide it from us or we will kill you. And what did the king say to you?' Then you must say to them, 'I was making a supplication to the king, that he not to send me back to Jonathan's house to die there.'" (Jer. 38:14, 17–22, 24–26)

Zedekiah did believe that Jeremiah was a prophet, but his faith was not strong enough to act on what Jeremiah said. For a long time, he had been caught in a dilemma. Two factions had struggled for control in Jerusalem. The one faction believed in continued submission to Babylon and evidently had been behind Jehoiachin's decision to surrender. This faction was "pro-Babylonian" in the sense that they believed Babylon's power to be irresistible and that Judah could for the time being survive only as a vassal of Nebu-chadnezzar. In the aftermath of Jehoiachin's surrender, however, there was widespread bitterness in the city over his deportation and imprisonment, and a pro-Egyptian faction became dominant. This group had been supportive of Jehoiakim's rebellion and believed that Egypt, having proven in 601 that they had the strength to turn back the Babylonians, made for a better suzerain.

In his decision to rebel against Nebuchadnezzar, therefore, Zedekiah was heavily influenced (and intimidated) by the pro-Egyptian group. Once the rebellion had begun and the army of Babylon appeared in Judah, some members of the pro-Babylonian faction fled the city and gave themselves up to the Babylonians. We know that these were not just commoners because Zedekiah feared that the Babylonians would hand him over to these men if he surrendered. This could be a possibility only if their number included ranking members of the aristocracy—men who would have access to the Babylonian officials and a degree of freedom to do as they pleased in the Babylonian camp. Thus, after the siege began, the pro-Egyptian party completely dominated the political scene, and effectively had Zedekiah as their puppet. Any people in the city who still supported surrender to Babylon were regarded as traitors and accused of weakening the morale of the people; both accusations were hurled at Jeremiah (Jer. 37:13; 38:4). Lachish Letter 6 also appears to contain a complaint about nobles who weakened the resolve of the people to resist Babylon.[8] Zedekiah feared the pro-Egyptian party because they had shown themselves to be willing to commit murder to achieve their goals. The palace women in Jeremiah's prophecy at 38:24–26 represent people with access to aristocratic circles. They had inside information about palace conflicts but had little power to influence the outcome. They would only suffer the consequences. The women recognized that the pro-Egyptian party had no real loyalty to Zedekiah and in their arrogance had brought disaster upon the dynasty. In the end, the pro-Egyptian faction, exploiting the weakness of Zedekiah, insisted upon the adoption of policies that would destroy them-selves and their city.

After a prolonged siege, the army of Nebuchadnezzar overcame Jerusa-lem's defenses. As the city was falling, Zedekiah and a small group of soldiers attempted an escape from the trap. He was captured and taken to Nebuchad-nezzar. The last thing he saw was the execution of his sons; after that, his eyes were gouged out. He was taken to Babylon and died there (Jer. 52:6–11).

---

8.   Di Vito, "Lachish Letters," 128.

CHAPTER 3

THE LIFE OF JEREMIAH:
FROM JOSIAH TO JEHOIACHIN

N
o other prophetic book of the Old Testament tells us as much about the experiences and internal struggles of its eponymous prophet as does Jeremiah. However, details are scattered throughout the book and are often not dated. We must, therefore, sift through the data to reconstruct his biography as best we can. For a chronological summary of Jeremiah's life and times, see appendix 2.

BIRTH AND COMMISSION

We do not know the precise year of Jeremiah's birth. However, he received his commission from YHWH to be a prophet in the thirteenth year of Josiah's reign, in approximately 627 BC (Jer. 1:2). At this time, Jeremiah protested that he was only a "boy" (נַעַר [na'ar], a word that can refer to subordinates of any age [Gen. 14:24; Num. 22:22] but that, as a measure of age, usually refers to a child or adolescent [Gen. 22:12; 1 Sam. 20:35; 2 Kings 5:14; Job 29:8]).[1] Assuming he was roughly thirteen years old when God spoke to him, he would have been born around the year 640. This was the year that King Amon of Judah was assassinated. Josiah, who was himself but a child of eight years, replaced him (2 Kings 22:1).

An alternative view, championed by William Holladay, is that Jeremiah was born in 627 BC. He gives seven arguments in favor of this: (1) None of Jeremiah's oracles can be dated to between 627 and 622, the time of Josiah's reform. (2) It is not clear that Jeremiah was a vocal supporter of the reform when it started. (3) The earliest dated message of Jeremiah is his temple sermon, which Holladay dates to 609/608. This is a late date for his first

---

1.   *HALOT* s.v. "נַעַר" 707.

message if Jeremiah received his call in 627. (4) The identity of the enemy from the north (1:15; 4:6; 6:1, 22; 10:22) is problematic for the earlier date for Jeremiah's ministry, since these references occur before Babylon was a real threat. (5) God's command that Jeremiah remain celibate (16:1–4) must therefore have been given to him after Jehoiakim burned the scroll (usually understood to have happened in December of 604, but which Holladay implausibly dates to December 601), since that command demonstrates that YHWH's decision to destroy Jerusalem was irrevocable, and thus that trying to raise a family was folly.[2] (6) Jeremiah's recollection, "Your words were found, and I ate them" (15:16), refers to the discovery of the scroll in the temple (in 622 BC). Considering Jeremiah's testimony in 1:9 that God put his words in Jeremiah's mouth, this must have happened before Jeremiah received his prophetic call. (7) "Before I formed you in the womb, I knew you" (1:5) implies that the call of God, as a theological event, took place in the year of his birth (with Jeremiah's verbal response coming later).[3] None of these arguments can withstand scrutiny.

(1) Dating Jeremiah's first awareness of his commission to be a prophet to 627 does not imply that he would have immediately begun preaching from the moment of his calling. Even his awareness that God had placed words in his mouth and had told him not to use youth as an excuse for avoiding the prophetic burden (Jer. 1:5–8) does not mean that he immediately began a public ministry. The fact that his call was in two separate stages (as described below) suggests that the initial message he received in 627 was meant to make him aware of his life's task and to set him to ruminating over what this would mean and what he would say. It does not mean that he, as a thirteen-year-old, would move to Jerusalem and start preaching messages. By analogy, Jesus came to a special awareness of his identity and task at age twelve, but he remained at home in Nazareth and lived in obscurity until he was about thirty years old (Luke 2:42–52).

---

2.   The MT places the reading of the scroll in the ninth month of Jehoiakim's fifth year, but the parallel text at LXX 43:9 places it in the eighth year. Holladay prefers the LXX because it is the more difficult reading, but that is a slender basis for making such an argument. Holladay, *Jeremiah 1: A Commentary on the Book of the Prophet Jeremiah, Chapters 1–25*, Hermeneia (Philadelphia: Fortress, 1986), 4. Holladay (pp. 1–2) is also following a scheme that asserts that Jeremiah's major messages occurred every seven years in conjunction with a public reading of Deuteronomy; he dates these readings to 608, 601, 594, and 587 BC, and so he wants to date this incident to 601. But this scheme is entirely unsupported by any evidence from the book. Jack R. Lundbom bluntly states that the LXX date is "a reading with nothing to commend it." Lundbom, *Jeremiah 21–36: A New Translation with Introduction and Commentary*, AB 21B (New York: Doubleday, 2004), 596.

3.   Holladay, *Jeremiah 2*, 25–26. Holladay notes that he is not the first or only scholar to take this view of the chronology of Jeremiah's life, citing Friedrich Horst and J. Philip Hyatt.

(2) In 622, when the reformation began, Jeremiah still would have been quite young (perhaps nineteen) and probably would still have been living in Anathoth. As young scion of a rural, priestly family, it is doubtful that he would have had meaningful support in the upper circles of Jerusalem society or that his messages would have been recorded in any document. Huldah was the recognized prophetess at this time, and members of the court sought out her when they needed a word from YHWH (2 Chron. 34:22). On the other hand, as Holladay observes, Jeremiah's recollection of having joyfully received YHWH's word after it was "found" (15:16) probably does refer to the discovery of the law in the temple (2 Kings 22:8). This implies that Jeremiah knew of and enthusiastically supported Josiah's efforts.

(3) If the temple sermon was preached around 609 BC, Jeremiah would have been around thirty years old at the time. As noted above, this is comparable to what we know of Jesus's public ministry. But in fact, the temple sermon is only the first dated sermon we know of; we do not have any reason to suppose it was his first sermon. Jeremiah 2–20 contains a great many undated excerpts from his preaching, and some of this was probably from earlier messages. The temple sermon is not likely to have been the opening salvo of his ministry. It is highly negative and condemnatory; it is more likely to have been given after he had already gained some recognition as a prophet but also after having experienced some rejection and hostility from his fellow countrymen. Indeed, 3:6 introduces a message that was given at some unspecified time in the reign of Josiah. It condemns the nation's apostasy, but it also holds out the hope that Jerusalem will repent and be saved (3:22–25; the message is described more fully below). This more optimistic tone, and not the sterner tone of the temple sermon, is what one would expect from the earliest period of his ministry. Also, the serious and alarmed response to Jeremiah's temple sermon (26:7–9) implies that he was already widely recognized as a prophet of YHWH when he gave it. This was not the first time he ever preached.

(4) Jeremiah 1:15 is certainly the first reference to a northern enemy in Jeremiah's career, and it no doubt refers to Babylon. But it was a word from God. One does not need to assume that Babylon was ascendant and recognized as a superpower at the time Jeremiah received the oracle. It is prophecy, not political analysis.

(5) There is no reason to suppose that Jeremiah received the command not to marry only after Jehoiakim burned the scroll. To the contrary, for the command to have had maximum impact on Jeremiah, it probably was given to him well before he was utterly disillusioned with Jerusalem and its leaders. That is, Jeremiah's celibacy was not something he embraced out of anger and despair. It was a word from God that served to help bring him

to the realization that there was no hope for his people. It was part of the process of moving him toward his final acceptance of YHWH's decrees of judgment against his city.

(6) There is no reason whatsoever for thinking that Jeremiah's joyful response to the discovery and reading of the law was prior to his call to be a prophet. God's statement in 1:9, that he put his words in Jeremiah's mouth, refers to prophetic inspiration and not to the book of the law.

(7) Holladay's interpretation of "Before I formed you in the womb, I knew you" (1:5), that it implies that the call of Jeremiah came to him on the day of his birth, is unnatural and implausible. Holladay takes 1:2, "The word of YHWH came to [Jeremiah] in the thirteenth year of the reign of Josiah son of Amon king of Judah," to mean that this was the year of both his birth and prophetic call. To the contrary, 1:2 refers to the moment Jeremiah for the first time consciously received a divine revelation, and it has to have come many years after his birth. It is comparable to the experience of the boy Samuel (1 Sam. 3:1–10).

We may thus conclude that Jeremiah was born in or around 640 BC and received his first divine calling in 627. He was from a priestly family, and his father's name was Hilkiah (1:1). This family may have been descendants of Abiathar, a high-ranking priest whom Solomon banished to Anathoth as punishment for his support of Adonijah (1 Kings 2:26). The high priest who announced the discovery of the law to Josiah was also named Hilkiah (2 Kings 22:8), but this was probably not Jeremiah's father. If his father had been the high priest, it is unlikely that 1:1 would identify him simply as "[one] of the priests who were in Anathoth."

A curious fact is that Jeremiah's priestly background is rarely evident in his messages. By contrast, Ezekiel frequently demonstrates his training as a priest. He is profoundly concerned about the ritual defilement of the temple (Ezek. 8), and when he deals with an issue, he works through it didactically, as one would expect of someone with priestly training (as in Ezek. 18). His great vision of restored Israel has at its center a temple, and a river of life flows from that temple (Ezek. 40–48). Jeremiah preaches against reliance on the temple as though it were a great talisman, but he shows little interest in purely cultic matters beyond what any educated Israelite would be familiar with. It may be that, because he received his call to prophetic ministry while he was still young, he did not receive extensive training in the priestly duties.

The narrative at Jeremiah 1:4–19 records two revelations to Jeremiah. The first revelation (1:4–10) is God's announcement to Jeremiah that he has been chosen to be a prophet, and it includes Jeremiah's initial objections and God's responses. The second revelation (1:11–19) is introduced by "The word of YHWH came to me," marking it as a separate episode. This text briefly tells him what his message will be and warns him to be prepared to face profound hostility. At the core of his ministry will be the prophecy that Babylon will destroy Judah (1:11–16). The people of Jerusalem will not accept this but will be extremely hostile to him. God will have put armor around his soul to enable him to withstand their attacks (1:17–19). The second revelation probably took place when he was old enough to take it in, at least several years after the revelation of 1:4–10. The significance of his call narrative is explored more thoroughly in chapter 9.

MINISTRY UNDER JOSIAH

All of Judah was aware of Josiah's reformation and of the sweeping changes he was making to the religious landscape (2 Kings 23:1, 8). Anathoth was very close to Jerusalem, and Jeremiah was part of a family of priests. Even as an adolescent, he certainly followed the events of the reformation. He was devout, and being eight years younger than Josiah we can imagine that he looked upon the king as a hero and as the leader of a new generation of faithful Israelites who would eschew all idols and faithfully keep the covenant. Both the discovery of the law and Josiah's public renewal of Israel's covenant with YHWH (2 Kings 22:8–23:3) would have thrilled him and given him hope that Judah could be transformed and enter a time of peace and prosperity under YHWH not seen since the days of David. This does not mean that he was blind to the spiritual problems of Judah; his support for Josiah's work implies that he knew that many were unfaithful to YHWH and that, against all opposition, he wanted to support the king in bringing about spiritual renewal.

Messages from Josiah's Reign

Although it is difficult to be completely certain about the historical background of any text in chapters 2–20, Jeremiah 3:6–4:4 is probably a good example of his preaching when he reached early manhood, late in the reign of Josiah. Verse 6 begins the passage:

> And in the days of King Josiah, YHWH said to me, "Have you seen what apostate Israel has done? She has been going up on every high hill and under every green tree and has committed adultery there."

As for a date, this only tells us that YHWH spoke to Jeremiah at some point in Josiah's reign. But we can probably assume that it was late in Josiah's reign. It is unlikely that he would receive such a sexually laden message while he was but a boy, although the fact that this message occurs so early in the book makes it more reasonable to assume it is one of Jeremiah's first prophetic oracles. Also, YHWH asked if he had seen how Judah had committed adultery against her lawful husband, YHWH. This may imply that it was given while Jeremiah was still young enough to have been somewhat dazzled by Josiah's reformation and perhaps living under the illusion that covenant fidelity was now triumphant over paganism in Israel. To paraphrase very loosely, the question is, "Yes, Josiah's reformation has been in full swing for some time, but do you see how things really are in the religious life of the Israelites?" This was YHWH's wake-up call to Jeremiah, informing him that although Josiah was sincere and to be commended, the reformation had failed.

The oracle also asserts that Judah learned such behavior from her sister Israel (Jer. 3:6–10). This concise metaphor of two adulterous sisters demonstrates both how Jeremiah drew upon the writings of an earlier prophet and how he was the inspiration for a message by a later prophet. The metaphor of Israel as wayward wife, engaging in prostitution with the gods of the nations, alludes to Hosea's portrayal of Samaria in his marriage to the unfaithful Gomer (Hos. 1–2). Jeremiah borrowed this imagery and spoke of Israel as the sister whom Judah imitated. And just as Israel was destroyed for its infidelity, so too disaster awaited Judah if she did not repent. But the metaphor of the two faithless sisters was only briefly developed in Jeremiah; Ezekiel took it up and created the much more elaborate story of the two whoring sisters Oholah and Oholibah (Ezek. 23).

The oracle complained that faithless Judah had only made a formal, pretended repentance and had not in fact returned to YHWH with her heart or abandoned her adulterous behavior (Jer. 3:10). This too reflects the situation late in Josiah's reign, when the people had formally abandoned their idols but had done so only under compulsion. True renewal had not yet occurred:

> I thought how I would set you among children, and I would give you a pleasant land, the most beautiful inheritance of all the nations. And I thought you would call me, "My Father," and would not turn back from following me. (Jer. 3:19)

The reminiscences introduced with "I thought" are spoken in YHWH's name but reflect the prophet's youthful and naïve optimism. He had believed that Josiah's reformation would bring in a golden age for Jerusalem, and now he was seeing reality more clearly.

Still, an abiding hope for renewal is reflected in his offer of salvation if the people would turn from their sin:

> Return, apostate children, I will heal your apostasy. [Return, saying,] "Look, we come to you! For you are YHWH our God. What we get from the hills, that crazed worship in the mountains, is really a lie. The salvation of Israel is really in YHWH our God." (Jer. 3:22–23)

These words of repentance and devotion to YHWH reflect Jeremiah's dream; he put the words he longed for the people to say into their mouths. He was not unaware of how thoroughly many of them despised what Josiah had done, but he stubbornly clung to the possibility that the nation would change. What remained of his hope, however, was quickly shattered.

Another prophecy from an earlier period and probably from Josiah's reign is 11:1–5. The text briefly exhorts the people to obey the terms of the covenant and reminds them of how YHWH delivered Israel from Egypt. It holds to the possibility that Jerusalem may repent and be spared exile from the land, and it includes Jeremiah's hopeful and enthusiastic response:

> Obey me and do all the things I command you, and you will be my people, and I will be your God, so that I may fulfill the oath I swore to your ancestors, to give them a land flowing with milk and honey, where you are today. And I said, "Amen, YHWH!" (Jer. 11:4b–5)

Clearly, Jeremiah at this stage still believed such a thing was possible.

Jeremiah the Celibate

According to Jeremiah 16:1–4, the prophet received a command from YHWH not to take a wife or have children. There was no future for Jerusalem, and raising a family would be impossible:

> For thus says YHWH concerning the sons and daughters who are born in this place, and concerning the mothers who bear them and the fathers who beget them in this land: They will die of fatal diseases. They will not be mourned, and they will not be buried. They shall become like dung on the surface of the ground. They will die by the sword and by famine, and their corpses will become food for the birds of the air and for the wild animals of the earth. (Jer. 16:3–4)

The text is not dated, and its placement in the book can only be determined by literary and thematic considerations. Although we cannot be sure when this took place, because Jeremiah was probably born around 640 BC, it is unlikely that it was given to him any later than 610 BC. By that time, he would have been about thirty years of age, and one would assume that he would have been married by that time if he had not been forbidden to do so. We can probably date this prohibition to around 615–610 BC, late in Josiah's reign, when Jeremiah was beginning his prophetic ministry.

The content of the prohibition is dire, as it seems to leave no room for Jerusalem to escape destruction. However, prophecy can seem to be fixed, with no possibility of alteration, and yet be modified if circumstances change (specifically, whether or not the people repent). For another example of an apparently irrevocable promise that was reversed, see 34:1–7.[4] Jeremiah probably received the command as a statement of how bad the moral environment had become and believed that Jerusalem's fate sat on a knife's edge, but we need not assume that he already considered the situation hopeless.

---

4.   See the discussion in Garrett and Pearson, *Jeremiah and Lamentations*, 320–21.

Even so, the oracle would have been doubly traumatic for him. First, Israel had no tradition of "clerical celibacy," and to live without wife and children was regarded as a cruel fate. He was deprived of the domestic happiness that was all but universal in Israelite society. Also, this would have increased the people's disdain for him; he was to them a strangely isolated man, a weird prophet who shunned marriage and children. Second, both in the command not to marry and in the explanation for it, he saw that Jerusalem was facing unbearable suffering and death. While this probably added urgency to the fulfillment of his prophetic calling, as he struggled to avert this calamity it also pushed him at times to near-despair.

Jeremiah's Abiding Devotion to Josiah

In Jeremiah 22:10–17, Jeremiah's attitude toward Josiah and his reform is set in stark contrast to that of the people of Jerusalem. This text contains oracles spoken against Jehoahaz (Shallum) and Jehoiakim. The messages were evidently first given in the early years of Jehoiakim, after Josiah had been slain by Pharaoh Necho II and after Josiah's son Jehoahaz had been crowned and then deposed by Necho and carried into exile in Egypt. Jeremiah exhorted the people not to weep over Josiah but over Jehoahaz, saying that he would never be restored to his homeland:

> Do not weep for [the king] who is dead, and do not grieve for him!
> But weep bitterly for him who goes away,
> For he shall return no more to see the land of his birth.
> For thus says YHWH concerning Shallum [Jehoahaz] the son of Josiah,
> king of Judah, who became king after his father Josiah, who departed
> from this place: He will never return here, but there, in the place where
> they took him into exile, he will die, and he will never see this land again.
> (Jer. 22:10–12)

Jeremiah contrasts the death of Josiah with the exile of Jehoahaz, treating the former as a noble ending to a life lived well and the latter as an ignoble, meaningless, and dreary life. This implies that the people thought the reverse. They believed that Josiah's sudden demise was proof that he was not under God's favor and that his reformation should be abandoned (see also Jer. 44:17–18). Jeremiah's stark assertion that Jehoahaz would die in Egypt implies that some held out the hope that he would soon return.

This popular conception was further encouraged by an apparent return to prosperity under Jehoiakim, who had resumed committing the "abominations" that Josiah had purged (2 Chron. 36:8). Jehoiakim was able to refurbish the royal palace with splendid decoration in cedar and vermilion (Jer. 22:14) and to resume sumptuous feasting. To some, Jehoiakim's apparent wealth and success were proof that he was under God's favor, unlike Josiah, who had died in battle. Jeremiah would have none of this:

Do you [Jehoiakim] behave like a king by being obsessed with cedar? Did not your father eat justice and righteousness and drink justice and righteousness and perform justice and righteousness?[5] Then it went well for him! He carefully judged cases involving the poor and needy. Then it went well! Is not this to know me? So says YHWH. (Jer. 22:15–16)

The idea that Jehoiakim was a better man than Josiah, who ate and drank righteousness, was absurd. Jeremiah's insistence that things "went well" for Josiah when he wholly followed God's law is an implied response to the belief that Jehoiakim's reversion to paganism and to a ruthless exploitation of his aristocratic privileges had been vindicated by his ostentatious wealth. Even so, Josiah's death and Jehoiakim's cancellation of the reformation showed Jeremiah that his earlier hope had been misplaced. There would be no spiritual renewal.

MINISTRY UNDER JEHOIAKIM

The major theme of Jeremiah 11:1–20:18 is the movement from an earlier period in Jeremiah's ministry, when he prayed fervently for God to spare Judah, to a later period, when he ceased to make intercession and began to make imprecations against his people, calling on God to punish them.[6] Intercession for sinners was, indeed, a critical element of a prophet's purpose. Following the examples set by Abraham in Genesis 18:16–33 and by Moses in Exodus 32:9–14, prophets were supposed to be agents of salvation, not only preaching but actively praying for the people under their ministry.[7] For Jeremiah to not pray for Jerusalem would seem to be proof that he was no true prophet, and the book must explain the surprising change that took place in his prayers. A key moment was when God told him he was prohibited from praying for his nation (11:14–17). But there is more to it than Jeremiah yielding to a divine command; he had himself concluded that the people of Jerusalem were hopelessly evil and that continuing to pray for them would be to no avail. Although we cannot know the precise sequence of events, the following synopsis provides a general chronology of key events in the reign of Jehoiakim that brought about this transformation in Jeremiah's thinking.

The Drought
Early in Jeremiah's ministry, possibly during the latter part of Josiah's reign and certainly in the early years of Jehoiakim's reign, Judah was hit with a major

---

5.   On the translation of Jer. 22:15, see Garrett and Pearson, *Jeremiah and Lamentations*, 235.
6.   The discussion here attempts to unravel the historical sequence of events in Jeremiah's life that brought him to abandon praying for Jerusalem. For a discussion of the structure of 11:1–20:18 as a literary unit within the book, see ch. 3 below.
7.   For further discussion, see Duane A. Garrett, *The Problem of the Old Testament: Hermeneutical, Schematic, and Theological Approaches* (Downers Grove, IL: IVP Academic, 2020), 273–85.

drought and famine. Jeremiah 3:3a speaks of the drought: "Therefore, the show-ers have been withheld, and the spring rain has not come." Jeremiah 3:1–5 is from early in the prophet's ministry (cf. 3:6, from the reign of Josiah, which develops the theme of 3:1–5). It may be that Judah suffered less than normal rainfall for several years, with the worst period of drought early in Jehoiakim's reign.

We see many verbal echoes of the drought in Jeremiah. In 14:22, Jeremiah prays, "Are the useless idols of the nations able to bring rain?" This implies that the people are turning to Baal or storm gods for rain, and none is coming. In chapter 17, Jeremiah declares that the wicked will be like a plant in the "parched places of the desert" (17:6), while the righteous would be like a tree planted by water (17:8). In 17:12–14, Jeremiah prays as follows:

> Throne of glory!
> Lofty height [that has existed] from the beginning! The place of our sanc-
> tuary!
> The hope (and water reservoir) of Israel: YHWH!
> All who abandon you are put to shame (and dry up).
> And my weeds in the land will be recorded [as follows]:
> That they abandoned the spring of living water: YHWH![8]
> Heal me, YHWH, and I will be healed!
> Save me and I will be saved!
> For you are the one I praise.

In this text, Jeremiah makes use of two wordplays. First, the word mean-ing "hope" has a homonym that means "water reservoir." Exploiting this, he calls YHWH the "hope (and water reservoir) of Israel," meaning that YHWH is the only hope for relief from the drought. Second, drawing on the similarity between two verbs that respectively mean to "be ashamed" and to "dry up," he states, "All who abandon you are put to shame (and dry up)." This implies that those who trust in some other god will be chagrined that their god has failed and suffer continued drought.[9] Those who abandon YHWH are like scrubby weeds that can scarcely survive and bear no fruit. When they turn from YHWH, they forsake the "spring of living water." This fixation on water metaphors implies that at the time water was a very scarce and precious commodity. It is important to note, however, that Jeremiah is in these contexts praying for God to give some relief to Judah. He says, "Are you not YHWH our God?" This is not a declaration that YHWH is rightly punishing Jerusalem and that the people deserve it. It is an appeal for help. Similarly, "Heal me, YHWH, and I will be healed!" in 17:14 is not a prayer for himself; it is a prayer for Judah. This implies that the drought,

---

8.   For notes on the translation of 17:13, see Garrett and Pearson, *Jeremiah and Lamentations*, 198.

9.   The word that can mean either "hope" or "water reservoir" is מִקְוֶה. See *HALOT* s.v. "626 מִקְוֶה." The word בּוֹשׁ means "to be ashamed," but it is similar to יבשׁ, which means "dry up." See *HALOT* s.v. "בּוֹשׁ" 116; s.v. "יבשׁ" 384.

or at least the first part of it, took place early in Jeremiah's career, before he was prohibited from praying for Judah. We can conclude that the drought probably became severe in the second or third year of Jehoiakim's reign, prompting Jeremiah's intercessory prayer. He knew that Jerusalem was under divine judgment, but he still held on to hope and still prayed for his nation.

The Sermon at the People's Gate

Jeremiah 17:19–27 contains a message Jeremiah delivered at what was called the "People's Gate, by which the kings of Judah enter and by which they go out." He then gave the same message at Jerusalem's other gates (17:19). The date of this sermon is not provided. Although it rebukes the people for a specific fault—failure to keep the Sabbath—the message overall is quite encouraging. The prophets certainly did not regard Sabbath-breaking as insignificant (Amos 8:5), but it was a sin that could be easily remedied: The people only needed to rest every seventh day. The hopeful tone of the message implies that it is from an earlier period. It includes a promise of a happy future for Jerusalem if they will only observe the Sabbath:

> But if you really obey me, says YHWH, by bringing in no burden by the gates of this city on the Sabbath day, by sanctifying the Sabbath day, and by doing no work on it, then kings who sit on the throne of David and officials shall enter by the gates of this city. They will be riding in chariots and on horses, they and their officials, along with the people of Judah and the inhabitants of Jerusalem. And this city shall be inhabited forever. (Jer. 17:24–25)

In this portrayal of a possible idyllic future, kings and high officials occupy a prominent place. It is a promise of an orderly and well-established government. This implies that at the time the message was given, Jerusalem was in the opposite state, and Jeremiah wanted to assure them that recovery was possible. Things were in upheaval politically, and people were distressed about the future of the royal house. The most likely time for such a setting was at the beginning of the reign of Jehoiakim. Everything seemed to have gone wrong. Their valiant King Josiah had been slain by an Egyptian; their preferred choice, Jehoahaz, had been deposed and exiled; and suddenly they found themselves under a man whom the Egyptians had placed over them, Jehoiakim. Jeremiah, still hoping for repentance and renewal in Jerusalem, promised them a glorious future under the house of David if only they would keep their covenant with God.

The Rechabite Incident (35:1–19)

Another important episode fairly early in the reign of Jehoiakim was the Rechabite incident. This encounter served as the basis for a condemnation of Jerusalem, and also showed Jeremiah how corrupted his people had become.[10]

---

10.   This section draws upon, but modifies, Garrett and Pearson, *Jeremiah and Lamentations*, 323–25.

The Rechabites were a subgroup of Kenites (1 Chron. 2:55). They identified themselves as "sojourners" in the land of Israel (Jer. 35:7), although their Yahwistic names (such as Jaazaniah, "YHWH will hear") imply that they had adopted Israelite religion. They sometimes roamed in the north, as indicated by 2 Kings 10:15–23. They were committed to maintaining the ideal of the nomadic, pastoral life. Thus, they would not settle into houses or plant crops but moved constantly with their flocks.

Jeremiah invited a group of Rechabites to a room in the temple complex and encouraged them to drink wine. They flatly refused and explained that their founder, Rechab, had prohibited the drinking of wine (Jer. 35:6). This was not because of concerns over sobriety. For them, drinking wine was a step toward the sedentary life of dwelling in houses and planting vineyards. To do this was to abandon their nomadic ideals and become settled farmers:

> We do not drink wine, because our father Jonadab son of Rechab commanded us, "Neither you nor your descendants must ever drink wine. Also, you must not build houses, nor sow seed, nor plant vineyards. You will never have any of these things but must always live in tents so that you will live a long time in the land where you are nomads." (Jer. 35:6–7)

Vine cultivation is labor-intensive and requires years of work before the first usable crop comes in. The lure of viniculture was a strong temptation to take up an agricultural lifestyle. For that reason, wine was prohibited to the pastoral and nomadic Rechabites. After they rejected the wine, Jeremiah gave a sermon comparing the stubborn disobedience of Jerusalem to stubborn loyalty of the Rechabites, and he warned that YHWH would bring disaster upon the city (35:12–17).

Not all scholars hold to the standard view of the Rechabites. An alternative position is that they were a group of itinerant metalworkers.[11] This depends heavily on a peculiar reading of 1 Chronicles 4:12–14, emending "Recah" in 4:12 to "Rechab," and linking this to the end of 4:14, which states, "they were craftsmen." The textual evidence is weak, and the case for emending is too tenuous to use as a basis for a hypothesis on the identity of the Rechabites.[12] Also, it is not likely that metalworkers of ancient Israel were itinerant. Blacksmithing requires furnaces and heavy equipment, making an itinerant life unlikely. First Samuel 13:20 implies that people traveled to blacksmiths rather than the reverse. There is no logical reason to forbid metalsmiths from building houses and settling in one place. But if itinerant shepherds transitioned

---

11. For a defense of this position, see Frank S. Frick, "Rechab," *ABD* 5:630–32.

12. LXX Vaticanus and the Lucianic recension do attest to רכב, but LXX Alexandrinus reads Pηφα. Ralph W. Klein emends to רכב, but Gary N. Knoppers stays with the MT רכה. See Klein, *1 Chronicles: A Commentary*, Hermeneia (Minneapolis: Fortress, 2006), 124; Knoppers, *I Chronicles 1–9: A New Translation with Introduction and Commentary*, AB 12 (New York: Doubleday, 2003), 340.

to a permanently stationary existence, it would be the end of their whole way of life. An argument given for why metalsmiths would need to abstain from drinking wine, so that they would not divulge the secrets of their craft, is far-fetched. The traditional view that they were shepherds is more persuasive.[13]

But this passage contains another and more vexing problem: its chronology. Jeremiah was prohibited from entering the temple precincts some time prior to the ninth month of the fifth year of Jehoiakim, December of 604 (36:9), and he presumably remained in that status until Jehoiakim's death. Since the Rechabite episode took place at the temple, it must have occurred prior to the prohibition. The narrative, however, appears to contradict this. The Rechabites state in 35:11 that they fled to Jerusalem to escape the Babylonian army under Nebuchadnezzar and the Syrian army. We know that Nebuchadnezzar captured Jerusalem at the end of Jehoiakim's reign, in February of 597. Some scholars date the beginning of the siege to as early as 599, but even this is too late to agree with Jeremiah's exclusion from the temple.[14] Jehoiakim banned Jeremiah from the temple at the latest in December of 604, at least four years before the siege. The chronological data seem impossible to reconcile.

There are other difficulties. Second Kings 24:2 says that Syrians and Chaldeans ravaged Judah, an event that can be no earlier than 602 BC. The Rechabites claimed that they fled from the Syrians and Chaldeans. Therefore, this too appears to reflect a time after Jeremiah had been expelled from the temple. A more minor problem is that there seems to be a self-contradiction in the narrative. By dwelling in Jerusalem, the Rechabites were violating their own rule requiring them to live in tents (Jer. 35:7). This could imply that the story is a fabrication or a composite of several narrative strands.

The above problems make it appear that the Rechabite episode is at best dated too early and at worst is not historical. But neither conclusion is necessary. From the survey of Babylonian history in chapter 1, we can see that Babylonian forces were in the Levant or were a threat to Jerusalem on many occasions, and in fact that Jerusalem first submitted to Nebuchadnezzar in the year 605–604. This implies that the Rechabites could have been near Jerusalem, fleeing the Babylonian threat, before Jeremiah was prohibited from entering the temple in December of 604. Nothing in Jeremiah 35 implies that Judah was under attack at the time of this episode. In 35:11, the Rechabites explain why they came to Jerusalem:

> But it turned out that when Nebuchadnezzar king of Babylon invaded the land, we said, "Come on! Let's go to Jerusalem [to get away] from the army of the Chaldeans and the army of the Syrians." And so, we stayed at Jerusalem.

---

13. For further options and discussion, see Thomas G. Smothers, Gerald Lynwood Keown, and Pamela J. Scalise, *Jeremiah 26–52*, WBC 27 (Dallas: Word, 1995), 195–96.
14. E.g., Holladay, *Jeremiah 2*, 246.

In the narrative, the "land" that Nebuchadnezzar invaded was wherever the Rechabites were prior to their setting out for Jerusalem. It was not Judah; it was somewhere in the Levant to the north of Judah. Also, the verse does not even imply that Nebuchadnezzar was personally present with the army. For comparison, the Bible routinely speaks of Nebuchadnezzar as the conqueror of Jerusalem, as though he were there when it fell, when in fact he was in Syria when the city was taken and destroyed.

The Rechabites do mention that they were fleeing "from the army of the Chaldeans and the army of the Syrians." This could be taken to imply that the episode took place in the years 602–600, the period in which "bands of the Chaldeans, bands of the Arameans, bands of the Moabites, and bands of the Ammonites" were harassing Judah (2 Kings 24:2). However, the harassment of Judah by various forces in 602–600 is probably not relevant to the Rechabite episode. If these hostilities had been going on at the time of the Rechabite movement, they probably would have tried to avoid Judah altogether, since this was a focal point of hostilities and they were trying to escape the conflict.

Furthermore, the Rechabites do not say that the Chaldeans and Syrians were allied with each other or that a united army was behind them and pressing toward Jerusalem, as might have been the case sometime after 602, when the Babylonians began to press southward to deal with Jehoiakim's rebellion. When Pharaoh Necho II fought Nebuchadnezzar, he had Syrian allies. It is reasonable to surmise that some Syrian states went over to the Babylonian side. After the battle, Syria did supply auxiliary troops for Babylon's army. It was, to say the least, a chaotic and violent environment. But Jeremiah 35:11 implies nothing about the relationship between "the army of the Chaldeans and the army of the Syrians." It says only that the Rechabites fled from both. In other words, the Rechabites found themselves uncomfortably close to a war zone where two of the combatants were Syrians and Chaldeans. The Rechabites were not allied to either, but their livestock and families would have been easy plunder for armies, and they wanted to get out of the military theatre. As such, they headed south. They could have begun their southward trek in 605, even before the Battle of Carchemish.

Most significantly, they never imply that Jerusalem was under imminent threat of attack from the Babylonians, as would have been the case in the period 602–597. If it were, they certainly would not have moved toward Jerusalem. The last thing nomadic shepherds would want to do is let themselves be trapped inside the very city that a ravaging army was marching upon, as is implied if one dates the episode to after Jehoiakim had begun his rebellion. It may be that reports about Nebuchadnezzar's military prowess brought by the Rechabites helped to convince Jehoiakim to become a vassal of Babylon. Or, if Jehoiakim had already submitted when the Rechabites arrived, this could explain why they felt that Judah would be a safe place. Nebuchadnezzar would not attack a state that already belonged to him.

As noted above, some interpreters assume that the Rechabites camped inside the city and that this violated their nomadic vows. Jack Lundbom counters this by arguing that the Rechabites could have maintained their traditions by pitching tents within the city.[15] Prima facie, however, this makes for an implausible scenario. Unless their flocks were small, it is unlikely that they would have been able to settle en masse inside the city (unlike major Greco-Roman cities, Jerusalem had no large, open square inside the city limits). Their natural inclination would be to keep moving since their purpose was to put as much distance between them and the warring factions as possible. In fact, the Rechabite statement does not require that they took refuge inside the city walls. "Jerusalem" in Jeremiah 35:11 refers to the general location of the city.[16] It is likely that the Rechabites were near but not inside the walls, that they were in tents and among their sheep, and that they would soon be on their way.

In summary: The Rechabites had been somewhere in the north during the upheaval of Nebuchadnezzar's early campaigns, prior to his enthronement. At some time around the Battle of Carchemish and Nebuchadnezzar's return for his Hatti campaign, they fled south to escape the turmoil and plunder-hungry armies. In 605, they encamped near Jerusalem, where people were aware of the growing power to their north. But the city was not under attack or facing an impending Babylonian siege. Jeremiah, not yet excluded from the temple, brought some of them to one of its chambers and tested them with wine. He may have already known of their traditions. Their fidelity to an ancestral custom was in stark contrast to Judah's infidelity to the covenant YHWH had made with Israel's ancestors. Sometime after this episode, the Rechabites no doubt folded their tents and moved on. Jehoiakim, either just before or soon after the Rechabite episode, sent a formal submission to Babylon that included hostages.

The Temple Sermon

The temple sermon represents a turning point in Jeremiah's ministry under Jehoiakim. It is so called because it was delivered at and concerned the Jerusalem temple. Jeremiah 26:1–19 gives a biographical account of the sermon, stating that it was delivered "At the beginning of the reign of King Jehoiakim son of Josiah of Judah" (26:1). This is not chronologically precise; it does not necessarily mean the first year of Jehoiakim's reign. In the summation of the sermon, Jeremiah called on the people to repent and warned them that if they did not heed the warning, "then I will make this house like Shiloh, and I will make this city a curse-formula for all the nations of the earth" (26:6). By reminding them of how Shiloh, the former location of YHWH's sanctuary had been destroyed, he made the point that

---

15. Lundbom, *Jeremiah 21–36*, 570.
16. The expression בִּירוּשָׁלַ͏ִם need not mean "inside Jerusalem." The preposition here only implies the general geographic location. If the text had meant to specify that they were within the walls of the city, it would have used an expression such as בְּתוֹךְ יְרוּשָׁלַ͏ִם, which more properly means "inside Jerusalem."

possession of the temple was no guarantee that God would protect Jerusalem.[17] They had to abandon the idea that the temple was a great amulet that would protect them from all disaster. But the message was given at a time that repentance and salvation still seemed possible:

> Perhaps they will listen, and everyone will turn from his evil ways, and then I can relent from inflicting on them the disaster that I was considering, a disaster brought on by the evil they have done. (Jer. 26:3)

Even so, the sermon did not go well. The religious leadership was enraged and demanded that Jeremiah be put to death:

> The priests and the prophets and all the people laid hold of him, saying, "You shall die! Why did you prophesy in YHWH's name, 'This house shall be like Shiloh, and this city shall be laid waste and left without inhabitant'?" (Jer. 26:8b–9a)

But this more biographical account gives only the most minimal summation of what Jeremiah said in the temple sermon. An account focused on the message (rather than on the biographical and chronological details) is found in Jeremiah 7:1–15. We can tell that the two texts concern the same event because of the following correlations. First, the temple sermon was given from the "courtyard" of the temple (26:2), and the message of 7:1–15 was given at the "gate" of the temple (7:2). These are not two separate locations; the gateway was in or directly in front of one of the courtyards; it may have been a gate between an outer and inner courtyard. Second, the sermon attacked reliance on the temple, specifically comparing it to the earlier shrine at Shiloh, which was destroyed; both passages refer to this (7:12, 14; 26:6, 9). Third, Jeremiah 7:5–7 specifically promises that if the people change their ways and return to God, they will be safe and can dwell in the land indefinitely:

> For if you genuinely amend your ways and your behavior, if you genuinely carry out justice one with another, if you do not oppress the alien, the fatherless, and the widow, or shed innocent blood in this place, and if you do not go after other gods, which only brings harm on yourselves, then I will dwell with you in this place, in the land that I gave to your ancestors forever and ever.

---

17. The destruction of the Shiloh sanctuary probably took place at the same time as the capture of the ark by the Philistines and the death of Eli (1 Sam. 4). The Samuel narrative does not mention the destruction of the sanctuary, but that is because the story focuses on the fall of the house of Eli and on the story of the travels of the ark. Psalm 78:60 refers to the destruction of Shiloh. Archaeology attests to the violent destruction of the site by fire in Iron I. See Israel Finkelstein, "Shiloh," *NEAEHL* 4:1368–69.

This optimism suggests that the message of 7:1–15 was given early, and it agrees with a similar statement of hope that the people might repent in 26:3.

As mentioned, the temple sermon changed everything for both the prophet and his audience. It was direct and somewhat severe, but it essentially only set out to correct a theological error. The people of Jerusalem thought that because they had within their city the temple, the house where YHWH dwelt, it could never be taken. It was, for them, a gigantic charm protecting them from all harm. It is likely that they had come to believe that YHWH had destroyed Sennacherib's forces in the time of Hezekiah because Jerusalem possessed the temple. They had forgotten the humility and devotion Hezekiah had displayed at that time (Isa. 37). Jeremiah mocked their attitude, noting how they recited a mindless mantra to invoke YHWH's protection:

> Do not entrust yourselves to deceptive words by saying, "The temple of YHWH! The temple of YHWH! The temple of YHWH!" (Jer. 7:4)

He reminded them that Shiloh, which had also been the site of YHWH's shrine, had been destroyed (7:12, 14). But this was not an irrevocable word of condemnation; it was a warning that if they failed to obey what YHWH commanded, the possession of the temple would do them no good.

The response of the people was ferociously hostile, declaring that Jeremiah must die. But this reaction indicated something more: They had become not just apostate but religiously perverse. They declared Jeremiah's warnings to be blasphemy. Possessed with zealous certainty about the righteousness of their own actions and beliefs, they would never be open to Jeremiah's appeals. There would be no repentance and no change of heart because they believed themselves to be righteous and orthodox.

Jeremiah at the Potter's House

Jeremiah 18:1–10 records an undated incident that is transitional, moving Jeremiah further away from any lingering optimism about Judah. It is an object lesson taken from the work of a potter.

> The word that came to Jeremiah from YHWH: "Get up and head down to the potter's house. I will announce my message to you there." And I went down to the potter's house, and there he was working at the wheel. But the vessel that the potter was shaping by hand with the clay was disfigured. And the potter went back and remade it into another pot, doing to it whatever was right in the eyes of the potter. And the word of YHWH came to me: "Can I not do to you, House of Israel, as this potter does?" YHWH says, "Like clay in the hand of the potter, so are you in my hand, House of Israel. At one time I may speak concerning a nation or a kingdom, intending to uproot, tear down, and slay it. But if that nation should turn away from its evil, which I spoke against, then I will relent from

carrying out the disaster I had planned for it. But at another time I may speak concerning a nation or kingdom, intending to build it up and plant it. But if it does evil in my sight by not obeying me, then I will relent from doing the good I had planned for it."

The basic meaning of this visual parable is self-evident: As the potter has the freedom to change his plans and abandon an earlier project when the vessel he is making does not take shape as he had intended, so God has the right to change his plans regarding any nation when it does not behave as it had before. The people of Judah were acting as though God, having entered into covenant with Israel and the house of David, could never bring judgment down upon them. They believed that, by an unalterable divine decree, Jerusalem was impregnable. To Judah, the sign of the potter meant that God could alter his plans and bring down the city, monarchy, and temple. To Jeremiah, the sign meant that he may have no hope to offer them for the immediate future. He may need to steel himself to reject their appeals to pray for their deliverance from their enemies.

The Prohibition Against Intercession for Judah

At last, when Jeremiah came to understand that there would be no salvation for Jerusalem, God prohibited him from continuing to pray for his people. Two passages imply that this came in the context of the drought. The first is 11:14–17:

> And you [Jeremiah], do not intercede for this people or lift up an outcry or prayer in their behalf, for I am not listening when they call upon me concerning their trouble.
> What is there in my house [the temple] for my beloved [Jeremiah]
> While she [Jerusalem] is carrying out her plan?
> The throngs of people and the holy [sacrificial] meat!
> They will depart from you [Jerusalem] because of your evil.
> Then will you be so exultant?
> "Green olive tree made beautiful by shapely fruit."
> [That is what] YHWH called your name.
> But with the sound of a great storm, he will set fire to it,
> And its branches will suffer.
> And YHWH Sabaoth who planted you has pronounced a disaster against you on account of the evil of the house of Israel and of the house of Judah. They did this of their own accord to provoke me by making offerings to Baal.[18]

---

18. This translation is taken from Garrett and Pearson, *Jeremiah and Lamentations*, 162–63. The Hebrew, especially at 11:15, is regarded as all but untranslatable by a number of scholars, such as Holladay, *Jeremiah 1*, 354. But the text makes more sense if one pays close attention to the gender and person of various nouns and pronouns. Jerusalem in this text is feminine, but "beloved" (יְדִיד) at 11:15 is masculine, implying that it refers to Jeremiah, not to Jerusalem.

The above text contains two hints about the date of the prohibition against intercession. First, it indicates that it took place soon after Jeremiah had been prohibited from entering the temple: "What is there in my house [the temple] for my beloved [Jeremiah]?" Jerusalem's depravity being what it is, Jeremiah should be neither surprised nor distressed that he is not welcome in the temple. Second, the text speaks of Judah as a "green olive tree" that would be consumed in fire. This metaphor alludes to the drought, when conditions were so dry that wildfires were common and even the hardy olive trees were at risk. The reference to Baal worship may also reflect the time of drought, as desperate people prayed that the Canaanite storm god would come to their rescue.

The second recording of the prohibition is at Jeremiah 14:22–15:2:

Are any of the worthless idols of the nations bringers of rain, or do the skies send showers [in response to these idols]? Is it not you, YHWH our God [who sends rain], and do we not set our hope on you? For you are the one who does all this. But YHWH said to me: Even if Moses and Samuel were to stand before me, my heart would not be moved for this people. Send them away from my presence and let them depart! And if they ask you, "Where shall we go?" tell them, This is what YHWH says: Those destined for death, to death; those destined for the sword, to the sword; those destined for starvation, to starvation; those destined for captivity, to captivity.

The opening of this text tells us that Judah was experiencing severe drought and that the people were hoping that Baal, a storm god, could give them rain. This was probably several years into Jehoiakim's reign, when the prolongation of the drought had made matters desperate. For his part, Jeremiah was praying to YHWH for relief from the drought. But YHWH tells him it is of no use. Even Moses and Samuel could not by their prayers avert YHWH's determination to punish Jerusalem. More than that, God has already determined that they should suffer death by disease, plague, starvation, and military violence, saving only those whom God would send into exile. The prohibitions recorded in chapters 11 and 14 probably took place at or near the same time.

By this time, Jeremiah had been made to realize how implacably hostile his people had become, in that they responded to his preaching with ferocious hostility. Still, he was distraught at the command to abandon praying for them. He still believed that the hatred directed at him came from an ignorant mob that had been misled and provoked by a few of the more corrupt aristocrats and religious leaders. He thought that there was still a sizable body of the population who believed in his message and feared YHWH, and no doubt he did know some among the nobles, priests, and commoners who supported his message (the book attests to the existence of such people). But right after the prohibition in 11:14, YHWH disabused him of continued optimism:

But YHWH made it known to me, and then I knew. It was when you
[YHWH] showed me their evil deeds. And I had been like a gentle
lamb led to the slaughter. And I did not know that they were devising
schemes against me, saying, "Let us destroy the tree with its fruit! Let us
cut him off from the land of the living, so that his name will no longer
be remembered!" But you, YHWH Sabaoth, who judge righteously, who
test the heart and the mind, let me see your punishment upon them, for
to you I entrust my case. Therefore, thus says YHWH concerning the
men of Anathoth, who seek your life and say, "You must not prophesy in
the name of YHWH, or you will die by our hand!" Therefore, thus says
YHWH Sabaoth: Look! I am about to punish them! The young men will
die by the sword! Their sons and their daughters shall die by famine! And
they will not even have a remnant. For I will bring upon the people of
Anathoth disaster, the year of their punishment. (Jer. 11:18–23)

It is difficult to overstate the importance of this moment in Jeremiah's
biography. First, he realized how foolish he had been to have any hope that
the people of his generation would repent. He had supposed that only some,
and especially the politically and religiously privileged classes, had rejected
him. But now he knew that even his own family and friends in Anathoth
were determined to kill him if they heard another prophecy come from his
mouth. Second, he here turns from intercession to imprecation, calling on
God to punish his enemies, including the men of Anathoth. God responded
positively to this prayer: Anathoth would be entirely wiped out.

The Burning of the Baruch Scroll
According to Jeremiah 36:1–2, YHWH in the fourth year of Jehoiakim
(605 BC) commanded the prophet to get a scroll and write on it a summation of all the prophetic oracles YHWH had given him up to that time. Since
the scroll was both inscribed and publicly read by Jeremiah's scribe Baruch, we
can call it the Baruch scroll. This was to be in one sense the culmination of his
prophetic ministry, the final indictment on Jerusalem. Although the command
to write out the words of Jeremiah came in Jehoiakim's fourth year, the scroll
was not finished and publicly proclaimed until the ninth month of the fifth year
of Jehoiakim's reign, in December of 604 (36:9). Thus, there was approximately
a year between the command to write the scroll and its public proclamation.
The chapter is in three parts. First, there is a summary of everything that
happened from the time God commanded Jeremiah to produce the scroll
until it was publicly read (36:1–8). Second, there is a detailed account of
what happened on the day the scroll was read (36:9–26). Third, there is a
summary of the aftermath, when Jeremiah and Baruch in hiding produced a
new copy of the scroll (36:27–32). But because verses 1–8 are a summary of
what happened over the course of about a year, we cannot be sure about the
precise chronology of the events they recount. Thus, Jeremiah's assertion that

he was not permitted to go to the temple (36:5) may not have been made until late in 604; it does not tell us precisely when the prohibition was issued. His forlorn expression of hope that the people might still repent (36:7) does not reflect any true optimism or expectation of change and thus does not imply that he still entertained any notion that Jerusalem could yet be spared.

It is at least clear that when the scroll was finally read in December of 604, Jeremiah had already been forbidden from entering the temple precinct, and thus Baruch took the scroll to the temple and publicly read it (36:8). This happened during a time of fasting, when the people were making an outward show of piety toward YHWH and when the temple district would have been especially crowded. The fast may also imply that the drought presupposed in Jeremiah 14–15 was ongoing. Baruch read the scroll at one of the temple gates, where people would have had to pass by in large numbers. A certain official, Micaiah son of Gemariah, heard Baruch read the scroll and immediately reported this to a group of other officials, and these men had Baruch brought to them to give them a private reading of its contents. The scroll alarmed them, and they knew they had to report the matter to the king (being inevitable that he would hear of it anyway). At least some of the men still had respect for the prophet and told Baruch that he and Jeremiah had to go into hiding. They then took the scroll to Jehoiakim in his winter residence, and a scribe named Elishama read it to the king. As he did so, the king would from time to time take what he had just read, cut it from the scroll, and throw it into a fireplace. Thus Jehoiakim had disdainfully burned the word of God:

> The king and all his servants who heard all these words showed no fear, and they did not tear their clothes. (Jer. 36:24)

The public release of the contents of the scroll and Jehoiakim's reception of it marked the fact that Jerusalem's destruction was now truly irrevocable. The people would not turn away from their apostasy and immorality, and YHWH would not turn away from his decision to destroy the city. This moment created an irreversible theological division in Jerusalem, with the prophet on one side, and the king, priests, and people on the other. It was not the beginning of the process of Jeremiah's alienation from his people and his abandonment of praying for them; it was the culmination. We should assume that this took place sometime after Jeremiah was forbidden from making intercession for the city. Having seen how Jehoiakim received the message of the scroll, Jeremiah fully accepted the justice of the prohibition against intercession.

After the burning of the scroll, Jeremiah and Baruch were in hiding for an unstated period in an unstated location. They produced a new copy of the scroll, and it grew as new oracles were added to it (36:32). This implies that the scroll became the foundational document for what would eventually become the book of Jeremiah, an issue that will be explored further in chapter 7. Jeremiah

25:1–13 concludes the original Baruch scroll, and the bleak contents of that passage tell us something of why Jehoiakim and his men were so alarmed:

> Listen! I am sending to retrieve all the tribes of the north and King Nebuchadnezzar of Babylon, my servant, says YHWH. And I will bring them against this land and against its inhabitants, and against all these nations around. I will obliterate them and make them an object of horror and of hissing and of unending disgrace. (Jer. 25:9)

Jeremiah in Hiding

Jeremiah 36:19 states that at the time of the reading of the Baruch scroll, officials sympathetic to the prophet and his scribe were alarmed for their safety: "Go off and hide, you and Jeremiah, and let no one know where you are!"

The book does not directly state how long Jeremiah and Baruch were in hiding or where they were. It is difficult to find a message of Jeremiah during Jehoiakim's reign that may be dated to after the burning of the scroll, and it is likely that they remained away for some eight years, until Jehoiakim died in 597. They were probably outside of Jerusalem and likely even outside Judah.

Jeremiah 26:20–23 briefly relates the story of how Uriah, a prophet whose messages agreed with Jeremiah's, fled to Egypt to escape the retribution of Jehoiakim. However, Jehoiakim's agents managed to extract him from Egypt. After he was returned to Jerusalem, he was executed with a sword. We are not told precisely when this happened, except that it was in Jehoiakim's reign. The book places the story of Uriah's death immediately after the account of Jeremiah's temple sermon (26:1–19), but this is a literary and not a chronological placement. It is meant to show the reader that the threats against Jeremiah's life were not frivolous matters; his murder was a real possibility.

At the time of the temple sermon, the more devout men were able to persuade the secular and religious aristocracy that they would only bring guilt on themselves if they murdered Jeremiah, and they noted that the prophet Micah had said things similar to what Jeremiah had preached but had not been killed for it (26:17–19). Also, Jehoiakim was not involved in the threats against Jeremiah at the time of the temple sermon. But by the time of the reading of the Baruch scroll, no one was able to dissuade Jeremiah's opponents from committing violence, and the king was the driving force behind the efforts to slay him. So too, the king was personally involved in persecuting Uriah:

> Also, another man who prophesied in the name of YHWH was Uriah son of Shemaiah from Kiriath Jearim. And he prophesied the same things against this city and this land as Jeremiah did. And King Jehoiakim and all his officers and officials heard his words, and the king was determined to kill him. But Uriah heard about it, was scared, and fled to Egypt. But King Jehoiakim sent some Egyptians, along with Elnathan son of Akbor and [some other Judahite] men [to find him]. They brought Uriah out of

Egypt and took him to King Jehoiakim, who had him executed by sword and had his body thrown into the burial place of the common people. (Jer. 26:20–23)

Interestingly, Lachish Letter 3 mentions a delegation to Egypt: "And to your servant it has been reported that the general of the army, Coniah, son of Elnathan, has gone down to enter Egypt, and he has sent to fetch from here Hodaviah, the son of Ahijah, and his men."[19] The purpose of this delegation would have been to plead for Egyptian help; it would not have been the same delegation that extracted Uriah from Egypt. However, if Coniah's father Elnathan was the same Elnathan son of Akbor who went after Uriah, it tells us that the family of Elnathan had friends in high places in Egypt and were prominent members of the pro-Egyptian faction in Jerusalem.

The execution of Uriah probably occurred after the reading of the Baruch scroll, as this was the incident that caused the king's rage to boil over. The execution demonstrated that any prophet who supported Jeremiah instead of the king did so at the risk of his life. This implies that Jeremiah and Baruch, like Uriah, fled the country. It also shows how deep Jehoiakim's hostility toward Jeremiah had become; it was not likely to subside with the passing of a few years. Therefore, the conclusion that Jeremiah and Baruch were well away from Jerusalem until Jehoiakim was out of the picture, an exile of some eight years, is reasonable.

As noted above, the book does not specify Jeremiah's place of exile. However, one baffling problem in the book may shed light on this. For some reason, the oracle concerning Moab (48:1–47) is far longer than any other oracle against a foreign nation except for the one directed at Babylon (50:1–51:58), which is understandably the longest, since Babylon was the world power that destroyed Jerusalem. At forty-seven verses, however, the oracle against Moab is considerably longer than the oracle concerning Egypt (46:2–26), despite the fact that Egypt played a much greater role in Judah's history at this time than Moab did. Apart from being strangely long, the oracle displays precise geographical knowledge of the nation, naming the following sites: Nebo, Kiriathaim, Heshbon, Horonaim, the ascent of Luhith, Dibon (referring to the Amorite Dibon-gab, not the Dibon in Edom), Aroer, the Arnon River, Holon, Jahzah, Mephaath, Beth-diblathaim, Beth-gamul, Beth-meon, Kerioth, Bozrah, Kir-heres, Sibmah, Jazer, and Eglath-shelishiyah. This list is astonishing for its sweeping inclusion of such an array of names of locations, and has no parallel in the oracles against other nations. The oracle against Moab's neighbor Ammon (49:1–6), for example, names only the Ammonite capital Rabbah. The oracle against Moab is also a good deal more personal than the others, reflecting both Jeremiah's disgust at the attitude of some Moabites but also his appreciation for the land. An example is Jeremiah 48:30–32:

---

19.   Di Vito, "Lachish Letters," 127.

I know, says YHWH, his arrogance.
His boasts are not true. What he does is not true.
And so, I wail for Moab. I cry out for all of Moab.
I mourn for the people of Kir-heres.
More than for Jazer I weep for you, vine of Sibmah!
Your branches crossed the sea. They extended as far as Jazer.
A destroyer falls upon your summer fruit and your vintage.

This intimate and extensive knowledge of Moab suggests that this was where Jeremiah and Baruch were in exile for the remainder of Jehoiakim's reign. This supposition, in turn, explains why the oracle against Moab stands out from all the others. One may argue that if Jehoiakim was able to find and extract Uriah from Egypt, he surely would have been able to do the same for Jeremiah in nearby Moab. In reality, we know nothing specific about how or why the king was able to find Uriah but not Jeremiah. However, we know that Egypt sought to maintain good terms with Jerusalem because it wanted Judah as an ally and buffer against Babylon. For diplomatic reasons, Egypt would have been willing to grant the extradition of Uriah. We do not know if Jehoiakim had a good relationship with Moab. Jeremiah simply attributed his survival to divine protection:

And the king commanded Jerahmeel the king's son, Seraiah son of Azriel, and Shelemiah son of Abdeel to capture Baruch the scribe and Jeremiah the prophet. But YHWH hid them. (Jer. 36:26)

Wherever they went, Jeremiah and Baruch managed to avoid Jehoiakim's detection, unlike the unfortunate Uriah.

MINISTRY UNDER JEHOIACHIN

As already noted, the circumstances surrounding the demise of Jehoiakim are not entirely clear. But we know that at the end of his reign his kingdom was in rebellion against Babylon and that his son Jehoiachin followed him on the throne. The latter reigned only three months before surrendering to Nebuchadnezzar's forces and being taken with the exiles of 597 BC to Babylon (2 Kings 24:8–17). A brief oracle that directly concerns Jehoiachin is found at Jeremiah 22:24–27:

As I live, says YHWH, even if you, Coniah [= Jehoiachin] son of Jehoia-kim, king of Judah, were a signet ring on my right hand, I would still pull you off. I will deliver you into the hands of those who seek your life, into the hands of those you fear: into the hands of Nebuchadnezzar king of Babylon and into the hands of the Babylonians. I will hurl you and the mother who gave you birth into another country, where neither of you was born, and that is where you both will die. You will never come back to the land to which you will yearn to return.

Since Jehoiachin is addressed as king, the oracle comes from during his brief reign.[20] At the time of the oracle, he had not yet been taken to exile, as it is described as being in the future. Jeremiah evidently knew of the young king's bad character, and declared that even if Jehoiachin were YHWH's signet ring, his most precious possession, YHWH would yank it off and throw it away. We are not told anything of Jeremiah's circumstances when he gave this oracle. If he had been in Moab, he could have quickly returned to Jerusalem when Jehoiakim was no longer a threat. However, one wonders whether it would have been safe to enter the city while Jehoiachin was in control and the Babylonians were outside the gates. It is more likely that he sent the oracle in an epistle before personally returning to Judah, which he did only after Jehoiachin had been carried away to Babylon. The oracle speaks of Jehoiachin as a repugnant man, a ring that God wants to yank off of his hand, as though it were a loathsome bug. This implies that Jeremiah would have wanted to stay far from the man.

---

20. In the expression כָּנְיָהוּ בֶן־יְהוֹיָקִים מֶלֶךְ יְהוּדָה, the phrase מֶלֶךְ יְהוּדָה, "king of Judah," should be understood to be in apposition to כָּנְיָהוּ, not יְהוֹיָקִים. If the meaning were "Coniah, son of king Jehoiakim," we would expect to see בֶן־הַמֶּלֶךְ יְהוֹיָקִים. The formula וְכָנְיָהוּ בֶן־יְהוֹיָקִים מֶלֶךְ־יְהוּדָה is also used in 24:1, where it clearly refers to Jehoiachin as the king.

CHAPTER 4

THE LIFE OF JEREMIAH:
FROM ZEDEKIAH TO THE EGYPTIAN EXILE

T he experiences and oracles of Jeremiah from the reigns of Josiah to Jehoiachin tell us why Judah's destruction could not be delayed or avoided. In the reign of Zedekiah and its aftermath, we see the agonizing story of the city's destruction played out before us.

MINISTRY UNDER ZEDEKIAH

Two Baskets of Figs

Jeremiah 24 contains a single oracle of YHWH. It is introduced as follows:

> YHWH showed me two baskets of figs that were set before the temple of YHWH. This was after King Nebuchadnezzar of Babylon had deported King Jeconiah [= Jehoiachin] son of Jehoiakim of Judah from Jerusalem, together with the officials of Judah, the artisans, and the smiths, when he took them to Babylon. (Jer. 24:1)

While it is possible that his seeing the two baskets was purely a vision, it is more likely that Jeremiah actually saw these baskets among offerings at the temple and that YHWH spoke to him through what he was looking at.[1] The episode is thus placed early in the reign of Zedekiah, and indicates that Jeremiah was back in Jerusalem and once again permitted to enter the grounds of the temple. The new king, Zedekiah, was more deferential toward Jeremiah and recognized that he was a true prophet; for all his faults, he did not view

---

1. By contrast, when Ezekiel saw the temple in a vision, he clearly states that he was physically still in his home in Babylonia when the hand of YHWH touched him, enabling him to see what was happening in Jerusalem (Ezek. 8:1–2).

Jeremiah with the kind of implacable hatred that Jehoiakim (and probably Jehoiachin) did.

What Jeremiah saw was very simple: One basket contained excellent, succulent-looking figs, and the other contained disgusting figs. Perhaps they were overripe and rotting and partially devoured by vermin. The first would be accepted as a suitable offering to YHWH and the other would be rejected and thrown out. YHWH used this to give the prophet a counterintuitive message: Those who were taken to Babylon were accepted by God as the remnant and the basis for the survival of Judaism, while those who remained in Jerusalem were rejected and fit only for destruction. The people of Jerusalem would have regarded those taken away as the cursed and unhappy few whom YHWH had set apart for punishment, while those who remained were righteous in God's eyes. Or they would have thought that the Jehoiachin exile was only a temporary setback; Jehoiachin and all the others would soon be brought back and resume their rightful place in Jerusalem. But YHWH told Jeremiah that this was not so. Those taken to Babylon would live in relative safety while Jerusalem burned, and they would form the nucleus for a new Jewish culture that would survive and thrive. Knowing this, Jeremiah sent a letter to the exiles telling them not to entertain false hopes of a return from Babylon in their lifetimes.

Letters to the Exiles

Jeremiah 29 gives extracts of letters Jeremiah wrote to the Jehoiachin exiles along with a summary of the reaction his letter provoked. Jeremiah's message to the exiles contains four points. First, the Jews in Babylon must settle in for a long stay and not hold on to the hope of a swift return to Jerusalem. They are to build homes, establish businesses, raise families, and expect to see a second or third generation born in Babylonia (29:5–7). Second, they should disregard any so-called prophet who promises a quick end to the exile. Such men do not speak the authentic word of YHWH (29:8–9, 15). Third, after a seventy-year exile, when the people have learned to truly fear YHWH, he will bring them back and reestablish Jerusalem (29:10–14). Fourth, and concerning the people back in Jerusalem under King Zedekiah, there is nothing in their future but military disaster, plague, famine, and death. Jerusalem will be destroyed (29:16–23).

The oracle of the figs (24:1–10) took place before Jeremiah wrote to the captives in Babylon. This is evident because the letter alludes to the oracle. In 24:10, YHWH concludes his oracle over the bad figs:

> And I will send upon them sword, famine, and pestilence, until they are entirely eliminated from the land that I gave to them and their ancestors.

In the letter to the exiles, Jeremiah similarly writes:

> Thus says YHWH Sabaoth, I am going to let loose on them sword, famine, and pestilence, and I will make them like rotten figs that are so bad they cannot be eaten. (Jer. 29:17)

Jeremiah's letter offended a self-styled prophet among the exiles in Babylonia, Shemaiah, and an exchange of letters followed, summarized in 29:24–32.[2] Shemaiah, whose predictions of a quick return to Jerusalem Jeremiah contradicted, wrote to the priest Zephaniah in Jerusalem and demanded that Jeremiah be silenced and punished. Instead, Zephaniah read the letter to Jeremiah, who then pronounced judgment on Shemaiah, saying that none of his descendants would live to see the restoration of Jerusalem. Zephaniah's deference to Jeremiah shows that at least some in Jerusalem had high regard for Jeremiah, possibly because his predictions regarding Jehoiachin's swift demise had been vindicated.

Jeremiah's Yoke and Hananiah's Response

In this episode, Jeremiah suddenly appeared among a group of high officials and delegates from other states with a yoke on his neck (Jer. 27–28). He did this to symbolize how all the nations in the region would be made subject to the Babylonians. He then gave what was as much a political message as it was a sermon. He exhorted not only Zedekiah but also "the king of Edom, the king of Moab, the king of the Ammonites, the king of Tyre, and the king of Sidon" (27:3) to abandon all hope of resisting Babylon. These were the nations that Zedekiah hoped to draw into an anti-Babylonian alliance. But Jeremiah warned them that God, the maker of heaven and earth, had chosen to give dominion for a time to Nebuchadnezzar and his army (27:5–7). Therefore, the only prudent thing to do was to surrender to him. Those who did so would survive, and those who did not would suffer terrible calamities.

Hananiah made a counterprophecy to what Jeremiah had said: God was about to break the power of Babylon, so that "within two years" the Jehoiachin exiles would return. To emphasize his rebuttal to Jeremiah, he took the yoke from Jeremiah's neck and broke it (28:10–11). Jeremiah's response was "Amen! May YHWH do so!" (28:6), indicating he had no desire to see Jerusalem in ruins. But he issued a simple challenge:

> As for the prophet who prophesies peace, when the word of that prophet comes true, then that prophet will be known to be one that YHWH truly sent. (Jer. 28:9)

---

2.   His name is given as Shemaiah the Nehelamite (שְׁמַעְיָהוּ הַנֶּחֱלָמִי), but this is odd because no town named Nehelam is known to us. Of course, it is possible that the town's existence has disappeared from memory, but it may be that this is an artificial gentilic meant as an insult to Shemaiah. It appears to be a *niphal* form of חלם, to "dream" (the root is not extant elsewhere in the *niphal*, but it is possible that the form did exist with a meaning "dreamed"). If so, his name means something like "Shemaiah of Dreamtown." Note that Jeremiah especially mocks prophets who claim to have had a revelation in a dream (Jer. 23:25–32).

It would take two years to see if Hananiah's prediction about the fall of Babylon would come true, but it appears that most of the people believed Hananiah had decisively rebuked Jeremiah. His act would lead Judah again to rebel against Babylonian suzerainty, which would in turn cause incalculable suffering during the siege and fall of Jerusalem. But within two months of Hananiah's rebuke, Jeremiah received another message from YHWH. He was to go to Hananiah and tell him that Babylon would not fall and that the nations were going to be under an unbreakable iron yoke. Hananiah himself would soon die for having convinced the people to believe a lie (Jer. 28:15–16). This prediction was proven true: "And Hananiah the prophet died in that very year, in the seventh month" (Jer. 28:17). This is the only occasion when something akin to a miracle was attributed to Jeremiah.

When did this episode occur? Jeremiah 27:1 says that it happened "in the beginning of the reign of King Zedekiah." One might suppose that this was in the first year of Zedekiah's reign, in 597, but 28:1 more precisely dates the events of chapters 27–28 to the middle of Zedekiah's fourth year: "And in that year, at the beginning of the reign of King Zedekiah of Judah, in the fifth month of the fourth year. . . ."

Also, despite the present order of the chapters, the episode of Jeremiah's yoke (Jer. 27–28) happened after the letter to the exiles (Jer. 29). The fate of the exiles was a pressing concern both in Jerusalem and among the Jews in Babylon, suggesting that Jeremiah would have wanted to address it as soon as possible. If the letter to the exiles was not sent until the fourth year of Zedekiah at the earliest, after the events of chapters 27–28, the Jews in Babylon would have been in limbo all that time, not knowing what they were supposed to do. Another indication that the yoke episode came after the letters to Babylon is that both episodes deal with false prophets and their promise that Babylon would soon fall. Jeremiah's letter predicting a long exile was opposed by several the false prophets (29:15, 21, 24–28). And in his message concerning the yoke, Jeremiah declares:

> And you must not listen to your prophets, your diviners, your dreamers, your magicians, or your sorcerers, who say to you, "You will not serve the king of Babylon." (27:9; see also vv. 14–18)

By the time of the yoke episode, therefore, Jeremiah had already come into conflict with a gaggle of false prophets who had denied the long exile that Jeremiah had predicted in his letter.[3] Finally, we can account for the placement of chapter 29 after chapters 27–28: The prophecy of restoration in 29:10–14 anticipates the oracles of salvation in chapters 30–33.

---

3.   For a useful survey of the practices and functions of prophets outside of Israel in the ancient Near East, see R. R. Wilson, *Prophecy and Society in Ancient Israel* (Philadelphia: Fortress, 1980), 89–134.

Zedekiah's Request for Intercession

And so it was that Jerusalem foolishly took up arms against Babylon. As the noose began to tighten around Jerusalem, Zedekiah and his officials were prepared to humble themselves enough to ask that Jeremiah would intercede for them and pray for God to save the city from the Babylonians. There are two accounts of this embassy to the prophet: Jeremiah 21:1–10 and 37:10. In the former account the delegates are Pashhur son of Malchiah and the priest Zephaniah son of Maaseiah, and in the latter account they are Jehucal son of Shelemiah and Zephaniah son of Maaseiah. This is not a contradiction, however. It is unlikely that either account gives a full roster of all the delegates, and it is also unlikely that there were two separate delegations to Jeremiah making exactly the same request. Jeremiah 37:4–5 gives us two important details about the dating of this event:

> Now Jeremiah was still coming and going among the people, and they had not yet put him in prison. And the army of Pharaoh had come out of Egypt, and the Chaldeans who were besieging Jerusalem heard news of them, and [the Babylonians] pulled back from [besieging] Jerusalem.

This latter detail refers to the attempt by Pharaoh Apries (= Hophra) to come to Jerusalem's rescue during an early phase of the Babylonian siege. The precise date is disputed; it probably occurred sometime in between the latter half of 588 and early 587.

Zedekiah was evidently hoping YHWH would give victory to the Egyptians so that the Babylonians would be driven away or, failing that, was looking for a repeat of the spectacular miracle under Hezekiah, when God slew the Assyrian army attacking Jerusalem. A summary of Zedekiah's appeal is in Jeremiah 21:2:

> Seek YHWH's favor on our behalf, for King Nebuchadnezzar of Babylon is making war against us. Perhaps YHWH will perform a miraculous deed for us, as he has often done, and will remove him from us.

Jeremiah's response was decidedly negative: Hophra would be beaten back by the Babylonians, and there would be no divine intervention to save Jerusalem (37:6–10). The account in 21:8–10 includes an exhortation for the people to go out and surrender to the Babylonians right away, before they face catastrophic death and destruction.

The Breaking of the Earthenware Decanter

In Jeremiah 19, the prophet dramatically declares that God's decree that Jerusalem must be destroyed is fixed and irrevocable. In the narrative, he bought an earthenware decanter (a vessel that would be lighter and more delicate than a heavy jar) and took some of the civil administration and senior priests to the Ben Hinnom valley at the Potsherd Gate (19:1–2).[4] Before these men, he denounced the practice of child sacrifice that was carried out there and declared that Jerusalem was about to suffer catastrophic destruction:

> And I will nullify the plans of Judah and Jerusalem in this place, and I will make them fall by the sword before their enemies, and by the hand of those who seek their life. I will give their dead bodies for food to the birds of the sky and to the wild animals of the earth. And I will make this city into a horrifying desolation, a thing to be hissed at; everyone who passes by it will be horrified and will hiss because of all its destruction. And I will make them eat the flesh of their sons and the flesh of their daughters, and all shall eat the flesh of their neighbors in the siege, and in the distress brought on by their enemies and those who seek their lives. (Jer. 19:7–9)

Jeremiah then smashed the decanter so that it was beyond repair, as a visible parable of what would happen to Jerusalem, its leaders, and its people. The audience included a priest named Pashhur, the son of Immer, who was a high official in the temple and had a reputation as a prophet. He struck Jeremiah and had him put in stocks located at the upper Benjamin Gate near the temple. Jeremiah was confined there all night and released the next morning (Jer. 20:1–2). Jeremiah then pronounced another harrowing prophecy against Jerusalem and against Pashhur personally:

> YHWH has not called your name "Pashhur" but "Horror Everywhere." For thus says YHWH: I am making you a horror to yourself and to all who love you; and they shall fall by the sword of their enemies, and your eyes will see it. And I will give all Judah into the hand of the king of Babylon; he shall carry them captive to Babylon and shall kill them with the sword. I will give all the treasury of this city, all it has acquired, all its prized belongings, and all the treasures of the kings of Judah into the hands of their enemies. And they will plunder them, seize them, and carry them to Babylon. And you, Pashhur, and all who live in your house, will go into captivity and go to Babylon. There you shall die, and there you shall be buried, you and all your friends, to whom you have prophesied falsely. (Jer. 20:3b–6)

When did this incident take place? Because of the finality and horror of the message, some argue that it probably happened either in 597, just before the Jehoiachin exile, or in 587, just before the fall of the city.[5] However, the

---

4.   The vessel called a בַּקְבֻּק is a small decanter or bottle used for a holding and pouring a liquid (*HALOT* s.v. "בַּקְבֻּק" 149). The expression מִזִּקְנֵי הָעָם וּמִזִּקְנֵי הַכֹּהֲנִים, "some of the elders of the people and some of the elders of the priests," refers to civic officials and senior priests.

5.   E.g., Peter C. Craigie, Page H. Kelley, and Joel F. Drinkard Jr., *Jeremiah 1–25*, WBC 26 (Dallas: Word, 1991), 258.

earlier date is unlikely. Jeremiah was in exile until the demise of Jehoiakim, and it is doubtful that he could have openly entered the city in the few days of the reign of Jehoiachin and commanded an assembly of leading citizens to follow him. Also, Jeremiah was imprisoned in the final days before the fall of Jerusalem and was certainly in no position to have led a delegation of leaders out to the Ben Hinnom Valley. Thus, the event happened when the city was in grave danger of falling to the Babylonians but before Jeremiah's arrest.

Who was this Pashhur, son of Immer? Identifying him will allow us to fix more precisely the date of Jeremiah 19, and we must therefore give attention to his place in the story. Unfortunately, that name occurs several times in the book of Jeremiah, and it is difficult to determine just how many Pashhurs there were.

Besides Pashhur, son of Immer, there was also a Pashhur, son of Malchiah (Jer. 21:1; 38:2). In chapter 21, he was part of the delegation from Zedekiah that asked Jeremiah to pray that YHWH save Jerusalem from Babylon. In chapter 38, after hearing Jeremiah advise the king to surrender to Babylon, he asked the king for permission to kill Jeremiah. It is not clear if this Pashhur was a priest. In Jeremiah he is never designated a priest and appears to have been a member of the royal family.[6] Even so, assuming Jeremiah did not refer to the one Pashhur by two different patronyms, the son of Immer should not be identified as the same man as the son of Malchiah.

The other Pashhur is the father of another enemy of Jeremiah, Gedeliah (Jer. 38:1). This Pashhur may have been either the son of Malchiah or the son of Immer, but we do not know. Taking the simplest path, we will deal exclusively with the priest named Pashhur son of Immer and disregard the other two.

We know from Jeremiah 19:1 that Pashhur son of Immer was one of the senior priests, and in 20:1 he is called "a chief inspector in the house of YHWH,"[7] meaning that he was a ranking official in the temple hierarchy. Some have argued that he was deported in 597 with Jehoiachin and that his place was taken by Zephaniah son of Maaseiah (29:25).[8] If so, then the oracle of Jeremiah 19 happened in the reign of Jehoiakim. But this is unlikely. First, we do not know that Pashhur and Zephaniah had the precisely same office or that only one man at a time held this position (his title lacks the definite article, suggesting that it was not a unique office). In fact, Jeremiah 29:26 explicitly states that Zephaniah replaced not Pashhur but a certain Jehoiada and that there was a plurality of officers called "inspectors" in the temple. Second, Pashhur's fate, as described in Jeremiah's prophecy above, involved extreme violence. The first deportation was a peaceful affair; it came about

---

6. On the other hand, in 1 Chronicles 9:12 and Nehemiah 11:12, a Pashhur son of Malchiah is said to have been the grandfather of the priest Adaiah. If this is the same man as Jeremiah's Pashhur son of Malchiah, then he was a priest.

7. Hebrew: פָּקִיד נָגִיד בְּבֵית יְהוָה.

8. Thus, Nola J. Opperwall, "Pashhur," *ISBE* 3:673.

after Jerusalem surrendered and not after a violent overthrow of the city. Pashhur experienced the destruction of the city and not a quiet exile.

But Jeremiah 29 does give us an important clue. In 29:26, Shemaiah appealed to Zephaniah to punish Jeremiah as follows:

> YHWH has made you priest instead of the priest Jehoiada, so that there may be inspectors in the house of YHWH to control any madman who plays the prophet, by putting him in stocks and irons.

Shemaiah's letter was publicly known (Jer. 29:29), and it encouraged the temple "inspectors" to put Jeremiah in the stocks. This suggests that Pashhur son of Immer, another priestly inspector, was willing to do what Zephaniah was not. Enraged by Jeremiah's sermon in the Ben Hinnom Valley and sensing that it gave him plausible justification for giving the prophet a painful night in stocks, he did it. Thus, the episode of Jeremiah 19:1–20:6 took place after the letters to the exiles in Babylon but before Jeremiah was imprisoned later in Zedekiah's reign. Also, we know from Jeremiah 37:11–16 that Jeremiah was arrested during the time the Babylonian army was away from Jerusalem and dealing with Pharaoh Hophra. Therefore, we can surmise that the message of Jeremiah 19 occurred earlier. It angered members of the hierarchy enough to give him a night in the stocks, but they were not ready to place him in a permanent incarceration. It is reasonable, moreover, to suppose that the message was given soon after Zedekiah's delegation to Jeremiah. The prophet now knew that there was talk in the city, even in the king's court, of a dramatic, divine intervention. The smashing of the clay decanter was a sign that there was no hope for Jerusalem. It was pointless for anyone to seek a miraculous deliverance. The issue was settled.

The Covenant Concerning the Slaves
Around the same time, another episode took place that illustrated how little regard the ruling class had for keeping faith with YHWH, recounted in Jeremiah 34:8–22. The episode began during the initial siege of Jerusalem by Babylonian forces. Zedekiah and his staff, hoping to find a way to demonstrate to YHWH the sincerity of their devotion to the law, decided to liberate their slaves (see Deut. 15:12–18). The Israelites had never been careful about obeying this law (Jer. 34:14). The leaders of Jerusalem carried out a solemn covenant ceremony in which they walked between the pieces of a sacrificed calf, symbolically taking an oath that YHWH should do to them what had been done to this animal if they failed to free their slaves (34:18). And they did grant manumission to their Israelite slaves, offering YHWH a token of good faith in the hope that he would save them from Babylon. But they then abruptly and apparently en masse used the power at their disposal to round up all their former slaves and subject them again to slavery. Instead of giving YHWH a reason to relent and to reverse his judgment against the city, they had only increased their guilt:

And you repented recently and did what is right in my eyes by each one of you proclaiming freedom to your fellow citizens. And you made a covenant before me in the house that is called by my name. But now you have turned back and profaned my name. Each of you has reclaimed the male and female slaves you had sent away free to do as they please. You compelled them to become your male and female slaves again. And so, thus says YHWH: You were not obedient to me in your act of proclaiming freedom to your people and your fellow citizens. Well then, I now proclaim freedom for you, says YHWH: freedom to fall by the sword, plague, and famine! I will make you a horror to all the kingdoms of the earth. (Jer. 34:15–17)

They made this sudden about-face because they saw that Hophra had led his forces out of Egypt to fight the Babylonians, who were in turn forced to lift the siege of Jerusalem to confront this threat. Confident that Hophra would drive away the Babylonians and that the danger to their city was gone, the Jerusalem aristocracy felt free to disregard their newly made covenant with YHWH. For this, they received the most terrible denunciation, together with the promise that the Babylonians would soon be back:

And I will make the men who transgressed my covenant and who did not keep the terms of the covenant that they made before me like the calf that they cut into two parts and passed between them. And I will give the officials of Judah, the officials of Jerusalem, the eunuchs, the priests, and all the people of the land who passed between the parts of the calf over to their enemies and to those who seek their lives. Their corpses will become food for the birds of the air and the wild animals of the earth. And I will give King Zedekiah of Judah and his officials into the hands of their enemies and of those who seek their lives, and into the hand of the army of the king of Babylon, which has withdrawn from you. And look, I am issuing a command, says YHWH, and I will bring them back to this city; and they will fight against it, and take it, and burn it with fire. I will make the towns of Judah into a desolation without inhabitant. (Jer. 34:18–22)

The Jerusalem leadership had once again proven itself to be utterly beyond redemption.

Jeremiah's Arrest and the Field in Anathoth

Jeremiah 37–44 is generally understood to be a single, contiguous narrative that recounts a series of events in their proper historical sequence. This is generally true, but one must make two qualifications. First, at least one event is given out of sequence. In 39:15–18, there is an oracle given for Ebed-Melech, a eunuch in the royal palace. Jeremiah gave this oracle while he was a prisoner at the court of the guard before the city fell. However, the account occurs in the narrative sequence after the description of Jerusalem's fall. Second, parts of Jeremiah's story that are recounted in chapters 37–44 are not necessarily told in full; some of the details are found in other parts of the book. This is true of the event described below, Jeremiah's acquisition of a field in Anathoth. To fully understand what happened, one must read 37:11–21 in conjunction with 32:1–15.

The initial events are related in 37:11–16. Jeremiah received word that a piece of land that had been part of the estate of his extended family had fallen vacant, apparently because a senior member of the family had died, and that he should go there to deal with the settlement of the property. In the kinship hierarchy of the family, his relationship to the deceased was close enough that he had a right to at least part of the land. This may have involved "redeeming" the property; that is, he would purchase the land, keeping it in the family, and the money would go to support other family members. The summons to go to Anathoth came while the Babylonian army was away dealing with the Egyptians under Pharaoh Hophra, and thus travel outside the city was possible. When he tried to go out the Benjamin Gate, however, he was arrested on charges of treason, the claim being that he was deserting to join the Babylonians. He was beaten and put into the "cistern house," probably no more than a shack that covered a cistern, that belonged to Jonathan the scribe. This would have made for a wretched confinement. The cistern shack offered minimal protection, and he perhaps had to crouch or lie down at the edge of the cistern, risking death if he should fall into it. He was there for "many days" (37:16, 20).

Finally, Zedekiah sent for Jeremiah secretly, implying that he respected Jeremiah's prophetic office but was unwilling to take a stand against the leading citizens, who were implacably hostile to the prophet. This meeting took place in the royal palace. He asked if there was a word from YHWH, and was told that there was: "You will be handed over to the king of Babylon" (37:17c). Jeremiah pleaded to be placed in better quarters than the cistern house, and was moved to the court of the guard, where he was given a daily allowance of food until supplies in Jerusalem ran out (37:18–21).

At this point, we follow the course of events by turning back to Jeremiah 32. In the historical sequence of events, the events recounted at 32:6–15 took place after 37:11–16. In chapter 32, Jeremiah is imprisoned at the court of the guard, and he has another meeting with Zedekiah. The king complains to the prophet, asking why he always predicts disaster for Jerusalem instead of giving a favorable oracle (32:1–5). Jeremiah's answer to the king completes the story of the Anathoth land (32:6–15).

Jeremiah, now in prison, had apparently given up on, or even forgotten about, the matter of the land in Anathoth. But then he received a message from YHWH that his cousin Hanamel would come to him to tell him to "redeem" the Anathoth property. This would require Jeremiah to purchase it to keep it in the family. This event was undoubtedly related to his previous effort to go to Anathoth; it is highly unlikely that they are two unrelated incidents concerning land. In both cases the issue involved the settlement of real property in Anathoth, and in both cases Jeremiah had some obligation to be involved due to kinship ties. In other words, when he first was informed of the Anathoth land, Jeremiah tried to go there to fulfill his duty, but he was arrested and imprisoned. After some time, his cousin Hanamel visited in prison regarding the same issue, the redemption of the land.

Hanamel did indeed come as YHWH had predicted. Possibly Jeremiah's cousin had become impoverished because of the warfare and social turmoil, and he desired to sell the property to obtain some money. He or another family member had first contacted Jeremiah when the Babylonian army was away fighting Hophra and there was some possibility that the land could have value, should the Babylonians be permanently driven away. But Jeremiah was arrested and imprisoned, and Hanamel was left in charge of the estate. But when the Babylonians came back to renew the siege, Hanamel fled behind the walls of Jerusalem.

The land in Anathoth now had no value at all; the enemy army was devastating the whole region, and Jerusalem itself was in danger of being overrun. But being under duress, Hanamel contacted Jeremiah again, hoping to get some money to sustain himself. Although we know nothing of Hanamel beyond what is related here, he was probably using the duty of land redemption as leverage to force his cousin to buy it; certainly no one else would have had any interest in the property.[9] Also, Jeremiah's friends and relatives in Anathoth hated him and had threatened to murder him (Jer. 11:21), and Hanamel may have been among their number. At the very least, Hanamel was acting in his own interests and not Jeremiah's, and the prophet would have known this. But because of the forewarning he received from YHWH, Jeremiah knew it was God's will for him to purchase the land even though it was not in his financial interest:

> And Jeremiah said, "The word of YHWH came to me: Listen, Hanamel son of Shallum your uncle is coming to you to say, 'Acquire my field at Anathoth, because it is your right and duty to acquire it.' And my cousin Hanamel came to me, just as YHWH said, at the courtyard of the guard. And he said, 'Acquire my field at Anathoth in the land of Benjamin. For you have the obligation to take possession of it for its redemption. Buy it!'

---

9.   Jeremiah 32:7 tells us that Hanamel's father was named Shallum. Wilson suggests that this Shallum was the man of that name who was married to the prophetess Huldah (2 Kings 22:14), asserting that "there is no particular reason to deny this" (*Prophecy and Society in Ancient Israel*, 223). But there is no particular reason to affirm it, either. Smothers, Keown, and Scalise point out that the name Shallum was not rare (*Jeremiah 26–52*, 152). It was the birth name of Jehoahaz (Jer. 22:11; Jehoahaz was his throne name), and as many as fourteen men in the Old Testament had that name. See also Holladay, who notes that Huldah's husband and Hanamel's father appear to come from entirely different family circles (*Jeremiah 2*, 213).

I knew that this was the word of YHWH, so I bought the field at Anathoth from my cousin Hanamel and weighed out seventeen shekels of silver for him." (Jer. 32:6–9)

He thus handed over the stipulated price, signed the legal documents, and entrusted them to Baruch with instructions to put them in an earthenware jar so that they would last a long time. This purchase was obviously foolish. Jeremiah, more than anyone else, knew that the city would soon fall amid massive destruction and death. The whole region would be left desolate, the Babylonians would control everything, and Jeremiah's property rights would have no value. But his purchase was a prophetic sign, a token of the promise that the Jews would return and Jerusalem would be inhabited again (32:16–44). The act was analogous to Abraham's purchase of the cave of Machpelah, a token of the faith that someday Israel would take possession of all the land (Gen. 23).

Jeremiah Almost Murdered

A group of ranking officials, including Shephatiah son of Mattan, Gedaliah son of Pashhur, Jucal son of Shelemiah, and Pashhur son of Malchiah, decided to do away with Jeremiah once and for all (Jer. 38:1–6). Context implies that this took place while he was imprisoned at the court of the guard (see 37:21; 38:26), but 38:1 says that these aristocrats "heard the words that Jeremiah had been speaking to all the people."[10] This does not mean that the imprisoned Jeremiah could go out before the people and continue making public speeches. Before he was arrested and locked up, his message was widely known throughout Jerusalem, as indicated by the anger directed at him when he tried to leave the city (37:13–15). Many people probably believed or feared that Jeremiah's predictions would prove true, and his imprisonment did nothing to convince them that he was wrong. Also, he probably was visited by the occasional delegation (apart from the private visits by Zedekiah), and he would have repeated his warning to them as well. Word would have gotten out that his message of doom was unchanged.

Lachish Letter 3 contains an enigmatic report about "the prophet" in the correspondence of the officers. It is possible (but not provable) that this prophet was Jeremiah, who probably had sufficient stature to simply be called "the prophet." The letter cryptically quotes someone as having said, "Beware!" If the prophet is Jeremiah, "Beware" may summarize his message opposing seeking an alliance with Egypt. Or it could be from a member of the pro-Egyptian faction, warning the readers to beware of listening to the discouraging messages of Jeremiah.[11]

---

10. Neither the verb וַיִּשְׁמַע nor the participle מְדַבֵּר imply that Jeremiah was giving sermons during his imprisonment. The pluperfect translation "had been speaking" is reasonable.

11. But Di Vito cautions, "it is impossible to specify the object of this laconic warning" ("Lachish Letters," 127).

The essence of Jeremiah's discouraging oracle is given in 38:2–3:

Thus says YHWH: Whoever stays in this city will die by the sword, by famine, and by plague, but whoever goes out to the Chaldeans will live and will hold on to his life as his share of what can be snatched from the disaster.[12] And he will live. Thus says YHWH: Beyond any doubt, this city will be given into the hand of the army of the king of Babylon and be captured.

One can see why Jeremiah was called a deserter in 37:13 and why the leaders thought that his message was "discouraging the men who are left in this city." Like all tyrants, they could not tolerate any message that contradicted official government policy; Jeremiah was undermining their propaganda. They equated blind obedience to their decrees with patriotism, and so they considered him and anyone who listened to him a traitor. Although subsequent events showed that Zedekiah was coming to believe that Jeremiah spoke the truth, he lacked the courage to oppose these men and told them, "All right, he is in your hands" (38:5). They then put Jeremiah into a nearby cistern, in the court of the guard, by lowering him down with a rope (38:6), and left him there to die of starvation and exposure. The cistern was empty except for mud at the bottom. A cistern is not a well; it is a bulbous-shaped, underground, artificial reservoir. After men dug it out and sealed it with plaster to limit leakage, it would be filled during the rainy season. But this one was almost entirely dry (Judah had recently had a severe drought).

One may wonder, since their intent was that Jeremiah would die, why they did not kill him outright or physically toss him into the cistern instead of lowering him safely with ropes. Probably they had enough fear of his prophetic reputation that they did not want to commit direct violence against his person. They supposed that they could escape guilt if he died quietly and out of sight. They might have also wanted to have some kind of plausible deniability before the public; they could claim, "We did no violence to him."

Happily, Jeremiah was saved from his plight. An Ethiopian eunuch named Ebed-Melech heard what they had done to him and immediately went to the king to report on it. We can only speculate about this man's background. Perhaps he had been acquired as a slave and brought to Jerusalem. But if so, he had proven himself to be a capable man and had been manumitted to serve the royal house. He had access to the king and the freedom to bring an item to his attention; it is unlikely that a slave could have done this. His name, Ebed-Melech, is certainly not his given name; it simply means "king's servant." The

---

12.   More literally, וְהָיְתָה־לּוֹ נַפְשׁוֹ לְשָׁלָל means, "and his life will be his plunder," but the idea is that although this person may lose everything else as plunder for the Babylonians, he will be able to come away with his life.

term "servant," however, does not imply that he was a slave. Every high official was said to be a "servant" of the king.

When Ebed-Melech told Zedekiah how the aforementioned high officials had put Jeremiah in a cistern to kill him, the king ordered the eunuch get three men and pull Jeremiah out (38:10). One wonders why the king, who previously had been so obsequious before Shephatiah son of Mattan and company, suddenly acted against them, as he surely knew that they would quickly learn what he had done. Probably this kind of disgraceful treatment of the prophet was more than the king could bear. More than that, the book portrays Zedekiah not as a determined enemy of Jeremiah, as his brother Jehoiakim had been, but as weak and vacillating man, only occasionally rising up to do the right thing. The narrative adds that when Ebed-Melech pulled Jeremiah up from the cistern, he first found some rags for him to put under his arms so that he would not suffer rope burns during the process. This demonstrates that Ebed-Melech was concerned even for relatively minor matters related to the prophet's suffering.

After he was saved, Jeremiah was returned to the court of the guard (38:13), and evidently the officials made no other effort to take Jeremiah's life. This suggests that there was still enough regard for (or fear of) Jeremiah in Jerusalem that they could not risk word getting out that they had tried to kill him twice.

During his second stay at the court of the guard, Jeremiah received a word from YHWH promising a reward to Ebed-Melech for his heroic action: He would escape retribution from the Jerusalem nobility and would survive the fall of the city (39:15–18). As noted above, this passage is chronologically out of sequence (the rest of ch. 39 describes events at the fall of Jerusalem), unlike what we generally see in chapters 37–44. Therefore, 39:15–18 is in its present context for literary and theological reasons. The prior text, 39:11–14, describes how after taking the city, the Babylonians liberated Jeremiah from captivity and their commander Nebuzaradan gave him freedom to go wherever he chose. By setting the oracle for Ebed-Melech here in chapter 39, the reader is reminded that the two people who showed Jeremiah respect and kindness were an Ethiopian eunuch and a Babylonian general. The Israelite hierarchy, by contrast, were routinely hostile to him. This is analogous to the story of the Rechabites (ch. 35), which also contrasts the fidelity of outsiders with the faithlessness of the people of Jerusalem.

Sometime after this, Zedekiah (who, for his part, did not want to risk being seen doing anything else that would offend the officials) had another private conversation with Jeremiah (38:14–26). Jerusalem was now approaching its last days, and Zedekiah wanted to know if there was anything he could do to save himself and his family (this meeting is discussed below).

A Note on the Rhetorical Strategy of Narrative in Jeremiah
The episode of the purchase of the land at Anathoth illustrates the difficulty in reconstructing the life of Jeremiah. A single episode can be split into

two parts, and those two parts can be inserted in the book out of sequence. Sometimes a single episode can be mentioned several times, or there can be several accounts of similar but distinct episodes.

In Jeremiah 37:15–16, Jeremiah is put in the "cistern house" of a certain scribe named Jonathan. In 38:6, he is put in a cistern belonging to Malchiah, the king's son, where he nearly dies. In this case, it is clear we are dealing with two separate episodes. Apart from the cisterns in question belonging to different people, Jeremiah's deliverance from his plight in the two accounts is entirely different. Still, two narratives that speak of Jeremiah being confined in or near a cistern illustrate how parallel accounts can confuse the reader.

There are four accounts of Zedekiah having a private meeting with Jeremiah. We have already seen two of these in 32:1–5 and 37:17. A third account is recorded in 34:1–7, and a fourth is in 38:14–28. Did Zedekiah have four private meetings with the prophet, or could it be that we have variant accounts of only one or two episodes?

The episode in chapter 37 took place soon after Jeremiah was arrested and while he was kept confined in a cistern house of Jonathan the scribe, just before he was transferred to the court of the guard. Since all the interviews with the king took place while Jeremiah was confined, this one, which happened soon after his arrest, was the first episode.

Jeremiah 32:1–5 contains a statement made by Zedekiah, although most of what he says is a citation of Jeremiah's prophecy. He does this to complain to Jeremiah about how harsh his messages are:

> The word that came to Jeremiah from YHWH in the tenth year of King Zedekiah of Judah, which was the eighteenth year of Nebuchadnezzar. At that time the army of the king of Babylon was besieging Jerusalem. And Jeremiah the prophet was confined in the court of the guard of the royal palace of Judah, where Zedekiah king of Judah had imprisoned him, saying, "Why are you prophesying, 'Thus says YHWH, I am about to give this city into the hand of the king of Babylon, and he will capture it. And Zedekiah king of Judah will not escape from the hands of the Babylonians, for he will certainly be given into the hand of the king of Babylon, and he will speak with him face to face and see him eye to eye. He will take Zedekiah to Babylon, where he will remain until I deal with him, says YHWH. If you fight against the Babylonians, you will not win.'"

This was in the year 587, during the final siege of the city, after the Babylonians had driven away the forces of Hophra of Egypt.[13] Zedekiah was highly distressed at how things had taken a turn for the worse. Jeremiah was a prophet who only gave bad news, and the king implicitly blamed him for what had happened (Jeremiah had refused Zedekiah's earlier request, when

---

13.   See Lundbom, *Jeremiah 21–36*, 502; Smothers, Keown, and Scalise, *Jeremiah 26–52*, 151.

he sent delegates asking the prophet to pray for the salvation of the city). In a direct response to the king, we read in 32:6–7, "And Jeremiah said, 'The word of YHWH came to me: Listen, Hanamel son of Shallum your uncle is coming to you.'" This leads into the full account of the land purchase after Hanamel's visit, as described above, and into a lengthy oracle of salvation.

It is obvious that the interview of chapter 32 was separate from and after the interview of chapter 37. The episode of Jeremiah 37 came just after Jeremiah was arrested, while he was kept in the cistern house and while the Babylonians were away from the city; but the one in Jeremiah 32 came after the Babylonians had resumed laying siege to the city and Jeremiah was kept in the court of the guard. Furthermore, the message of Jeremiah 37 is pessimistic; it asserts only that Jerusalem will fall. In Jeremiah 32 it is Zedekiah who, in his complaint, recites the account of the prophecy of doom. In fact, Zedekiah's complaint echoes the earlier word of condemnation given in 37:17: "You [Zedekiah] will be given into the hand of the king of Babylon" (in Zedekiah's complaint cited above, he twice repeats the prophecy that he would be "given into the hand of the king of Babylon"). Jeremiah, however, does not respond with further promises of death and exile. Beginning in 32:6, he moves from recounting the story of Hanamel's visit to an extended message of future salvation for Israel—a response to Zedekiah's implied complaint that Jeremiah never offers any hope. Therefore, chapter 37 is Zedekiah's first encounter with Jeremiah after his arrest, and chapter 32 is his second encounter, which took place after Jeremiah was moved to the court of the guard and after Hanamel's visit.

The account in 38:14–28 is the most extensive. In this meeting, Zedekiah stresses to Jeremiah that the conversation must be kept quiet because he fears the power of the aristocrats who are implacably determined to kill Jeremiah. This meeting did not take place at the court of the guard; Zedekiah had him brought out to "the third entrance to the temple of YHWH" (38:14). The reason they met there is not stated, but it probably was meant to hold the conversation away from people who might report on what was said to the ranking nobility. Zedekiah instructed Jeremiah that, if asked what the two of them had talked about, Jeremiah should say that he met with the king to plead not to be sent back to the cistern house of Jonathan the scribe (38:26). This implies that he was at this time confined at the court of the guard but that he could be put back into the cistern house. This would mean that the meeting was sometime during Jeremiah's first or second confinement in the court of the guard. However, the series of events in chapter 38, in which the conversation with the king comes soon after Ebed-Melek saved Jeremiah from the cistern, is by all appearances historically sequential and not merely a literary connection. This implies that the meeting took place during Jeremiah's second confinement at the court of the guard.

In this meeting, Zedekiah does not complain about Jeremiah's predictions of disaster for Jerusalem. It appears that by the time of this meeting, he had come to accept Jeremiah's prophetic authority. He is instead seeking a way to preserve himself and his family. This interview is not dated but clearly took place late in the process. Jerusalem was in dire straits, and the king knew that he and his family were in mortal danger. Jeremiah tells him, "This is what YHWH God Sabaoth, the God of Israel, says: If you will just go out [in surrender] to the officers of the king of Babylon, your life will be spared, and this city will not be burned down. You and your family will live."

Is it possible that chapters 32 and 38 describe the same encounter? This is not likely. Though not explicitly stated, chapter 32 implies this interview happened either at the court of the guard or the palace, while that of chapter 38 happened at the temple. Jeremiah 32 is connected to the visit of Hanamel, and chapter 38 is connected to the rescue from the cistern. Also, the hope Jeremiah gave the king in chapter 32 was, as we would term it, eschatological, expressing the great hope for redeemed Israel after God has regathered them. The interview in chapter 38 is personal, concerning the safety of the royal family. Thus, the accounts of chapters 32, 37, and 38 concern three separate interviews with the king.

The interview in 34:1–7 also took place late in the siege of the city. Both verses 1 and 7 assert that Nebuchadnezzar's full military power was set against Jerusalem. Jeremiah 34:7 adds that apart from Jerusalem itself, only Lachish and Azekah still remained of Judah's fortified cities. This places the interview of 34:1–7 in the same general context as 32:1–5 and 38:14–28. Does chapter 34, therefore, represent the same event as either of these two passages? In favor of tying it to the interview of chapter 32, the prophecy of 34:2–3 is almost identical to what appears in 32:1–5. Compare that text, cited above, to 34:2b–3:

> Thus says YHWH: I am going to give this city into the hand of the king of Babylon, and he shall burn it with fire. And you will not escape from his hand, for you will certainly be captured and handed over to him. You will see the king of Babylon eye to eye and speak with him face to face. And you will go to Babylon.

This suggests that the interview of chapter 34 was either the same as that recorded in chapter 32 or took place prior to it. Furthermore, there are no specific verbal connections between 34:1–7 and 38:14–28.

Against this, however, two things in chapter 34 stand out. First, 34:2a says, "Thus says YHWH, the God of Israel: Go and speak to King Zedekiah of Judah and say to him. " But Jeremiah was confined. How could he "go" to Zedekiah? A possible solution is that he had been summoned to meet the king in the temple, as described in chapter 38. Second, 34:4–5 contains a promise that Zedekiah can still avoid coming to a bad end:

> But hear the word of YHWH, Zedekiah, King of Judah! Thus says YHWH concerning you: You will not die by the sword. You will die in peace. And as spices were burned for your fathers, the earlier kings who were before

you, so they will burn spices for you and mourn for you, saying, "Alas, lord!" For I have spoken the word, says YHWH.

This is entirely out of place in the interview of chapter 32, with its eschatological focus, but fits well with chapter 38, where Zedekiah is most concerned for his own fate and that of the royal house. Thus, it appears that 34:1–7 is an oracle Jeremiah received from YHWH after he was summoned to meet the king at the temple. He was to repeat the prophecy that defeat was inescapable and that, one way or another, Zedekiah would be taken as a prisoner to Nebuchadnezzar (34:2–3). But there is also a promise that Zedekiah can still attain a good end to his life, which agrees well with the promise in 38:17 that the king's life would be spared if he surrendered.

When one reads 34:1–7 in connection with 38:14–28, taking the two texts to refer to a single event, a mystery is resolved. The promise that Zedekiah would die "in peace" (34:5) is difficult because in reality he came to a wretched end. He was captured while trying to escape, saw his sons slain before him, was blinded, and then was carried away to Babylon (Jer. 52:7–11). But from the account in chapter 38, we know that the well-being of Zedekiah and his family depended upon whether he would listen to Jeremiah and quickly capitulate to Babylon. He did not do this.

The sequence of meetings was thus as follows:

- Jeremiah and Zedekiah first meet while he is confined at the cistern house of Jonathan. Jeremiah tells the king that defeat is certain but pleads to be confined in a better place (37:15–16).
- Zedekiah visits Jeremiah during his first confinement at the court of the guard and complains of how Jeremiah has no hope to offer. Jeremiah recites the story of the visit of Hanamel and promises eschatological salvation for Israel (32:1–5).
- Not long before the fall of Jerusalem and while Jeremiah was in his second confinement at the court of the guard, Zedekiah met Jeremiah at the temple and pleaded for some way to save himself and his family. Jeremiah replied that he could come to a good end if he surrendered to Nebuchadnezzar immediately (34:1–7; 38:14–28).

Each account has its own purpose in its context.

- The account in chapter 37 is biographical, telling us why Jeremiah was arrested and when his first encounter with Zedekiah occurred. It also adds that he used it as an opportunity to appeal to the king to be moved away from the cistern house.
- Zedekiah's complaint in chapter 32 is used as a segue into the oracle account at 32:6–44, the purchase of the field of Anathoth and the oracle of eschatological salvation.

- The account in chapter 34 indicates YHWH was willing to show some compassion to Zedekiah and his house if he would have faith in the word of the prophet Jeremiah. Instead, the next episode in the book is the story of the faithless covenant regarding the slaves in 34:8–22. The two texts are set side by side for literary and theological (not chronological) purposes, to show that Zedekiah and the officials around him were beyond hope. Even when offered a way out of his dilemma, Zedekiah was not able to receive it. We should note that chapter 34 implies no historical or sequential connection between verses 1–7 and 8–22 (the breaking of the covenant occurred earlier, while the Babylonians were away dealing with Pharaoh Hophra; and the offer to Zedekiah came just before the fall of the city).

- In chapter 38, Zedekiah is offered the possibility of lenient treatment at the hands of Nebuchadnezzar. But this would only happen if Zedekiah had the courage to face down the nobles in his court who hated Jeremiah and were determined to resist Nebuchadnezzar to the bitter end. Against the fervent opposition of his peers, Zedekiah should surrender immediately. Instead, Zedekiah was a coward, telling Jeremiah to lie about the reason for their interview and refusing to make the hard decision. In the sequence of the narrative, the next event is the fall of Jerusalem (ch. 39). The implied message is that Zedekiah's lack of moral courage had disastrous results for him, his family, and Jerusalem.

A Second Message of Hope from Prison

As described above, Jeremiah gave an extended prophecy of Jerusalem's future restoration in chapter 32 as an explanation of the meaning of his purchase of the field at Anathoth. He gave another prophecy of eschatological hope for Israel soon after that, as recorded in chapter 33.[14] This prophecy is given no context beyond the fact that he received the oracle while he was imprisoned and that it came after the message of chapter 32:

And the word of YHWH came to Jeremiah a second time while was still confined in the court of the guard. (Jer. 33:1)

Since this chapter focuses on a future, righteous Davidic king, the prophecy may have been given after Jeremiah had been disappointed by Zedekiah's feckless behavior. The name Zedekiah means "Righteousness of YHWH,"

---

14. As described below in chapter 7, it may be that 33:14–26 was originally given on a different occasion. Jeremiah 30–31, the other major set of optimistic prophecies, are undated. They are probably a compilation of several messages from different times.

and Jeremiah promises that the messianic king will be named "YHWH is our righteousness" (33:16).

A Summary of Messages from the Time of Jeremiah's Imprisonment

Not surprisingly, we do not have any public sermons from the time of Jeremiah's imprisonment, but we do have several messages from that time. We have already noted that there are four accounts of Jeremiah giving private oracles to Zedekiah. There was also a private oracle for Ebed-Melech (39:15–18). The oracle condemning Jerusalem after the breaking of the covenant to free the slaves (34:8–22) may come from Jeremiah's time under confinement. We know that this episode took place while the siege of Jerusalem was temporarily lifted, when Hophra tried to relieve the city, but we do not know if it happened before or after Jeremiah was arrested. The two dated prophecies of hope, promising that God would recall Israel from exile and renew the nation (Jer. 32–33), also come from the time of Jeremiah's imprisonment.

It is possible that one prayer comes from this time. In 18:19–23, Jeremiah gives an extended imprecation against his persecutors:

> Hear me out, YHWH, and then listen to what my adversaries say!
> Is evil a proper recompense for good? But they dug a pit for my life.
> Remember how I stood before you to speak good for them,
> And to turn your wrath away from them.
> Well then, give their children over to famine!
> Cast them out to the power of the sword!
> Let their wives become childless and widowed!
> Let their men die by pestilence!
> Let their young men be slain by the sword in war!
> Let a cry be heard from their houses when you bring plunderers swiftly upon them!
> For they dug a pit to catch me, and they set snares for my feet.
> And you, YHWH, know all their plans to kill me.
> Do not forgive their iniquity or erase their sin from your sight!
> Let them stumble before you! Deal with them in your anger!

This curse was obviously given after Jeremiah had ceased making intercession for Judah and had begun praying against them. It could have been given at the same time as the revelation of the plot by the men of Anathoth (see Jer. 11:18–23), but there is a clue that it came from the time of Jeremiah's near death in the cistern: He twice speaks of how they "dug a pit for me" (11:20, 22). This is a standard biblical metaphor for the plots of the wicked against the righteous, and so it could have no bearing on the date of the prayer. However, in Jeremiah's case, the "pit" was more than a metaphor. Jeremiah's enemies really did put him in a hole in the ground in the hope that he would die there.

As such, it is plausible to date this prayer to Jeremiah's time in the cistern. This may explain the prayer's harsh language.

THE FALL OF JERUSALEM

The account of Jerusalem's fall is found in Jeremiah 39:1–14. Verses 1–2 state that the siege began in the tenth month of the ninth year of Zedekiah's reign, and that the walls were breached and the city taken on day nine of the fourth month of the eleventh year of his reign. There are two alternative chronologies for determining the date of the fall of the city. The "lower" and more traditional chronology dates it to the ninth of Tammuz (in July) of 586, and the "higher" chronology, followed by many scholars today, dates it to the same day in 587.[15] The whole siege took a little over fifteen months. Zedekiah and his remaining army fled the city but were caught at Jericho. Zedekiah was taken to Nebuchadnezzar at Riblah in Syria (Nebuchadnezzar had not been physically present at the siege of Jerusalem). Zedekiah watched his sons being executed and then had his eyes gouged out, and was taken in chains to Babylon. A certain Nebuzaradan, who seems to have been the equivalent of the commander of the Babylonian military police, oversaw the governance of Jerusalem in the aftermath of the fall of the city.[16] On instructions from Nebuchadnezzar himself, Nebuzaradan released Jeremiah from prison and gave him the option of either accompanying the exiles to Babylon or staying behind; he was free to go wherever he pleased. Jeremiah chose to remain (39:10–14; 40:1–6).

It is not surprising that Nebuchadnezzar knew about and respected Jeremiah. Babylonian intelligence services would have been keen to gather all the information they could about factions in Jerusalem, and Jewish deserters who fled to the Babylonians would have informed their captors of the words of the prophet. Indeed, many of those deserters would have abandoned the city precisely because of the warnings that Jeremiah gave, and these people would have regarded Jeremiah as a true prophet and have conveyed their admiration

---

15. See Jack R. Lundbom, *Jeremiah 37–52: A New Translation with Introduction and Commentary*, AB21C (New York: Doubleday, 2004), 84. Lundbom notes that an alternative method, using the lower chronology but following a Tishri (autumnal) calendar has the siege last two and a half years. For a detailed account of the complexities involved in resolving this problem, see Mordechai Cogan, "Chronology, Hebrew Bible," *ABD* 1:1007–8. See also Paul K. Hooker, who dates the fall of Jerusalem to 586. Hooker, "Chronology of the OT," *NIDB* 1:40.

16. Nebuzaradan's title was רַב־טַבָּחִים, which seems to be literally "commander of the cooks" (the LXX has ἀρχιμάγειρος, "chief cook," at LXX 47:1). See *HALOT* s.v. "טַבָּח" 368. But high officials could be given titles that translated literally appear to be no more than roles for domestic servants; cf. the use of "cupbearer" and "baker" in Genesis 40 for two men who were undoubtedly high officers in Pharaoh's court. The title רַב־טַבָּחִים is often translated as something like "captain of the guard" (NRSV), but he had a higher administrative role than seeing to the king's personal safety. Nebuchadnezzar's personal guard would have been present with him in Riblah and not at Jerusalem.

of him to the Babylonians. In fact, Nebuzaradan was able to quote Jeremiah's own message to Jeremiah and the Jewish survivors after the fall of the city:

> And the commander of the military police took Jeremiah and said to him,[17] "YHWH your God threatened this place with this disaster, and YHWH has brought it and did as he warned, because you [people of Jerusalem] sinned against YHWH and did not obey his voice. Therefore, this thing [he warned of] has come upon you." (Jer. 40:2–3)

MINISTRY DURING THE EXILE

The Gedaliah Assassination

Nebuzaradan, an agent of Nebuchadnezzar, appointed Gedaliah son of Ahikam son of Shaphan as governor over the province of what had been Judah to manage the Jews who remained behind in the land (39:14; 40:7). In the MT, Gedaliah first appears at this point (and in the parallel passage in 2 Kings 25). However, in the LXX 43:25, it is possible that Gedaliah's name appears among the men pleading with Jehoiakim not to burn Jeremiah's scroll (= MT 36:25, which gives the name as Delaiah). However, the name Delaiah/Gedaliah of MT 36:25/LXX 43:25 has no patronym, and so we cannot be sure if it is the same man. There is a Delaiah son of Shemaiah in both the MT 36:12 and LXX 43:12, and it is reasonable that the Delaiah of MT 36:25 is this man and not the later governor Gedaliah. Still, it is likely that Gedaliah did have some administrative experience. A seal impression belonging to a certain Gedaliah appears at Lachish dating from ca. 600 BC, and this may have been the same person.[18]

Gedaliah's official residence was at Mizpah. Unlike Jerusalem, it had not been destroyed by the Babylonians. This was the Benjamite Mizpah located north of Jerusalem (not the lesser known Mizpah of Judah, located in the Shephelah of western Judah [Josh 15:33, 38]). Benjamite Mizpah had been a somewhat prominent town in Israel's history; for example, Samuel called for an assembly here (1 Sam. 7). The survivors came before Gedaliah at Mizpah, and he assured them that they could dwell safely in the land without fear of further hostilities from the Babylonians and that they should resume agricultural work. They did as he said, and Jews who had fled to Moab, Ammon, Edom, and other nearby countries heard that things were returning to normal and returned to join the Mizpah community of Jews. Gedaliah was evidently

---

17.   Jeremiah 40:2–5 conflates what Nebuzaradan said to the Jewish survivors, as indicated by the plural verb חֲטָאתֶם ("you [people] sinned") in 40:3, with what he said to Jeremiah personally, as indicated by the comment in 40:4. Jeremiah 40:5 is also somewhat complex and further indicates the conflated nature of this text. It begins with an inserted comment from the narrator, וְעוֹדֶנּוּ לֹא־יָשׁוּב ("And still he [Jeremiah] would not return [with them to Babylon]"), and then resumes Nebuzaradan's comments to Jeremiah, וְשֻׁבָה אֶל־גְּדַלְיָה ("then you return to Gedaliah . . .").

18.   Robert Althann, "Gedaliah (Person)," *ABD* 2:923–24. Althann also provides a survey of various scholarly proposals that attempt to identify Gedaliah more precisely.

a capable and just administrator; the people resumed farming and had a good crop of wine and fruit (Jer. 40:9–12).

There were several other men who had been of some importance in Judah, as attested by the listing of their names in 40:8. Among them was a certain Ishmael son of Nethaniah. This man was a member of the royal family and had served in Judah's army (41:1). He had been residing in Ammon under King Baalis with a small band of former Judahite soldiers. Another man who had been an officer in the army, a certain Johanan son of Kareah, came to Gedaliah at Mizpah and warned him that Ishmael, acting as an agent of Baalis, was coming to assassinate him. He even offered to handle matters himself by going and killing Ishmael before he could get to Gedaliah. Apparently, the former officers traded information among themselves, and Ishmael's plot could not be kept hidden (Ishmael may even have tried to recruit Johanan). He warned, with some prescience, that if Gedaliah were murdered the small community around him would scatter. Gedaliah did not believe Johanan and rejected the plan entirely. But in the seventh month, around October, Ishmael and ten men came to Gedaliah at Mizpah and during a meal assassinated him, other Jews who were with him, and even some Babylonian soldiers who were stationed there (40:13–41:3). This could have happened in the same year as the fall of Jerusalem (since Jerusalem fell in the fourth month of the year), but the process of regathering Jews under Gedaliah could have taken time. If so, the assassination was probably a year later.

It is difficult to ascertain the motives of all the men involved. We have no reason to doubt Johanan's claim that Ishmael was acting as the agent of Baalis of Ammon, who would not have wanted a thriving Jewish community on his doorstep. But it is hard to believe that Ishmael, a member of the royal house of Judah, was acting purely on behalf of Ammon. He probably believed that anyone who cooperated with the Babylonians was a traitor and deserved to die. Baalis may have even encouraged him with an empty promise that he would help restore the house of David to power with Ishmael on the throne. Regardless, the narrative depicts Ishmael as a thoroughly dishonorable man (thus, perhaps, explaining Johanan's eagerness to kill him). Against all the rules of hospitality, Ishmael murdered his host at a common meal. The narrative further implies that Gedaliah was as naïve a man as he was decent.

But Ishmael was not done committing atrocities. The next day, a group of eighty Jewish pilgrims was heading toward the remains of the temple to mourn its destruction. Ishmael, weeping as if himself a mourner, went out to them and encouraged them to turn aside and for a brief stay with Gedaliah at Mizpah. When they did so, he murdered them all except for ten men who bargained for their lives by promising to give Ishmael and his men a stash of food they had hidden. Ishmael let these men live, but unceremoniously threw his victims into a cistern (41:4–10). He then rounded up a group of hostages among the Jews at Mizpah, including some of the "king's daughters," and began to drive them toward Ammon. This latter detail suggests that he did in fact aspire to claim the throne for himself. He may have wanted to marry one or more of the women to try to establish his claims to being the legitimate king.

If so, his plan was soon thwarted. Johanan and his men soon heard of the carnage, set off in pursuit of Ishmael's troop, and caught them at the Pool of Gibeon northwest of Jerusalem; this was the place where David's men under Joab defeated Abner's men (2 Sam. 2:12–17). The people whom Ishmael had taken looked upon Johanan's men as their saviors and happily ran to them. In the mayhem, however, Ishmael and eight of his men escaped and fled to Ammon (Jer. 41:11–15). This is the last we hear of Ishmael; we know nothing of the remainder of his life. But if he was aiming for greatness and power, he never got it. Sadly, Johanan's warning to Gedaliah about the scattering of the Jews proved entirely true. Even worse, Johanan would himself play a major role in bringing this about.

Jeremiah Taken to Egypt

Not surprisingly, Johanan was terrified that the Babylonians would be enraged at what had been done to their appointed governor and their men. He assumed that they would come down on the Mizpah community in force and without regard for who was guilty and who was not. He forcibly gathered the people, including Jeremiah and Baruch, and fled south, intending to go to Egypt. They paused at an otherwise unknown place near Bethlehem, Geruth Kimham. At this point, at least some in the group wondered if they were doing the right thing, and Johanan along with another ranking member of the group, Jezaniah son of Hoshaiah, led a delegation to ask Jeremiah for divine direction:

> Give attention to our request and pray on our behalf to YHWH your God. Pray on behalf of this entire remnant! For we are just a small remnant, as you now see us, though we were many. And may YHWH your God tell us the road we should take and the thing we should do! (Jer. 42:2–3)

Jeremiah responded that he would take up the matter with God and give them the answer (42:4). To this, they responded with an unsolicited vow of obedience:

> Let YHWH be a true and honest witness against us if we do not do in accordance with the message that the YHWH your God sends us through you! Whether it is good or bad, we will obey the voice of YHWH our God, to whom we are sending you, in order that things will go well for us. For we will obey the voice of YHWH our God! (Jer. 42:5–6)

For some unstated reason, it took a full ten days for Jeremiah to get an answer from YHWH. It may be that this was a cooling-off period, allowing them a chance to get over their initial panic. Or it may have been a test of faith. But at last, Jeremiah gave them as unambiguous an answer as they could have hoped for:

> Thus says YHWH, the God of Israel, to whom you sent me to give atten-
> tion to your request: If you will just remain in this land, I will build you
> up and not destroy you. I will plant you and not uproot you. For I do feel
> grief over the disaster that I brought upon you. Do not fear the king of
> Babylon . . . for I am with you to save you and to rescue you from his hand.
> I will give you compassion, act compassionately upon you, and return
> you to your land. But if you say, "We will not stay in this land," disobey-
> ing the voice of YHWH your God, and say, "No! We will go to the land of
> Egypt, where we shall not see war or hear the alarm-shofar or be hungry
> for bread! And that's where we will stay!" Well then, hear the word of
> YHWH, remnant of Judah! Thus says YHWH Sabaoth, the God of Israel:
> If you are determined to go to Egypt, and you do go to sojourn there, the
> sword that you fear will catch up with you there in the land of Egypt! And
> the famine that scares you will cling to you all the way to Egypt! And that
> is where you will die. . . . Just as my anger and my fury were poured out
> on the inhabitants of Jerusalem, so my fury will be poured out on you
> when you go to Egypt. . . . YHWH has spoken to you, remnant of Judah:
> Do not go to Egypt! And make sure you understand that I have warned
> you today that you are making a fatal mistake. Because you sent me to
> YHWH your God with the pledge, "Pray on our behalf to YHWH our
> God, and whatever YHWH our God says, tell us! And we will do it." Well,
> I have told you today, but you do not obey the voice of YHWH your God
> in anything that he sent me to tell you. So now, know for a fact that you
> will die by the sword, by famine, and by pestilence in the place where you
> desire to go and settle. (Jer. 42:9–16, 18–22)

As Jeremiah perceived, Johanan and the other leaders did not obey his oracle:

> You are lying! YHWH our God did not send you with the message, "Do
> not go to Egypt to sojourn there!" But Baruch son of Neriah is provoking
> you against us to put us in the hands of the Chaldeans to kill us or take us
> into exile in Babylon! (Jer. 43:2–3)

Instead, they took all the community, including Jeremiah and Baruch, to Egypt. As indicated in the citations of the text above, this tale is told in great detail and with the words of the various players fully quoted; it could have been told in far fewer words. There is a reason for this fulsome treatment of the episode in the book. It again demonstrates that YHWH and his prophet were justified in their evaluation of the spiritual condition of the people of Judah. Even after the trauma of the fall of Jerusalem and the exile, when Jeremiah's message had been fully vindicated, they still refused to believe him. Their stubbornness, even when it meant disregarding Jeremiah's proven record as a prophet, is on full display in this text. Also, their behavior in promising to obey the oracle and then angrily declaring that it was a lie and that they would disregard it uncannily echoes the behavior of the Jerusalem aristocracy, who made a covenant before God promising to free their slaves and then repudiating it (34:8–22).

JEREMIAH IN EGYPT

The Oracle at Tahpanhes

There are two recorded oracles of Jeremiah from his time in Egypt. The first was given at Tahpanhes apparently soon after they arrived there. Tahpanhes was an outpost on the eastern edge of the Egyptian Delta, close to the Sinai Peninsula. There is clear evidence that the site, located at modern Tell ed-Defenna, was occupied during the Saite period (664–526 BC) when Jeremiah and the company of Jewish refugees arrived. There was a building called "Pharaoh's House" in the town (43:9). This was probably a fortress and administrative center and perhaps served as the pharaoh's temporary residence when he was venturing beyond the borders of Egypt into Asia. Archaeologists have discovered a large rectangular building, probably the fortified governor's residence, in the Tahpanhes of the Saite period. Against several translations (e.g., NIV, NRSV), however, this should not be considered "Pharaoh's Palace" in the sense that we normally understand the term—a magnificent building meant to be the ruler's primary or secondary residence and capital.[19] When W. M. Flinders Petrie excavated it in 1887, the ruined site of this building was known by locals as the "The Fortress of the Jewish Woman."[20] Some Jewish refugees evidently stayed in Tahpanhes for a time.

Jeremiah gave an oracle of YHWH to the refugees at Tahpanhes, probably soon after they arrived. He was told to bury some stones beneath the brick pavement before the government building and give the Jews this warning:

> Thus says YHWH Sabaoth, the God of Israel: I am going to summon and bring my servant King Nebuchadnezzar of Babylon, and he will set his throne above these stones that I have buried, and he will spread his canopy over them. And he will come and strike the land of Egypt, giving those who are destined for death by plague to death by plague, and giving those who are destined for captivity to captivity, and giving those who are destined for the sword to the sword. He will set fire to the temples of the gods of Egypt and burn them. And he will carry off [their gods] as captives. And he will pick at the land of Egypt, as a shepherd picks at his

---

19. The term בֵּית־פַּרְעֹה could refer to the pharaoh's palace, but it need refer only to a structure that was directly controlled by the royal house and used for official functions.

20. See Richard N. Jones and Zbigniew T. Fiema, "Tahpanhes," *ABD* 6:308–9.

garment. And he will depart from there safely. He will shatter the obelisks of Egyptian Beth-Shemesh; and he will burn down the temples of the gods of Egypt. (Jer. 43:10–13)

The essential message, that Egypt will provide no haven from the Babylonians, is clear. The metaphor, that Nebuchadnezzar is a shepherd who picks at his garment to remove fleas (an inevitable part of working with livestock all day), shows how insignificant Egypt was before Babylon. They were no more than a nuisance, and they certainly could not protect people who fled inside their borders.

There is, however, a problem. The oracle seems to imply that Babylon would conquer all of Egypt as it had conquered Judah and would burn all its temples as it had burned Jerusalem and its temple. But this never happened. Nebuchadnezzar probably never made a deep incursion into Egypt, and he certainly did not conquer it. He did not burn and plunder Egypt's temples. A special problem presents itself in the common translation of 43:13a, as in, for example, the ESV: "He shall break the obelisks of Heliopolis, which is in the land of Egypt." Heliopolis was located at the southern end of the Nile Delta, near modern Cairo, and we can be confident that Nebuchadnezzar neither made it that far into Egypt nor plundered Heliopolis. But before we dismiss Jeremiah's oracle as an error, we should consider several factors.

First, the common translation of 43:13a is probably wrong. It should be, as above, "Egyptian Beth-Shemesh" and not "Heliopolis, which is in the land of Egypt." There was a Beth-Shemesh in the Shephelah of Judah, and the qualification "Egyptian" is meant to clarify this is an Egyptian site and not the place Jeremiah's audience was familiar with.[21] We do not know where this Egyptian Beth-Shemesh was, but it is reasonable to suppose it was a nearby settlement with a shrine to an Egyptian god.[22]

Second, when the prophets gave oracles against a location, they tended to use formulaic and often hyperbolic language. For example, Ezekiel used formulaic language when he spoke of Nebuchadnezzar's assault on Tyre, saying that the Babylonians would come against it with horses, chariots, cavalry, and a

---

21. The Hebrew בֵּית שֶׁמֶשׁ is literally "house of the sun" or Beth-Shemesh. This is widely taken to refer to Heliopolis, where the Egyptians had an ancient temple of the sun-god Re. The name Heliopolis is Greek for "city of the sun," a name that recognized the prominence of this temple. The Egyptian name for Heliopolis was *Iwnw*, and the name is transliterated into Hebrew in Ezek. 30:17 as אָוֶן. The interpretation of בֵּית שֶׁמֶשׁ as Heliopolis in Jer. 43:13 is based on the LXX, which translates it as Ἡλίου πόλεως, "of Heliopolis." But the Biblical Hebrew name for Heliopolis (besides Ezekiel's transliteration of the Egyptian name to אָוֶן) is עִיר הַחֶרֶס, a minor emendation of עִיר הַהֶרֶס in Isa. 19:18 (against the ESV, this should not be translated "City of Destruction"). See Hans Wildberger, *Isaiah 13–27*, trans. Thomas H. Trapp, CC (Minneapolis: Fortress, 1997), 261–62; and note that הַחֶרֶס means "the sun" in Job 9:7. Jeremiah qualifies בֵּית שֶׁמֶשׁ with אֲשֶׁר בְּאֶרֶץ מִצְרָיִם, "which is in the land of Egypt," meaning that this is Egyptian Beth-Shemesh as opposed to the other. No such explanatory note is needed for עִיר הַחֶרֶס.

22. The NIV translates בֵּית שֶׁמֶשׁ as "temple of the sun." This is probably not precisely correct, since is בֵּית שֶׁמֶשׁ a proper name, but the idea that it refers to a cultic site is reasonable.

powerful army (Ezek. 26:7). This was conventional language for land warfare, but it was not a literal possibility for an attack on Tyre, which was on an island. Isaiah provides an example of hyperbolic language in his oracle against Babylon, in which he speaks of the Medes heaping up a massive slaughter of Babylonian men, women, and children and declares that Babylon will be left like Sodom and Gomorrah, never to be inhabited again (Isa. 13:17–20). Babylon did indeed fall to the Medes and the Persians, but it was a quick and relatively bloodless conquest, and Babylon remained a great city for centuries. When Jeremiah spoke of the burning of temples in Egypt, it may sound like a massive destruction of the whole country, but the prophecy could have been fulfilled by a brief incursion into the eastern delta. The Babylonians could have delivered a military rebuke to Egypt without engaging in a full invasion and conquest. The use of hyperbole is a rhetorical technique and not a literal prediction.

The similarities between the oracle against Tahpanhes and earlier oracles against Judah are another indication that Jeremiah is deliberately using stylized language. He says Nebuchadnezzar will subject Egypt to plague, captivity, and the sword; also, "He will set fire to the temples of the gods of Egypt." These are comparable to his prophecies against Judah, as at Jeremiah 7:14; 21:7, 9; 24:10; 27:8; 29:18; 32:29, 36; and 34:17. That is, Jeremiah is making the point that Egypt will be no safe refuge. As God had punished them while they were in Judah, so he could reach them in Egypt. Even the reference to "Egyptian Beth-Shemesh" may be a glance back to what happened in Judah: Beth-Shemesh of Judah was destroyed by the Babylonians under Nebuchadnezzar, and it never recovered.[23] If Beth-Shemesh of Judah was not safe, neither would Egyptian Beth-Shemesh.

Taking formulaic language, hyperbole, and allusion to the fall of Judah into account, all that is necessary for this prophecy to have been fulfilled is for Nebuchadnezzar to have brought his forces to the edge of Egypt, camped at Tahpanhes, and plundered some temples as a show of force and a warning to the pharaoh. Our knowledge about late Babylonian campaigns against Egypt is sparse, and as stated above, he did not conquer (or even try to conquer) all of Egypt. But he may have come to intimidate the Egyptians in 582 and again in 568. The first of these may be most pertinent for this text. Lundbom states:

> Josephus (*Against Apion* i 133; *Ant* x 181–82) reports that Nebuchadrezzar in his twenty-third year, i.e., 582 B.C., occupied Syria, made war on the Moabites and Ammonites . . . and then invaded Egypt, killing the Egyptian king and appointing another, after which the Jews living in Egypt were exiled to Babylon. The killing of the Egyptian king is widely discounted, but if an invasion did occur in this year, an exile of Jews living in Egypt could have taken place. In this year there was a third deportation from Judah (Jer. 52:30).[24]

---

23.   Shlomo Bunimovitz and Zvi Lederman, "Beth-Shemesh," *NEAEHL* 1:251.
24.   Lundbom, *Jeremiah 37–52*, 208.

If the information in Josephus is correct, then the Babylonians may well have both come to Tahpanhes and taken away some of the Jewish refugees there.

The Oracle of the Queen of Heaven

Jeremiah 44 reports how the prophet gave an oracle to all the Jewish expatriates throughout Egypt. It was for "all the Jews living in Lower Egypt, including those in Migdol, Tahpanhes, and Memphis, and [the Jews] in Upper Egypt" (44:1). The location of Migdol is uncertain, but because it is paired with Tahpanhes here and in Jeremiah 46:14, it was probably in the eastern delta. Migdol was clearly in Lower Egypt (the delta, in the north) because in Ezekiel 29:10 it is made out to be at the opposite end of the country from Aswan, in the far south. Memphis was just south of modern Cairo, at the southern tip of the delta. Some of the Jews whom Jeremiah addressed were members of his party, who had just arrived in Egypt at Tahpanhes, but those in other locations had probably been in the country for years or even generations. They had fled the encroachments of first the Assyrians and then the Babylonians.

Famously, there was a Jewish community on Elephantine Island on the Nile in Upper Egypt, in the Aswan region at the very southern border of pharaonic Egypt. A significant trove of Jewish letters, official documents, and literary texts was discovered in southern Egypt; most were found in the late nineteenth and early twentieth centuries and were part of a larger collection of documents called the Elephantine Papyri. These texts came from various periods of antiquity and were written in several languages (one papyrus contains a copy of an Egyptian hieratic text from the Sixth Dynasty of Egypt in the third millennium), but the Aramaic Jewish texts have attracted the most attention.[25] They tell us a great deal about the beliefs and practices of the Egyptian Jews. The physical papyri date to the fifth century BC, but the Jewish community that produced them was probably significantly older. Some Elephantine Jews may have come from Judah as refugees from Nebuchadnezzar, but the community was probably founded by refugees from Samaria who fled the Assyrian invasion in the late eighth century.[26] The Elephantine community practiced a syncretistic religion that combined Yahwism with pagan beliefs.

Jeremiah's oracle to the Egyptian refugees probably involved sending a letter to the Jewish settlements. It is not likely that he visited every Jewish colony in Egypt. However, the heated exchange recounted in Jeremiah 44

---

25.   For a survey of the documents found here, see Bezalel Porten, "Elephantine Papyri," *ABD* 2:445–55. For a full translation of the texts, see Porten, *The Elephantine Papyri in English: Three Millennia of Cross-Cultural Continuity and Change*, DMOA 22 (Leiden: Brill, 1996); the introduction (pp. 1–29) contains an extensive discussion of the discovery and characteristics of the papyri.

26.   For a good survey of what may be considered conventional opinions about Elephantine, see Sami Said Ahmed, "The Jewish Colony at Elephantine," *Iliff Review* 22, no. 2 (1965): 11–19. By contrast, Karel van der Toorn argues that a core element of the Elephantine community came from Samaria. See van der Toorn, *Becoming Diaspora Jews: Behind the Story of Elephantine*, ABRL (New Haven, CT: Yale University Press, 2019).

implies that he gave it to some of the Jews orally in a face-to-face meeting, and 44:15 indicates that this encounter took place in Pathros (that is, in Upper Egypt). From this, we can infer that he made it at least as far south as Memphis. In the oracle, he castigates the refugees as severely as he ever chastised the apostates of Jerusalem:

> Thus says YHWH Sabaoth, the God of Israel: You saw all the disaster that I brought upon Jerusalem and upon all the cities of Judah. Consider that today they are a desolation, and no one dwells in them. This was because of the evil that they committed, provoking me to anger, by going to make offerings and serve other gods that neither they, nor you, nor your fathers knew. But I sent to you all my servants the prophets, and did so persistently, and said, "Do not do this abomination that I hate!" But they did not listen. . . . And my wrath and my anger were poured out and burned in the cities of Judah and in the streets of Jerusalem, and [those cities] became a waste and a desolation, as at this day.
>
> And now thus says YHWH. . . . Why do you do this great evil against yourselves, which will cut off from you man and woman, infant and child, from the midst of Judah and leave you no remnant? Why do you [act] to provoke me to anger with the works of your hands by making offerings to other gods in the land of Egypt? . . .
>
> Therefore, thus says YHWH Sabaoth, the God of Israel: Look, I am setting my face against you for harm, to cut off all Judah. And I will take the remnant of Judah who were determined to come to the land of Egypt to sojourn there, and they will all perish. In the land of Egypt, they will fall. By the sword and by famine they will perish. From the least to the greatest, they will die by the sword and by famine, and they will become an oath, a horror, a curse, and a taunt. . . . And there will be no fugitive or survivor from the remnant of Judah who came to sojourn in the land of Egypt. None will return to the land of Judah, to which they desire to return and inhabit. For they will not return, except for a few fugitives. (Jer. 44:2–8, 11–12, 14)

The oracle states that they were carrying on the same kind of paganized worship that they had practiced in Jerusalem and that they would receive the same response from YHWH. Jeremiah's audience, however, and particularly the women, understood his fierce condemnation to be directed especially at their veneration of the Queen of Heaven:

> That message that you spoke to us in the name of YHWH: We are not going to listen to you! No, we are going to do absolutely everything that

we vowed, by making offerings to the Queen of Heaven and by pouring out libations to her, just as we, and our fathers, and our kings, and our officials did in the towns of Judah and in the streets of Jerusalem. And at that time, we had plenty of food, and we prospered, and we experienced no disaster. But as soon as we stopped making offerings to the Queen of Heaven and pouring out libations to her, we lacked everything and perished by the sword and by famine. And yes, we are making offerings to the Queen of Heaven and pouring out libations to her! And do we make cakes for her without the involvement of our husbands, as we shape them for her and pour out libations to her? (Jer. 44:16–19)

The two sides reached what appeared to be a stalemate. Both agreed that that Jerusalem had fallen because of offenses against a deity, but while Jeremiah claimed that YHWH was the offended God, the Jews in Egypt—and especially their vocal wives—claimed that it was the Queen of Heaven who became angry and punished them for their negligence. The refugees' protests represented the popular opinion that Josiah's reforms, which had involved shutting down all the shrines to the other gods, had been a disastrous mistake and was the real reason for the ruin that had befallen them. From their viewpoint, they were the religious conservatives, preserving core elements of the faith and practice that had been handed from their ancestors.[27] They thought that Josiah and Jeremiah were the apostate innovators who had brought down Jerusalem. On the surface, there was no empirical method for resolving this religious dispute. Jeremiah, however, declared that they would see hard evidence of how wrong they had been:

I am watching over them for harm and not for good. And all the people of Judah in the land of Egypt will perish by the sword and by famine, until all are gone. And refugees from the sword, few in number, will return from the land of Egypt to the land of Judah. And those Jews who are left of those who came to the land of Egypt to sojourn will know whose words will stand, mine or theirs! And this will be a sign to you, that you may know that my word against you will be carried out, says YHWH, for I am punishing you in this place: Thus says YHWH, I am going to give Pharaoh Hophra, king of Egypt, into the hands of his enemies, and into the hands of those who seek his life, just as I gave King Zedekiah of Judah into the hand of King Nebuchadnezzar of Babylon, who was his enemy and sought his life. (Jer. 44:27–30)

Two issues arise from this exchange. First, what evidence do we have of the religion of the Jewish refugees in Egypt? Second, what are we to make of

---

27. See Gard Granerød, *Dimensions of Yahwism in the Persian Period: Studies in the Religion and Society of the Judaean Community at Elephantine*, BZAW 488 (Berlin: de Gruyter, 2016), 325–26.

Jeremiah's prophecy that they would be obliterated except for a few survivors who would make their way back to Jerusalem? After all, Egypt hosted a thriving community of Jews for many centuries.

Regarding the first question, the Elephantine community vividly illustrates the syncretism of the Egyptian Jews. A recently discovered text from this period, Papyrus Amherst 63, draws upon Psalm 20 but in addition to the deity "Yaho" (a version of the name YHWH), the text refers to other deities they honored: Nabu, Nanay, Bethel, Banit, and Anat. Analyzing this and related documents, Karel van der Toorn comments,

> In the Jewish quarter of Elephantine Island, there was a temple of Yaho. The Hermopolis letters refer to temples in Syene for Nabu and Banit, on the one hand, and for Bethel and the Queen of Heaven, on the other. The goddess Banit is none other than Nanay . . . her name comes from the Babylonian word *bānītu*, 'Beautiful One,' an epithet of Nanay. The consort of Bethel is Anat (or Anat-Bethel); her epithet, 'Queen of Heaven,' was also familiar to the Jews of Egypt (Jeremiah 44).[28]

The Elephantine Jews had a temple to Yaho at the center of their community, but it had no legitimacy from the standpoint of orthodox Yahwism, such as Jeremiah championed. The "Yaho" of Elephantine was a syncretized YHWH, and the people also worshipped other gods.[29] The Elephantine Papyri do not mention the title "Queen of Heaven," but she was certainly venerated there. "Given the general likeness between Nanay and Anat in the Amherst papyrus, it is to be expected that the goddess Anat who was venerated in the Jewish quarter of Elephantine would be viewed as Yaho's consort. In the nocturnal sky, god and goddess showed themselves as the moon and the Venus star. Yaho was king of the host of heaven, and Anat was the Queen of Heaven."[30]

Regarding the second question, Jeremiah's prophecy to some degree contains the same kind of formulaic and hyperbolic language that we see elsewhere. Furthermore, his words are directed at the syncretistic Jews and not at every Jew who ever emigrated to Egypt. The later Judaism we see reflected in the Letter of Aristeas and the writings of Philo was far more orthodox than that seen in Elephantine. And the Elephantine community and its temple were, in fact, violently destroyed. For reasons not fully understood, a major rivalry developed between the Elephantine Jewish community and the nearby temple of the Egyptian god Khnum. In the struggle that followed, the priests of Khnum prevailed. The Jewish temple was razed, and their community was eliminated around 410 BC. If it were not for the discovery of the papyri, we would today know nothing of this Jewish colony or the syncretistic Judaism

28.   van der Toorn, *Becoming Diaspora Jews*, 66.
29.   See van der Toorn, *Becoming Diaspora Jews*, 100–114.
30.   van der Toorn, *Becoming Diaspora Jews*, 113–14.

that they practiced. And all the other Jewish refugees in Egypt who shared the same outlook as the Elephantine community appear to have suffered the same fate. As Jeremiah predicted, they were utterly wiped out, and they had no lasting impact on the course of the development of the Jewish religion. Also, as Jeremiah predicted, Hophra was indeed slain by his enemies, although it was not the Babylonians but the Egyptians under the usurper Amasis II who overcame him and took his life.

THE DEATH OF JEREMIAH

We do not know when, where, or under what circumstances Jeremiah died. He could have been martyred by his foes, but if something as momentous as this had happened, we would expect that the book would not pass over it in silence. Furthermore, although the promise of divine protection given to Jeremiah at his prophetic commission is not necessarily a guarantee that he would not perish at the hands of his enemies, it seems implied:

> And they will fight you; but they will not prevail against you, for I am with you, says YHWH, to deliver you. (Jer. 1:19)

We may be confident that his two oracles against the Jewish refugees in Egypt (Jer. 43:9–44:30) are the last messages found in the book that he ever gave. Although it is possible that something from his undated promises of salvation for Israel (Jer. 30–31) or his oracles against the nations (Jer. 46–51) come from his Egyptian exile, there is no compelling reason to suppose they were not given while he was in Judah, before the exile. By all appearances, his work ended in Egypt with the oracle against the Queen of Heaven, and so presumably did his life.

This raises the question: Why doesn't the book give an account of Jeremiah's death? After all, the book gives us a wealth of information about his life. By comparison, the book of Isaiah provides little biographical information for its prophet; and the book of Ezekiel, although it does track the life of the prophet, primarily gives dates and accounts of divine commands but offers little about his personal interactions with people or about his inner life. The book of Jeremiah gives us a personal and even intimate view into the life of its prophet. We can suggest several reasons, however, why it does not mention his passing. First, no prophetic book contains an account of the death of its eponymous prophet. Second, as described in chapter 7 below, Jeremiah himself was probably alive when the first draft of his book was completed. Third, an account of his death would have been a distraction from a primary purpose of the book: to vindicate Jeremiah as a genuine prophet (see ch. 9 below). An account of his death, unless he had been heroically martyred, would not have enhanced the case that he, and not his opponents, truly spoke for God and correctly identified the reason for the fall of Jerusalem.

CHAPTER 5

RELATED HISTORICAL ISSUES
AND THE STORY OF BARUCH

I n addition to the geopolitical context of Jeremiah and the biographical details of his prophetic ministry, the book contains two important historical problems. Furthermore, the attention given to the scribe Baruch is noteworthy. He occupies a far more important place in the book than one might have expected.

OTHER HISTORICAL PROBLEMS

The Problem of Correlating Jeremiah and Daniel

When compared to what we see in Jeremiah and Kings, Daniel 1:1–2 is a problematic passage:

> In the third year of the reign of Jehoiakim king of Judah, Nebuchadnezzar king of Babylon came to Jerusalem and besieged it. And the Lord placed Jehoiakim king of Judah into his hand, along with a few items from the temple of God. And he took these to the temple of his god in Babylonia and deposited the items in the treasury of his god.

There are two difficulties with the Daniel text. First, it names Nebuchadnezzar as king in Jehoiakim's third year, contrary to Jeremiah 25:1, which says that the fourth year of Jehoiakim was the first year of Nebuchadnezzar's reign. Second, it speaks of a siege of Jerusalem that resulted in Jerusalem's capitulation and its loss of certain items from the temple. This sounds as though the author of Daniel is historically confused, supposing that the exile of Jehoiachin of 597 took place in the "third year" of Jehoiakim. Comparing the Daniel text to an account of the Jehoiachin exile, we can see similarities between the two. For example, 2 Kings 24:12–13 describes Jehoiachin's reign as follows:

King Jehoiachin of Judah, his mother, his officers, his officials, and his eunuchs surrendered to the king of Babylon. The king of Babylon, in the eighth year of his reign, took [Jehoiachin] prisoner, and he took away all the treasures of the house of YHWH and the treasures of the king's house. And he cut up all the items of gold found in the temple of YHWH that King Solomon of Israel had made, just as YHWH foretold.

The first problem, the apparent discrepancy between the third year of Jehoiakim against his fourth year, comparing Daniel 1:1 to Jeremiah 25:1, can be resolved. As is well known, there are two common methods for dating the reigns of kings from the ancient Near East. In the "accession year system," the time from a king's enthronement to the beginning of the New Year is called the king's "accession year." The year after New Year's Day is counted as the king's first year. Thus, using our calendar for the sake of simplicity, if a king were crowned on December 1, the month of December would be counted as his "accession year," and January 1 would begin the first year of his reign. In the "nonaccession year system," the time from a king's enthronement until New Year's Day is counted as his first year. Again, using our system for simplicity, if he was crowned on December 1, his "first year" would have been only one month long. The year after the first New Year's Day of his reign was counted as his second year.

It appears that Judah used a "nonaccession" system at the time of Jehoiakim's reign, but that Babylon used an "accession year" system. This means that what would have been called Jehoiakim's fourth year in Jerusalem was reckoned to be his third year in Babylon, where Daniel lived.[1]

Approximate Calendar Year	608	607	606	605	604
Babylonian system (Dan. 1:1)	Jehoiakim accession year	Jehoiakim year 1	Jehoiakim year 2	Jehoiakim year 3 = Nebuchadnezzar accession year	Jehoiakim year 4 = Nebuchadnezzar year 1
Jerusalem system (Jer. 25:1)	Jehoiakim year 1	Jehoiakim year 2	Jehoiakim year 3	Jehoiakim year 4 = Nebuchadnezzar year 1	Jehoiakim year 5 = Nebuchadnezzar year 2

The above table is approximate, not precise. It does not deal with the date of the new year in the ancient world, nor is it concerned with the complexities of the lunar calendar. Still, it provides a general picture of how the two systems can by correlated. Identifying Nebuchadnezzar in Dan. 1:1 as king of Babylon

---

1.   The chart below is taken from Garrett and Pearson, *Jeremiah and Lamentations*, 247.

merely provides a point of reference for the reader. By analogy, saying that President Kennedy was born in 1917 does not mean that he was president on the day he was born. Thus, to say what "King Nebuchadnezzar" did in Jehoiakim's third year does not necessarily imply he was already enthroned at that time.

The language of Daniel 1:1–2 may have been framed after a formulaic account of the taking of a city and the removal of treasures, so that one would speak of besieging the city regardless of how complete or lengthy this siege really was. Even so, the account in Daniel is in some ways markedly different from what we read in 2 Kings 24:12–13. The Kings version speaks of the forced deportation to Babylon of King Jehoiachin, his mother, and many of his high officials, and of the systematic plundering of the treasuries of the temple and palace. Daniel 1:1–2 implies only that Jehoiakim submitted to Babylon and that some valuable items were taken away as tokens of fealty. It does not indicate that high members of the royal court were exiled, and the removal of "some items" does not signify a thorough plundering of the treasury. The word "besiege" in Daniel 1:1 can be misleading. Although it can imply a prolonged assault on a city with a siege wall, an earthen siege ramp, and engines of war, events on the ground in a "siege" were not necessarily nearly so severe. To fulfill the account in Daniel 1:1, all that is really needed is for the Babylonians to have made a show of force sufficient to frighten Jehoiakim into submission. It may have been over quickly and with no formal siegeworks whatsoever. The fact that there was no royal deportation, but only the taking of some upper-class boys as hostages (Dan. 1:3–4), implies that there was a quick capitulation and no captivity analogous to what happened to Jehoiachin. The Babylonians felt no need to punish Jerusalem at that time.[2]

The story of Jeremiah's encounter with the Rechabites (35:1–19) is helpful here. As described above, the newly crowned Nebuchadnezzar in 605/604 was marching through the Levant, making a show of force, and bringing the various small states into submission. The Rechabites at this time were staying ahead of the armies to keep their flocks from falling into the hands of hungry soldiers. When they arrived at Jerusalem, the city was certainly not under siege, and the Rechabites did not take refuge behind its walls from an attacking army. However, the Babylonians were not so far away as to be disregarded. Soon after meeting with Jeremiah, the Rechabites no doubt continued to go south to remain out of harm's way. Around that same time, Babylonians demanded tokens of submission from Jerusalem and received them. Daniel and his companions were carried off as hostages who would work as scribes in the imperial administration. The account in Jeremiah 35 coheres well with what we find in Daniel 1.

The Problem of the Seventy Years

Jeremiah twice predicts that the Babylonian captivity would last seventy years. This is something of a problem because if one thinks of the captivity as

---

2.   See also Wiseman, *Nebuchadrezzar and Babylon*, 24.

beginning in 587/586 with the fall of Jerusalem, and as ending in 538 with the issuance of the Cyrus decree allowing the Jews to return home, the exile lasted only about fifty years.

The first prediction is in Jeremiah 25:11–12, in an oracle delivered in Jehoiakim's fourth year:

> All this land will become a ruin and a waste, and these nations will serve the king of Babylon seventy years. And after seventy years are completed, I will punish the king of Babylon and that nation, the land of the Chaldeans, for their iniquity, says YHWH, and I will make it a perpetual desolation.

The second prediction is in Jeremiah 29:10, in the letter Jeremiah wrote to the Jehoiachin exiles at the beginning of the reign of Zedekiah:

> For thus says YHWH: When what I predicted concerning the seventy years of Babylon are fulfilled, I will visit you and fulfill for you my good promise to bring you back to this place.

We also see references to the seventy-year captivity in Daniel and Zechariah. Writing in the first year of Darius the Mede, Daniel states:

> In the first year of his reign, I, Daniel, understood from the Scriptures that the ruin of Jerusalem would last seventy years, according to the word of YHWH given to Jeremiah the prophet. (Dan. 9:2)

Zechariah, writing in the second year of Darius I of Persia, records:

> And the angel of YHWH responded, "YHWH Sabaoth, how long will you withhold mercy from Jerusalem and the cities of Judah, with which you have been angry for these seventy years?" (Zech. 1:12)

And writing in the fourth year of Darius I of Persia, Zechariah addresses a group of people who have been observing regular seasons of ritualized lamentation over Jerusalem for many years. In Zechariah 7:5, YHWH instructs the prophet:

> Say to all the people of the land and to the priests: "When you fasted with lamentation in the fifth month and in the seventh for these seventy years, did you really fast for me?"

The first thing we should observe is that neither the beginning nor the ending of the seventy years has a fixed date. In Jeremiah 25:11–12, which speaks of the complete desolation of the land, the beginning of the seventy years must be reckoned to be when Babylon had razed all of Judah and Jerusalem, in approximately 586 BC. But in Jeremiah 29:10, the seventy years begins with the exile of Jehoiachin in 597. Without getting into the complexities of identifying Darius the Mede, we can assume the setting for Daniel 9:2 is the year Cyrus conquered Babylon, 539 BC. Thus, for Daniel, the date for ending the seventy years is when the Jews began their return to Jerusalem, which took place after the decree of Cyrus in 538. The two texts from Zechariah, however, speak of the end of the seventy years coming at or soon after the second and fourth years of Darius I of Persia, around 520 to 518 BC.

Since the "seventy years" do not have a precise beginning or ending, we must also consider what "seventy years" is meant to convey. This is, according to Psalm 90:10, the approximate maximum life span for all but the healthiest persons. Telling the people that the captivity would last seventy years was equivalent to saying that no one who was taken into exile as an adult would ever return to Jerusalem. They would all die before the deportation ended. This is most explicit in Jeremiah's letter to the exiles in 29:10, where he tells the recently deported Jews to abandon all hope of a return to Jerusalem in their lifetimes. They should settle down, raise families, and be prepared to live and die in Babylon.

For his part, Daniel dates the beginning of the exile with his own departure as a hostage to Babylon in 605/604 BC. Thus, his seventy years would end in approximately 535 BC, and contemplating Jeremiah's prophecy, he calculates in 539 BC that the time of exile is almost over. He prays in Daniel 9, therefore, that God will remember his people, forgive them, and restore them soon.

Zechariah 1–8, like Haggai, is dominated by the prophetic appeals for the people to rebuild the temple. For Zechariah, therefore, the seventy years represent the period of the temple's desolation, beginning in 587/586 BC. His oracles of the years 520–518 exhort the returnees to complete the task of building Jerusalem's second temple. This task was completed in the sixth year of Darius I, by around 515, according to Ezra 6:15. Zechariah would have calculated the seventy years that Israel was without a temple to have been roughly 586–515 BC.

BARUCH THE SCRIBE

His Family and Career

Baruch, Jeremiah's personal scribe, is mentioned in Jeremiah 32, 36, 43, and 45, with the latter entirely devoted to an oracle delivered to him personally. His father's name was Neriah, his grandfather was named Mahseiah (32:12), and he had a brother named Seraiah (51:59). Baruch's brother Seriah appears in 51:59–64, where Jeremiah commissions him to carry a prophetic text to Babylon while on a diplomatic mission there. Since Seraiah was part of so important a party (51:59 indicates that King Zedekiah himself was part of the mission), the brothers must have belonged to a prominent family. Seraiah was evidently in charge of the tribute. The text gives him the enigmatic title of "chief of the resting place,"[3] a term used nowhere else in the Bible. Several translations render this as "quartermaster" (ESV, NRSV), but it is hard to see a how a quartermaster, a person responsible for provisioning the army, would be part of a diplomatic mission (the NIV leaves the matter unsettled and simply gives him the generic office of "staff officer"). Lundbom translates the term as "caravan prince," but this has little to commend it.[4] The Aramaic targum, however, calls him the "chief of the offering," and the LXX similarly calls him the "chief of gifts."[5] This indicates that an emendation from "resting place" to the similar Hebrew word "gift" is warranted.[6] It implies that Seraiah was given the task for delivering Jerusalem's tribute to Babylon—an extremely important responsibility. We can therefore be sure that Baruch was from a family highly placed in the aristocracy.

Within the book of Jeremiah, Baruch is always subordinate to the prophet, and this gives the misimpression that he was a person of little significance—that he was essentially a humble clerk. But that was not how he was perceived in his lifetime. The position of his family implies that he, like his brother, had a high rank in society. More than that, it is striking that when the Mizpah Jews under Johanan rejected Jeremiah's message and said he was lying, they attributed this to the influence of Baruch:

> But Baruch son of Neriah is provoking you against us to put us in the hands of the Chaldeans, to kill us or take us into exile in Babylon! (Jer. 43:3)

Although it may be that they attributed the lie to Baruch because they wanted to soften their accusation against the prophet Jeremiah, they would not have said such a thing if they did not think of Baruch himself as a man of some authority. Certainly Baruch, like Jeremiah, had long believed that resistance to the Babylonians was hopeless, but the people did not perceive him as a lackey, writing whatever Jeremiah told him and mindlessly believing all of it. They recognized Baruch as a significant agent in his own right and probably understood that he was Jeremiah's partner in presenting a front against the royal and priestly leadership in Jerusalem. Rather than think that Jeremiah plucked Baruch from obscurity, we should look at it the other way around. Jeremiah, a member of a minor priestly family confined to the relative backwater that was Anathoth, became so prominent a prophet that even a man of Baruch's great stature was attracted to him.

Little is known of other biographical details of his life. We do not know when he entered Jeremiah's service. The first time we see him is in Jeremiah 36, where he writes out and then reads the scroll of Jeremiah's prophecies

---

3.   In Hebrew, שַׂר מְנוּחָה.
4.   Lundbom, *Jeremiah 37–52*, 507.
5.   The Aramaic is רב תוקרבא and the Greek is ἄρχων δώρων.
6.   I.e., an emendation from מְנוּחָה to מִנְחָה.

that Jehoiakim subsequently burned. After that, Baruch went into hiding with Jeremiah (and possibly, as suggested above, into exile in Moab). Along with the prophet, he was able to show his face again in Jerusalem after Jehoiakim was gone.

The next time we see him is in Jeremiah 32:13–16 (chronologically later than Jer. 36), where he writes up and stores the documents attesting to Jeremiah's purchase of the land in Anathoth. This indicates that Baruch was the keeper of Jeremiah's papers. It also implies that he could move about during Jeremiah's imprisonment, but we do not know where he was or what he was doing for much of that period. Nonetheless, he was with Jeremiah after the fall of the city and during the Mizpah episode. He was neither slain in the calamity nor taken into exile. This is somewhat surprising; as a professional scribe of high social standing, he was the kind of man the Babylonians would have carried into exile. Perhaps Jeremiah requested that he be permitted to remain with him in the land.

He was then forcibly taken to Egypt with the prophet. If, as seems likely, Jeremiah died in Egypt, Baruch may have survived him and preserved his documents. But he apparently did not remain in Egypt. The Letter of Baruch indicates that he made it to Babylon at the end of his life: "These are the words of the book that Baruch son of Neriah . . . wrote in Babylon in the fifth year, on the seventh day of the month, from the time when the Chaldeans took Jerusalem and burned it with fire" (Bar. 1:1–2). The book is apocryphal, but it probably preserves a genuine tradition that Babylon was his final home. If this notice reflects a genuine tradition, he may have only been in Egypt for about four years, perhaps until the death of Jeremiah, at which time he moved on to join the exiles in Babylon.

The Work of the Scribe

Baruch belonged to a highly respected professional guild: He was a scribe.[7] To appreciate Baruch's occupation and to better understand the narratives of Jeremiah 32 and 36, we should give some attention to the scribal art and the tools scribes used in preexilic Israel. To begin with, a scribe such as Baruch would have used the paleo-Hebrew script. This is essentially the same Hebrew alphabet we know today, but the shapes of the letters were entirely different. The Hebrew script we have in our Bibles today is derived from an Aramaic script, and it was not adopted into Hebrew before the fifth century BC. It probably did not become the standard script for Hebrew until around 250 BC.

The Israelites used a wide variety of media for writing. For monumental inscriptions, they could chisel letters into stone, but often stones were covered with plaster and inscriptions were set in the plaster. Walls, too, could have inscriptions set in plaster. Sometimes a black or red ink would be used for

---

7.   The following draws primarily on Ernst Würthwein, *The Text of the Old Testament*, rev. and exp. Alexander A. Fischer, trans. Erroll F. Rhodes, 3rd ed. (Grand Rapids: Eerdmans, 2014), 5–14, 303.

writing on the plaster. Small seals could have words carved into limestone or a semiprecious stone, such as quartz or amethyst. For making temporary notations and repeated use, a scribe could use a wooden tablet coated with wax. When the scribe had no further use for the text, he could simply rub it out and write something new, using a pointed stylus. Or, for a brief but durable note that could be easily transmitted, one could write with ink on a potsherd (ostracon). For example, the Lachish letters were written on ostraca. Words could be inscribed onto thin sheets of metal. This technique could be used with very small objects, such as the two tiny silver scrolls found at Ketef Hinnom. These date to approximately the sixth century BC and contain blessings in YHWH's name; they drew upon biblical texts, including Deuteronomy 5:10 and Numbers 6:24–26. Metal sheets could also be used for very lengthy texts, such as the Copper Scroll from Qumran. More than two meters (over seven feet) long, this is a list of hiding places used by the Essenes for items they treasured. Apart from the difficulties of opening and reading the scroll, it employed a kind of code for its various caches, and it has not enabled modern archaeologists to find the places it mentions.

For lengthier documents, ancient scribes wrote on papyrus or leather. Individual books were rolled into scrolls. The codex, a "book" as we know it, with the sheets bound together to a spine, did not come into use until about the second century AD. Indeed, the codex quickly became the preferred medium among Christians for biblical texts. On scrolls, the text was written in a series of columns on a lengthy, continuous sheet. As the reader worked through a book, he would turn the scroll so that a column he had read would be rolled up and a new column would be exposed for reading. This was the medium Baruch employed in Jeremiah 36, the account of the scroll Jehoiakim burned.

The Egyptians developed the process for creating a kind of paper from the papyrus stem in the third millennium BC. The pith of the stem was pressed into thin strips which were then laid out in a crisscross pattern, horizontal and vertical, to produce a durable paper. The sheets were glued into scrolls for the writing of books or important documents. Papyrus was widely used, but few Israelite samples have survived. Ernst Würthwein suggests that the scroll of Jeremiah 36 would have been written made of papyrus.[8] Scribes in Israel would typically roll a document into a scroll and then wrap a papyrus fiber around it to keep it tightly rolled. They would press a clay seal onto the outer layer of the scroll and over the fiber, keeping the text permanently rolled up until the seal was broken. This would identify the owner of the scroll and prevent tampering. These seals are called bullae (singular: bulla), and many of these have survived from antiquity even though the papyrus manuscripts they once held have long since decayed into dust. A scribe, upon rolling up the scroll, would have tied it with string and held it all in place with the bulla. He impressed on the bulla a seal upon which his name was engraved. A famous

---

8.   Würthwein, *Text of the Old Testament*, 8.

bulla purports to have come from the hand of Baruch himself. The impression reads, "Belonging to Berechiah [= Baruch], son of Neriah, the scribe." Unfortunately, this bulla may be a forgery.[9]

Leather was also used as a medium for documents. It lasted for a long time, but it was difficult to produce in quantity due to the complexity of the tanning process. It was, for that reason, quite expensive. By about the second century BC, tanners had developed a process for creating a soft, pliable, but durable material for writing called parchment. Because parchment was so valuable, scribes would often scrape off an old text and reuse the parchment for a new text. Such a manuscript is called a palimpsest. When modern scholars find a palimpsest, they will often use a sophisticated camera or X-ray technique to recover the erased text (the erased text may turn out to be of more value or interest than the secondary, visible text). Baruch, of course, would not have had access to parchment, but there are also palimpsests written on papyrus.

The writing tool a scribe would employ would depend upon what medium he was working with. To carve letters into stone would require a chisel. For papyrus or leather, ink was applied using a thin rush that had been frayed at the end. Ink was made from soot mixed with water and gum arabic or a vegetable oil.

Jeremiah 36:23 mentions a "scribe's knife" as the tool that the king used to cut off columns from Baruch's scroll before throwing them into the fire. There are at least three reasons why a scribe would want to have a good knife at hand. First, depending on the nature of his stylus, he might use the knife to trim it as needed. Second, he could use the knife when scraping off an old text to use the papyrus or leather as a palimpsest. Third, he could use the knife to trim the edges of the papyrus or leather sheets.

Scribes were highly respected members of society. They often came from influential families, and scribes often held high government positions. In one Egyptian text, a father exhorts his son to become a scribe, asserting that this is the path to success and that all other occupations are backbreaking jobs for the peasants.[10] But it is probably not correct to say that the scribes were the only "literate" people in Israelite society, although we must be careful about how we define literacy. The Hebrew alphabet has only twenty-two letters and is not difficult to master. Probably many people could read small, simple notes

---

9.   Nahman Avigad, "Baruch the Scribe and Jerahmeel the King's Son," *IEJ* 28, nos. 1/2 (1978): 52–56. See also Jack Lundbom, who lists the various bullae purported to be from Baruch. Lundbom, *Jeremiah 1–20: A New Translation with Introduction and Commentary*, AB21A (New York: Doubleday, 1999), 876–77; and Lundbom, *Jeremiah 21–36*, 606–7. Casting doubt on the authenticity of the Baruch bulla and a related seal is Christopher A. Rollston, who says, "But the seal used to make the Baruch Bullae is actually a modern forgery; therefore, the Baruch Bullae are modern forgeries as well." See Rollston, "The Bullae of Baruch ben Neriah the Scribe and the Seal of Ma'adanah Daughter of the King: Epigraphic Forgeries of the 20th Century," *ErIsr* 32 (2016): 83.

10.   The Egyptian text is called "Dua-khety or the Satire on the Trades." It can be found in William W. Hallo and K. Lawson Younger, Jr., *The Context of Scripture*, 3 vols. (Leiden: Brill, 2003), 1.48:122–25.

or scratch out a few words as needed on a potsherd (Egyptian hieroglyphs, however, were entirely the domain of specialists). But an ordinary Israelite probably could not write out a lengthier text without making many errors and similarly would have difficulty reading a longer text due to lack of practice. Even the king, although not illiterate, was not a practiced reader. Thus, Jehudi read Baruch's scroll to Jehoiakim; the king did not read it himself (36:23).[11]

The Scribe as Attorney

As the men who wrote out official, legally binding documents, scribes effectively served as attorneys in matters of property law. Jeremiah 32 gives us a good sense of how legal transactions, particularly the purchase of property, worked. Comparing 32:11 to 32:14, it is evident that the legal documents included at least two specific texts, the "sealed" document and the "open" document. There may have been another document containing the "provisions and terms" as mentioned in 32:11, but probably this material was included in the two aforementioned documents. We may surmise that normally the "open" document was a scroll that had not been sealed and thus was available for anyone to look at. Probably the purchaser of the land kept the open document as proof that he had lawfully acquired the land. The sealed document was probably in content identical to the open document; it was a duplicate. It would be kept in some agreed-upon location, something analogous to the county clerk's office. Should someone challenge the legality of the transaction or in a lawsuit claim that the purchaser had fraudulently modified the terms of the sale, the parties would retrieve the sealed document, break the seal (the "bulla"), and compare it to the open document to ensure that the two copies were the same. The hardened clay of the bulla provided the necessary security because it could not be removed without destroying the bulla, thus making it difficult for someone to tamper with the sealed copy.

In the case of Jeremiah's purchase of the Anathoth land, however, the prophet ordered Baruch to place both copies inside a clay pot and bury it somewhere. The pot would have had a lid that was sealed in place to make it relatively impermeable. This was precisely how the Qumran community preserved the texts we now call the Dead Sea Scrolls. The burial of the scrolls did not follow the normal procedure for handling the documents in a real estate purchase, because Jeremiah was not actually concerned about defending his legal ownership of the land. What he did was a prophetic sign-act testifying that someday the land would again belong to the Jews. He would soon die, and Jerusalem would soon be destroyed by the Babylonians. For that reason, his personal ownership of a parcel of land at that time was meaningless in the literal, normal sense. But as a symbol for the certainty of Israel's return to its ancestral land, it made a powerful statement.

---

11.   For further study on the world of the Israelite scribe, see Christopher Rollston, *Writing and Literacy in the World of Ancient Israel*, ABS 10 (Atlanta: Society of Biblical Literature, 2010).

The Prophecy for Baruch

Jeremiah 45, the shortest chapter in the book, is exclusively concerned with a prophetic oracle given privately to Baruch. It reads as follows:

> The message that Jeremiah the prophet spoke to Baruch the son of Neriah, when he wrote the words in a scroll at the dictation of Jeremiah, in the fourth year of Jehoiakim the son of Josiah, king of Judah: Thus says YHWH the God of Israel, to you, Baruch: You say, "Woe is me! For YHWH is adding sorrow to my pain. I am exhausted with my groaning, and I can find no rest." This is what you must say to him: Thus says YHWH! Consider! What I built I am breaking down, and what I planted I am uprooting, and [I am doing it] to the whole land. And are you seeking greatness for yourself? Do not seek it! For consider! I am bringing disaster upon all flesh, declares YHWH. But I will give you your life as plunder you can carry away to all the places where you go.

This oracle was given in the fourth year of Jehoiakim soon after the episode of the scroll of chapter 36, to which the heading in 45:1 refers. It probably was given after Jeremiah and Baruch had gone into hiding; as suggested above, they appear to have fled to Moab. The sorrow, pain, and exhaustion that Baruch expresses reflect his social ostracism, his fear of the king's wrath, and the laborious effort it would have taken for him and Jeremiah to escape the city and make their way to a hiding place in another land. He was a member of a prominent family and at this time probably still a young man, and he was distraught over having thrown away his career by associating with Jeremiah. The "greatness" that he aspired to but lost was not an idle dream; he would have had a realistic prospect of attaining a high rank in the government had he not taken the side of this despised prophet.

YHWH's response to Baruch ("What I built I am breaking down, and what I planted I am uprooting") alludes to the initial call given to Jeremiah: "Look, I appoint you this day over nations and kingdoms to uproot and tear down, to destroy and overthrow, to build and to plant" (Jer. 1:10). By making this allusion and applying it to Baruch's situation, he makes the scribe a partner with the prophet. And in this context, what YHWH had "built" and "planted" was Judah and Jerusalem; now he was destroying and uprooting them. Baruch had no future in Jerusalem because no one had a future there. The city was doomed.

The end of the oracle speaks of Baruch having his life as plunder wherever he goes. This implies that he would have to flee from one disastrous situation after another and that he would not be able to carry riches with him, like some greedy soldier snatching money from a household treasury. But he will have his life; that is the "plunder" God will allow him. Through all his trials and journeys, God will preserve him. The text further implies that at the time the oracle of Jeremiah 45 was given, Baruch had already begun his life of wandering. As argued above, he may have just fled to Moab when he received this message. He would return to Jerusalem after the ascent of Zedekiah, but then he would live through the demolition of the city. After a brief stay in Mizpah and the harrowing events surrounding the murder of Gedaliah, he would be carried off to Egypt. But he was a despised man among the Jewish refugees there, and after the death of Jeremiah made his way to Babylon (per the Letter of Baruch).

PART 2

THE STRUCTURE AND COMPOSITION OF THE BOOK

CHAPTER 6

THE STRUCTURE OF JEREMIAH

Given a casual reading, Jeremiah is almost devoid of any identifiable structure. After the account of Jeremiah's calling in chapter 1, it moves into a lengthy series of diatribes against Jerusalem, repeatedly denouncing the people for their behavior and promising that terrible destruction awaits them (ch. 2–20). Because it is unremittingly pessimistic, this makes for grim reading, but the most difficult thing is that the messages seem all mashed together. They are never dated and superficially look like a complete jumble. This is entirely unlike Ezekiel, which often dates its messages and keeps them all distinct from one another (Ezekiel was contemporary with Jeremiah). Next, Jeremiah gives a series of messages that are dated by the reigns of Judah's kings (ch. 21–29), but they are not in chronological order, which again contrasts with Ezekiel, which generally records its oracles in their historical sequence.[1] Jeremiah then gives a sudden and unexpected series of oracles predicting the eschatological salvation of Israel (ch. 30–33). This too differs from many other prophets, who typically concentrate their messages of salvation at the ends of their books. After that, Jeremiah works through a series of episodes and messages from the prophet's life (ch. 34–45). These are dated but are again out of sequence. This is followed by a series of oracles concerning various nations (ch. 46–51), and at the end, by an account of the fall of Jerusalem and of what became of Jerusalem's last kings (ch. 52). Although we can see a certain level of grouping of different kinds of texts here, the book is not easy to read through. One famous scholar called it a "hopeless hodgepodge thrown together without any discernible principle of arrangement at all."[2]

In fact, however, Jeremiah does have a specific and well-defined structure. It is not intuitive, and as will be argued in the next chapter, it took some time for

---

1. For a table of Ezekiel's dated messages, see Greenberg, *Ezekiel 1–20*, 8.
2. John Bright, *Jeremiah: With Introduction, Translation and Notes*, AB 21 (Garden City, NY: Doubleday, 1965), lvi.

Jeremiah and his scribe Baruch to settle on this arrangement for the book. At its heart, the book has seven sections that generally follow the description above:

    I.   Prologue: The beginning of Jeremiah's ministry (1:1–19)
    II. Two anthologies against Judah (2:1–20:18)
    III. Historically contextualized messages (21:1–29:32)
    IV. Eschatological salvation (30:1–33:26)
    V. Historically contextualized messages (34:1–45:5)
    VI. Two anthologies against the nations (46:1–51:64)
    VII.Epilogue: The end of the house of David (52:1–34)

For a full presentation of the structure of the book, see appendix 1.

THE PROLOGUE AND EPILOGUE

The first and last major sections (I and VII) create an *inclusio* structure. Section I is Jeremiah's call to deliver a painful message of judgment to Judah and section VII is an account of the fulfillment of that message in the fall of Jerusalem and the end of the monarchy. If not entirely parallel, the second text strongly echoes the first.

Section I begins by identifying Jeremiah as a member of a family of priests of Anathoth (1:1) and proceeds to identify the dates of his ministry, from the thirteenth year of Josiah to the eleventh year of Zedekiah (1:2–3). God tells Jeremiah that he set him apart to be a prophet even before he was born and assures him that he would be with him, so that Jeremiah need not fear (1:4–8). God then touched Jeremiah's mouth, saying he had given the prophet God's word and had appointed him both to overthrow and to build nations (1:9–10). After this, God tells Jeremiah that Jerusalem is doomed to be destroyed by a nation from the north (Babylon) and that God must armor Jeremiah against the many attacks he will face from the kings and officials of Judah (1:11–18).

Section VII begins by identifying Zedekiah as the king, naming his mother Hamutal, and stating that he did evil in YHWH's eyes (52:1–3a). It identifies the date of the beginning of the siege of Jerusalem and the date of its fall (52:3b–6, 12). It further describes the tragic end of Zedekiah, giving an account of how he was captured while in flight, saw his sons slain, and then had his eyes gouged out (52:7–11). It describes in detail the destruction and plundering of the city as well as the circumstances of the exile (52:12–30). As a kind of postscript, it describes how Jehoiachin was finally released from prison in Babylon (52:31–34).

Comparing the two, we see parallels throughout the two passages, except for the postscript at 52:31–34. Jeremiah is identified as a member of a priestly family, and Zedekiah is identified as king and by the name of his mother. Chapter 1 summarizes the dates of Jeremiah's ministry, and chapter 52 dates the major events of the fall of Jerusalem. Whereas YHWH declared he would be with Jeremiah and would fortify him against his enemies, he abandoned Zedekiah and handed him over to Nebuchadnezzar, who tortured him both emotionally and physically. God declared the destruction to be poured out on the city from Babylon to be the central prophecy of Jeremiah's ministry (1:13–15), and chapter 52 details how this took place. Thus, section VII mirrors and provides the fulfillment to opening of the book in section I.

ANTHOLOGIES AGAINST JUDAH AND AGAINST THE NATIONS

Sections II and VI also balance one another. Section II (2:1–20:18) is a collection of oracles against Judah and corresponds to section VI (46:1–51:64), a collection of oracles against the nations. Both are anthologies of many messages given at various occasions, and most of the messages are not dated. Both sections II and VI have two major segments.

Section II, the First Anthology Against Judah (2:1–10:25)

Section II has two distinct anthologies (2:1–10:25; 11:1–20:18). The first anthology (2:1–10:25) is in three parts: (a) an introduction summarizing the whole (2:1–4:4); (b) texts in 4:5–6:30 that alternate between passages describing the deceit that fills Judah with passages describing the invasion that will destroy it; (c) texts in 7:1–10:25 that alternate between passages describing the religious deceit that fills Judah with passages containing lamentation over the nation.

The First Anthology (2:1–10:25)	
Summarizing Introduction	2:1–4:4
First Set of Alternating Passages	4:5–6:30
Second Set of Alternating Passages	7:1–10:25

Thus, this anthology develops two thematic ideas: (1) Judah is filled with deceit, false hope, paganism, and a general disregard for the truth. (2) Babylon is an instrument of God's wrath and will soon heap destruction on the city.

The Alternating Themes of 4:5–6:30	
Judgment and Destruction for Jerusalem	Jerusalem Under Deceit and Delusion
Invasion from the north (4:5–8)	Bewildered and corrupt leaders (4:9–12)
The Babylonian storm (4:13)	Jerusalem, home of evil schemes (4:14)
The enemy approaches (4:15–18)	Senseless people and a world in turmoil (4:19–28)
The towns deserted (4:29)	A cosmetic solution (4:30)

| The Alternating Themes of 4:5–6:30 ||
Judgment and Destruction for Jerusalem	Jerusalem Under Deceit and Delusion
The helpless woman facing murderers (4:31)	A city of liars (5:1–5)
Babylon is a lion, wolf, and leopard (5:6)	Faithless to God and to marriage (5:7–9)
Ravaged vineyards (5:10)	Lying versus true prophets (5:11–14)
The all-devouring enemy (5:15–19)	Houses full of deceit (5:20–31)
Zion in flight; Jerusalem under siege (6:1–9)	Incapable of hearing the truth (6:10–11a)
Enemy takes all people and all property (6:11b–12)	Saying "Peace" when there is no peace (6:13–21)
The cruel army from the north (6:22–26)	Conclusion (6:27–30)

| The Alternating Themes of 7:1–10:25 ||
False Religion	Real Lamentation
Jerusalem's perverse religion (7:1–8:12)	Lamentation over a godless land (8:13–9:26)
Idolatry versus YHWH (10:1–16)	Lamentation over exile (10:17–22)
Transition to next anthology: Jeremiah's confession and imprecation (10:23–25)	

The following examples illustrate the kind of alteration we see in these passages, where a passage describing Judah's delusion and the collapse of all that once seemed fixed and secure has as its counterpart a text bluntly describing the coming Babylonian invasion.

For the first example, Jeremiah 4:19–28 describes the people's willful ignorance.[3] The prophet can foresee the approaching armies, but his people, like children at play, are blissfully unaware of all this:

> My pain! My pain. . . . How long will I see the battle standard? How long will I hear the [trumpeting of the battle] shofar? It is because my people are foolish. They don't know me. They are witless children. (Jer. 4:19, 20–22)

The world that they know is an illusion, and soon everything they take for granted will be gone. The seemingly reliable blessings of heaven and earth will disappear and what appears to be immutable will collapse:

> I saw the earth, and it was without form and void,
> And to the heavens, and they had no light. . . .

---

3.   For an account of the poetic structure of 4:19–28, see Garrett and Pearson, *Jeremiah and Lamentations,* 115–17. There is also a note investigating the unusual Hebrew of 4:19 on p. 116.

I saw that the fruitful land was a desert,
And all its cities were laid in ruins before YHWH [and] before his fierce
anger. . . .
For this, earth will mourn,
And heaven above will be dark.
For I have spoken; I have made it my purpose.
I do not relent, and I do not turn back. (Jer. 4:23–28)

The counterpart to this is 4:29, in which the text shifts from using cosmic
language to giving a straightforward prediction of invasion by enemy cavalry
and archers:

At the sound of cavalry and archers every city takes to flight.
They head into coverts and up into rocky terrain.
Every city will be forsaken, and no one will live in them.

Instead of the delusion of security, they will face the hard reality of
invasion.

A second example, in 4:30, portrays Jerusalem as a woman putting on
cosmetics and jewelry for her lovers:

And you, Desolation, What do you mean by dressing in scarlet,
By adorning yourself with gold jewelry,
[And] by shadowing your eyes with cosmetics?
In vain you beautify yourself.
Your lovers despise you. They seek your life.

The deceit here is twofold. First, the woman attempts to deceive her lovers
by artificially beautifying herself, a metaphor for Jerusalem (called "Desolation") trying to attract allies by pretending to be richer and more powerful
than it is. Also, the woman is herself deceived, thinking that her lovers, Jerusalem's allies and especially Egypt, will save her. The counterpart to this is
4:31, in which defeated Jerusalem is also portrayed as a woman:

For I hear a cry, like a woman in labor,
I hear anguish like that of a woman birthing her first child!
It is the cry of Daughter Zion!
She will gasp for breath! She will spread her hands,
"Woe is me! My strength is exhausted in the face of murderers."

For a third example, Jeremiah in 10:1–16 mocks the dread that idols
inspire in the Gentiles, observing that they are only the work of craftsmen
and are no more worthy of awe than a scarecrow. He praises YHWH as the

living God, in contrast with the dead, artificial gods of the nations. YHWH, unlike the gods, is maker of heaven and earth:

> Speak like this to them: "The gods who did not make heaven and earth will perish from earth and from under heavens."
> [YHWH] by his power is maker of earth.
> [He] keeps the world in place by his wisdom.
> And by his understanding he stretched out the heavens. . . .
> Every person is stupid and without knowledge. . . .
> For their images are a lie,
> And they have no breath.
> They are worthless; they are a travesty.
> When [YHWH] deals with them, they will perish.
> The portion of Jacob is not like these. (Jer. 10:11–16)

The counterpart to this is 10:17–22, in which Jeremiah laments the coming diaspora of Jerusalem:

> Pick up your pack from the ground,
> [You city] that sits under siege!
> For thus says YHWH:
> Look, this time, I am slinging out the inhabitants of the land. . . .
> Woe is me because of my hurt! My wound is infected. . . .
> A message, a report! A great upheaval comes out of the northland
> To make the cities of Judah a desolation, [and] a lair of jackals. (Jer. 10:17–19, 22)

Throughout the whole of 2:1–10:25, a specific message is developed. First, Judah is in the grips of deceit. The people lie, they cheat one another, and also deceive themselves. They have false hopes that help will come from some foreign power or that the presence of YHWH's temple in their city makes them invulnerable. Also, they show as much reverence toward idols as do the nations around them, viewing gods of wood and stone as able to protect and provide for them. Second, and against this, there is the reality that YHWH is the one God, and that the Babylonian army will soon be at their gates. The prophet can only mourn the people's delusion.

Section II, the Second Anthology Against Judah (11:1–20:18)

The second anthology (11:1–20:18) gives an account of Jeremiah's movement away from making intercession on behalf of his people and toward praying imprecations against them, calling on God to punish Judah. The two anthologies are thematically related. The first anthology focuses on Judah's self-deception, the belief that they could continue in apostasy and yet disaster would never strike them. The second anthology deals with Jeremiah's self-deception, the belief that there was hope for Judah's repentance and that if he just prayed fervently enough, revival and restoration would come. The second anthology, like the first, is divided into three parts: (a) an introduction summarizes the whole (11:1–23); (b) Jeremiah attempts to intercede for Judah (12:1–15:9); (c) Jeremiah harshly condemns Judah and makes imprecations against it (15:10–20:18).

The Second Anthology (11:1–20:18)	
Summarizing Introduction	11:1–23
Jeremiah's Earlier Intercession for Judah	12:1–15:9
Jeremiah's Condemnation of Judah	15:10–20:18

Section II, Second Anthology, Summarizing Introduction (11:1–23)

The introduction (11:1–23) is a proleptic summary; that is, it foreshadows what is going to happen in the following chapters. If the reader does not recognize it for what it is, the chapter seems incoherent. It jumps from one issue to another without any clear connections between them, but this is because it is only concisely describing what will be explained more fully in the chapters that follow. Also, chapter 11 looks odd if read sequentially with what follows, since it concludes with a divine command to cease praying for Judah, and yet Jeremiah prays repeatedly for Judah in the subsequent chapters. For example, 12:1–4 is an intercessory prayer in which he asks God to save Judah from its corrupt leaders. These prayers include several strong and direct appeals, such as 14:9: "You are among us, YHWH, and we are called by your name. Do not lay us aside!" These intercessory prayers should not be read sequentially with 11:14 ("But you [Jeremiah], do not intercede for this people!"), as though he were disobeying a direct command from God.

Chapter 11 provides four crucial details that explain why Jeremiah had to stop praying for Jerusalem. We have already looked at parts of this passage from the standpoint of where the events fit in the biography of Jeremiah. Here, we consider them in their literary context.

First, 11:1–5 comes from an earlier period in Jeremiah's career, perhaps during the reign of Josiah. It appeals to the people to be faithful to the covenant and promises them security and abundance if they will do so.

Second, 11:6–13 is a sterner condemnation. It asserts that the Israelites have always been prone to disobedience and apostasy, ever since the exodus. Now they are worse than ever, worshipping as many gods as they have towns (11:13). They are entirely incorrigibly unfaithful to God and to the covenant, and so intercession is pointless.

Third, 11:14–17 declares that Jeremiah must stop praying for Jerusalem because God has irrevocably decreed that it must be destroyed. As noted in the biographical review above, this text reflects the fact that Jeremiah has been excluded from the temple and that there is an ongoing drought (a translation of this difficult text is provided in ch. 3 above). But it is important to remember that in its literary context here, this is a summarizing and introductory text. Much of what is recounted in Jeremiah 12–14 took place prior to this text with its divine prohibition against continued intercession for Judah

Fourth, 11:18–23, an account of how the men of Anathoth, Jeremiah's hometown, plotted to murder him, has a thematic purpose in this context. This was an extreme betrayal, since ties of kinship and of a common local community were almost sacred, and they should have made the people of Anathoth the last to turn against him. The implication is that when apostasy reaches this extreme—so that God's messengers are not only hated but made to be the objects of murderous violence—a community has reached the point of no return. Jeremiah himself prays that he has done nothing to deserve such hostility and asks God to bring vengeance upon these people (11:19–20). This prayer and God's response (11:21–23) conclude the summary account of why Jeremiah stopped praying for Jerusalem. The event awakened Jeremiah to the level of hostility toward him and his message, and it helped him to understand that the nation was doomed and that continued prayer for its deliverance was misguided.

Thus, chapter 11 explains in summary fashion why continued intercession was fruitless. The story is told more fully in chapters 12–20. But again, this is a thematic and literary presentation, and it deals heavily with Jeremiah's inner life and his interactions with YHWH. It is not told as a linear, biographical account.

Section II, Second Anthology, Jeremiah's Earlier Intercession (12:1–15:9)

In 12:1–15:9, the story backs up to a time before Jeremiah received the prohibition against praying for Jerusalem, describing how he had been making intercession in their behalf. Some of this goes back to fairly early in Jeremiah's ministry, either late in Josiah's reign or early in Jehoiakim's reign.

Jeremiah's Earlier Intercession (12:1–15:9)	
Jeremiah's first intercession	12:1–17
Two object lessons	13:1–14
Jerusalem cannot repent	13:15–27
Jeremiah's second intercession	14:1–12
Jeremiah's third intercession	14:13–18
Jeremiah's fourth intercession	14:19–15:9

Jeremiah 12:1–17 is both Jeremiah's intercession and YHWH's response. It sounds as though he is praying an imprecation against the people, as at 12:3b:

Separate them [from the flock] out like sheep for the slaughter,
And set them apart for the killing day.

In reality, the hostile language in 12:1–4 is directed at those in Judah who have the power to exploit the people and not the whole nation. Jeremiah wants God to remove evil men from his flock to preserve the rest. This is a prayer for Judah, not against it. This probably reflects the early stage of Jehoiakim's reign, when the prophet was just coming to realize how corrupt the new king and his court were, and thus all his anger was directed at men in high office. But Jeremiah's language is somewhat harsh and challenging, implying that YHWH's is somewhat lax about doing his job of upholding justice. If God would just punish the wicked rulers, all would be well.

God's initial response is somewhat enigmatic: "If you have run with men on foot and they have exhausted you, how can you compete with horses?" (12:5). This is a lesser-to-greater argument. In this analogy, the corruption of certain officials, which is so common as to be expected, is the lesser. Jeremiah has seen the treachery of these government and religious leaders, and he can scarcely endure it. But this is only running with men. The greater thing, which Jeremiah at this point does not know but the reader does (from 11:18–23), is that the apostasy of the people is so deep that even his relatives in Anathoth will seek to kill him. God tells him that his closest companions have already turned against him and that he must not trust them (12:6; the events of 11:18–23, when Jeremiah directly experienced their hatred, occurred at a later time). Facing this harsh truth, for Jeremiah, will be like trying to outrun horses. In 12:7–17, YHWH concludes that the whole of Judah in incurably evil and must be destroyed.

Jeremiah 13:1–14 contains two object lessons. The first, in 13:1–11, involved Jeremiah carrying a loincloth to Perath, a village about three miles from his hometown of Anathoth.[4] The loincloth represented Israel's intimate covenant bond with YHWH. Jeremiah buried it under a rock near Perath and sometime later went back to retrieve it. Because of weather, dirt, and perhaps vermin, it was ruined and filthy. The message was that the relationship between YHWH and Israel was in tatters and could not be restored. The second object lesson, 13:12–14, was that wine jars had to be filled with wine. This seemingly pointless truism (the people would respond, 13:12, "Well, don't we know that every wine jar should be filled with wine?") pointed to the fact that a people must come to its destiny. The apostate people of Jerusalem were destined for drunkenness, for drinking the wine of God's wrath and, in the end, for being smashed as empty and useless jars. Both object lessons had a message not just for the people but

---

4.   Against the ESV and NRSV, he did not go to the Euphrates, which would have involved two round trips of about fourteen hundred miles, although the town Perath was chosen because its name sounded like the Hebrew for Euphrates. Cf. NIV.

also for the prophet. Jeremiah had to see the people for what they were and understand that there would be no spiritual renewal.

In Jeremiah 13:15–27, YHWH more prosaically asserts that Jerusalem is incapable of repentance. It opens with a lengthy appeal for them to turn away from their evil ways (13:15–21), which reflected Jeremiah's hope at this stage of his ministry but closes with a blunt assertion that they can no more change their ways than a leopard can change its spots (13:22–27).

Jeremiah 14:1–12 contains a lamentation over the drought from early in Jehoiakim's reign. Jeremiah made a prayer that confessed that Judah was sinful but appealed to YHWH to be merciful and grant them relief (14:7–9). YHWH responded that the people were incorrigibly evil and neither Jeremiah's prayers nor their sacrifices would cause him to lift the punishment. At this point, as foreshadowed in 11:14–17, YHWH told Jeremiah to stop praying for Judah:

> And YHWH said to me, "Do not pray for the benefit of this people. If they fast, I will not listen to their appeals. If they offer burnt offerings and grain offerings, I will not accept them. Instead, I will finish them off with the sword, famine, and plague." (Jer. 14:11–12)

Jeremiah's rejoinder in 14:13 is a direct response to God's command to stop praying for the people:

> But I said, "Oh, come on, Lord YHWH! Look here, the prophets keep telling them, 'You won't experience the sword or suffer famine. Indeed, I will give you lasting peace in this place.'"

Jeremiah's plea is not just a complaint that there are false prophets. It is an excuse for the people, claiming that they are doing wrong only because they are being misled by the religious leaders. It is a counterargument to God's harsh decree that all prayers for the nation should cease—and in that, it is another intercession. In his reply (14:14–18), God does not deny that the people are deceived by their preferred prophets. These are indeed false guides, and they will be proven to be liars when the men and women of Jerusalem lie dead in the streets. Still, the people are responsible for their abandonment of God and their embrace of false religious teaching, and they will suffer for it. The only thing God will allow Jeremiah to do is weep over the disaster that is about befall the nation (14:17–18).

Jeremiah 14:19–15:9 is a single episode containing a dialogue between Jeremiah and God. In 14:19–22, Jeremiah again admits that Jerusalem is guilty of great sin, but forcibly argues that God should still be compassionate and forgiving:

> Have you entirely rejected Judah? Do you loathe Zion? . . . Remember your covenant with us! Don't break it! (Jer. 14:19, 21)

His question in 14:22, "Among the worthless idols of the nations are there any that bring rain?" demonstrates that we are still in the context of the drought. But God's response is unyielding: "Even if Moses and Samuel stood [praying] before me, my heart would not be with this people" (15:1).

Moses had saved Israel by praying for them during the golden calf incident (Exod. 32); and Samuel had declared, "Indeed, as for me, far be it from me that I should sin against YHWH by ceasing to pray for you" (1 Sam. 12:23). But such prayers would no longer be accepted. Instead, YHWH gave Jeremiah a detailed account of how terrible the fall of Jerusalem would be (Jer. 15:2–9). This dialogue concluded the matter: Jeremiah had to stop praying for Jerusalem.

Section II, Second Anthology, Prophetic Imprecations Against Judah (15:10–20:18)

The boundaries of this anthology are set by an *inclusio*. It opens with Jeremiah lamenting that his mother gave him birth (15:10) and closes with him cursing the day of his birth (20:7–18). Forbidden from continuing to make intercession for Jerusalem, Jeremiah falls into depression and has an angry exchange with God. He does, however, come to see that people are implacably evil (17:5–11) and concludes that Jerusalem's destruction is both just and unavoidable. He finally gives an imprecation against Judah (17:18). Following this, sermons and imprecations against Judah illustrate how Jeremiah's outlook changed (17:19–20:18).

Prophetic Imprecations Against Judah (15:10–20:18)	
Jeremiah laments that he was born and complains	15:10–21
Two object lessons	16:1–9
Jerusalem cannot repent	16:10–17:4
A meditation on the human condition	17:5–11
Jeremiah's prayer of lamentation and imprecation	17:12–18
Messages at a gate and a house	17:19–18:17
Jeremiah prays a second imprecation	18:18–23
Messages at two gates	19:1–20:6
Jeremiah curses the day of his birth	20:7–18

Jeremiah 15:10–21 is a dialogue between YHWH and Jeremiah. Jeremiah first laments that his prophetic office has only made him the object of universal hatred (15:10), and YHWH responds that he will protect Jeremiah

and vindicate him before his enemies (15:11–14).[5] Jeremiah, however, responds with some anger. He fears God will abandon him, and remembers how when God's words were found he eagerly "ate" them. This looks back to early in his life when a copy of the law was found in the temple during Josiah's reformation (2 Kings 22:8). He eagerly supported what Josiah was doing and was thrilled to hear the law read. Now, the memory has only left bitterness in his mouth: Josiah was dead, revival would not come to Judah, and Jerusalem was condemned to the flames. Thus, his hope in God was disappointed. Even so, he could not join in the apostasy and mindless parties of his contemporaries:

> I do not sit among revelers and celebrate with them.
> I sit alone because your hand is on me, for you fill me with rage. (Jer. 15:17)

As such, he had no source of happiness at all, neither from his role as God's prophet nor from the pleasures his community offered. God, in whom he had placed all his hopes, turned out to be a "deceptive brook" (15:15–18). YHWH responds to this somewhat severely, telling Jeremiah he must repent and not utter such foolish words but assuring him that if he shows appropriate faith, God will protect him and see him through all his trials (15:19–21).

Jeremiah 16:1–9 contains other prohibitions that YHWH gave to Jeremiah. First, he must not marry or have a family (16:1–4), and second, he must not attend funerals or celebrations (16:5–9). These were probably not given in the same context as the prior dialogue with God. Since celibacy was not practiced in ancient Israel, he must have received the first command somewhat early in life (again, the structure here is literary, not chronological). All the prohibitions are signs of how terrible things will become: Soon enough, it will be impossible to have a normal domestic life. Death will be so common that proper funerals will be impossible to carry out, and parties at such a time are entirely inappropriate.

In Jeremiah 16:10–18, God asserts that Jerusalem must be destroyed because it is incorrigibly evil and serves other gods. Jeremiah responds in 16:19–20. He alludes to Josiah's reformation by declaring that idols are worthless (the eradication of idols had been a major objective of the reformation). In this, he affirms that YHWH is right in his actions and implies he continues to believe in what Josiah tried to do, even if the people were unwilling to follow. YHWH reaffirms that the nation is so thoroughly depraved that it must undergo the full force of God's anger (16:21–17:4).[6] Jeremiah 17:1–4,

---

5.   Jeremiah 15:11–14 is difficult in the Hebrew, but it is translatable. See Garrett and Pearson, *Jeremiah and Lamentations*, 191–92.

6.   Unfortunately, YHWH's portrayal of the incurable nature of the people's apostasy is almost lost in most translations of 17:1–4. For a discussion of this text, see ch. 8 below or Garrett and Pearson, *Jeremiah and Lamentations*, 195–96.

with its focus on how idolatry has corrupted the hearts of the people and made them hopelessly immoral, naturally leads into the next section, especially 17:9–10, which stresses that the heart is both obscure and evil.

Jeremiah 17:5–11 is a brief oracle on the human need for security, declaring that the only place of true safety is under the care of God. But people have twisted minds and try to find refuge in evil and in greed, and they only destroy themselves. The poems in 17:5–8 and 17:11 appear self-contained and may have come from different times in Jeremiah's ministry. They are set here because they appropriately continue the examination of human corruption in 17:1–4. All these passages affirm that people are incorrigible; Jeremiah should not expect to see repentance and renewal.

Jeremiah 17:12–18 is a prayer voicing a similar request to that found in 15:10–21; in both, Jeremiah is keenly aware of how isolated he is and asks that God will protect him from his enemies. These two passages thus create bookends to form the borders of 15:10–17:18. Jeremiah probably gave the latter prayer some time after the former but still during the crisis of the drought; both passages use metaphors involving water. However, 17:12–18 lacks the angry and despairing tone of 15:10–21. In 17:12–18, he does not complain that YHWH has been a "deceitful brook" (15:18) but confesses that he is the only reliable source of the water of life (17:13).[7] This closes with Jeremiah calling on God to bring "the day of disaster" down upon Judah, indicating he has fully accepted God's determination to obliterate the nation. He is ready to obey God's command to desist from interceding for them.

Following this, a series of passages demonstrate how Jeremiah recognizes that Judah is beyond all hope. Two distinct messages are placed side-by-side in 17:19–18:17. First, the sermon at the People's Gate, probably from earlier in Jeremiah's ministry, holds out the possibility of restoration if the people will keep the Sabbath (17:19–27). But this is followed by the sermon at a potter's house, which asserts that YHWH is free to annul his earlier good intentions for Judah and bring them to a "day of disaster" instead (18:1–17). In this context, the placement of the two messages implies that Judah once could have repented but their obstinance has made it impossible for God to save them. These are followed by another imprecation against Judah (18:18–23). After this, the book records two climactic messages of condemnation: the sermon at the Potsherd Gate, which declares that Jerusalem will be obliterated (19:1–15), and the denunciation of Pashhur at the Benjamin Gate (20:1–6). At the last, brokenhearted at how bleak and bitter his ministry has become, Jeremiah curses the day of his birth (20:7–18).

In summary, Jeremiah 2:1–20:18 condemns Judah in two anthologies. The first asserts that the people are deluded and will only see the truth when Jerusalem comes burning down around them (2:1–10:25). The second asserts that

---

7. For the translation and meaning of 17:12–13, 16, see Garrett and Pearson, *Jeremiah and Lamentations*, 198–99.

Jeremiah himself had been blindly optimistic, but YHWH opened his eyes to the profundity of Jerusalem's apostasy well before the end came (11:1–20:18).

Section VI, First Anthology Against the Nations (46:1–49:39)

As noted above, section VI, a series of undated oracles against the nations, is the counterpart to section II, a series of undated oracles against Judah. Both collections are divided into two major anthologies. In section VI, the two anthologies are (1) oracles against the nations that Babylon dominated, and (2) oracles against Babylon itself.

The first anthology is in ten parts, and it addresses the following nations: Egypt (46:2–26); Israel (46:27–28); Philistia (47:1–7); Moab (48:1–47); Ammon (49:1–6); Edom (49:7–22); Damascus (49:23–27); Kedar (49:28–33); Elam (49:34–39). As suggested above in chapter 3, the lengthy and geographically detailed oracle concerning Moab is best explained by the supposition that Jeremiah and Baruch were in exile there while evading Jehoiakim's attempts to murder them.

Section VI, Second Anthology Against the Nations (50:1–51:64)

This anthology concerns Babylon, the conqueror of all the above states. It has a major superscript (50:1), and this echoes the superscript at 46:1, which stands at the head of the oracles against the other nations. This is a signal to the reader that this begins a second anthology.

This anthology against Babylon is in two parts. The first is a straightforward oracle against the city (50:1–51:58). The second part (51:59–64) is an oracle set within a historical narrative. It describes a commission Jeremiah gave to Seraiah, brother of Baruch, to carry a scroll with a message condemning Babylon written on it. Seraiah was to read the message and then throw the scroll into the Euphrates as a sign that Babylon, too, would sink from the world stage. Although the first anthology has ten parts and the second has only two, they are surprisingly close in length: 46:1–49:39 has 121 verses and 50:1–51:64 has 110 verses.

HISTORICALLY CONTEXTUALIZED MESSAGES

Sections III (21:1–29:32) and V (34:1–45:5) both contain various dated messages and episodes from the life of Jeremiah, although the individual units are not arranged in chronological sequence. Both sections concern Judah's refusal to keep the covenant and its hostility to Jeremiah. Sections III and V each have two parts. Sections III and V also echo each other in significant ways, confirming that this arrangement is a deliberate editorial decision.

Section III, Part 1 (21:1–25:38)

This portion of the book groups together three dated messages. As one can see in the dates provided below, the messages are chronologically in reverse order.

The Messages of Jeremiah 21:1–25:38	
The delegation from Zedekiah in 588, and related denunciations	21:1–23:40
The good and bad figs, a message given in 597	24:1–10
Messages on YHWH's wrath, dated to 605	25:1–38

The thematic purpose of this body of texts is to show that the house of David is hopelessly corrupt and the dynasty must end. By arranging the messages in reverse order, this collection points out that the corruption of the last king, Zedekiah, is a continuation of the infidelity of his predecessors Jehoiachin and Jehoiakim. That is, one might assume that Zedekiah was especially evil because Jerusalem fell in his time. But in fact, his predecessors were as bad or worse. None of them lived up to the examples of Josiah or their more distant ancestor, David.

21:1–23:40

In this text, the delegation from Zedekiah came to ask Jeremiah to seek God's help against the Babylonians, hoping that Jerusalem could be saved by a miracle. Jeremiah rejected their request and said that God would fight against Judah (21:1–10). The passage then justifies God's opposition to Judah by citing a collection of earlier appeals for Judah and especially the royal house to repent (21:11–22:9), as well as other earlier oracles that condemned the kings Jehoahaz (22:10–12), Jehoiakim (22:13–23), and Jehoiachin (22:24–30). It concludes in two parts (23:1–40): first, a promise that someday there will be a Davidic king who will truly show the righteousness of YHWH (in contrast to the morally weak Zedekiah, whose name means "righteousness of YHWH"), and second, a denunciation of the false prophets who proclaim that YHWH will deliver Jerusalem from Babylon. This repudiation of the false promise of national deliverance (23:9–40) forms an *inclusio* with the initial request from Zedekiah for a favorable oracle (21:1–10), marking the end of this unit.

24:1–10

Jeremiah 24:1–10 recounts a message given soon after the deportation of Jehoiachin (called Jeconiah in 24:1) in 597. It is the account of the two baskets of figs, evidently left as offerings at the temple. One basket contained excellent fruit, but the other contained figs that were disgusting and inedible. YHWH's message, that the good figs were those that were taken to Babylon and the bad ones were those that remained behind in Jerusalem, is counterintuitive. One would have thought that those who suffered the punishment of deportation were the worst sinners, but in reality, the ones chosen for extreme punishment were those who were left in Jerusalem. Apart from encouraging the Jews in Babylon to prepare themselves for a long stay, it implied that Zedekiah and the men around him were worse than those who had been taken. God would entirely reject the part of the populace that remained in the city after the 597 exile.

25:1–38

Jeremiah 25:1–38 is in three parts. The first part, 25:1–14, cites a scroll (25:13) that pronounces a death sentence over Jerusalem, saying that the city will be left desolate for seventy years. The second part makes use of the familiar metaphor of the cup of YHWH's wrath (25:15–29). It declares that Jerusalem and many nations will have to drink from this cup and then stagger and fall. In the metaphor, Babylon is the cup from which they will drink. The third part (25:30–38) uses a series of other metaphors to describe the coming calamity: YHWH will roar like a lion, and he will be like a man treading out grapes, in which the juice represents the blood that will flow from the slain Israelites. YHWH will be like a man who formally accuses an adversary and sees to it that punishment is carried out. The coming disaster will be like a storm sweeping through the land destroying everything in its path. The slain bodies of Jerusalem's young men will be like dung in a field. Judah's rulers will be like shepherds who weep over a flock that a lion has ripped apart. The lion metaphor, coming in 25:30 and 38, serves to demarcate the boundaries of the third part. This series of messages, attached to the name of Jehoiakim, tells the reader that Jerusalem's fate was sealed by that king long before Zedekiah came to the throne.

Section III, Part 2 (26:1–29:32)

This portion of Jeremiah concerns the distinction between the true and false prophet. As a literary unit, it makes the point that the people despise the true word of God but eagerly embrace prophets who say what they want to hear. It has four distinct texts.

The Messages of Jeremiah 26:1–29:32	
A narrative account of the temple sermon	26:1–19
The martyrdom of the prophet Uriah of Kiriath-jearim	26:20–24
The false prophet Hananiah and the yoke	27:1–28:17
The false prophet Shemaiah the Nehelamite and letters to the exiles	29:1–32

The term "false prophet" is not actually found in Jeremiah; it is a New Testament term (e.g., Matt. 7:15; Mark 13:22; Acts 13:6; Rev. 16:13). But the concept of people who prophesy falsely in YHWH's name is an authentic idea in the Old Testament (e.g., Lam. 2:14 and Ezek. 13:9), and it legitimately applies to Hananiah and Shemaiah.

26:1–19

The first text, the temple sermon, gives only a brief account of what Jeremiah said (26:4–6). The gist of it was that it was folly to rely upon the temple as a guarantee of God's protection. It would be destroyed as surely as Shiloh had been. Rather, attention is given to the reaction of the people; they were so enraged at Jeremiah's blasphemy that they wanted him to be put to death. Reliance upon the temple was emblematic of false prophecy; it was a false teaching in the guise of orthodoxy that prevented people from truly turning to God.

26:20–24

The second text concerns Uriah son of Shemaiah of Kiriath-jearim. He had prophesied the same things as Jeremiah. Jehoiakim was determined to kill him, and he fled to Egypt. But Jehoiakim was able to have him extracted, and he slew him. This did not necessarily happen at the same time as the temple sermon incident of the previous text; the two episodes have been set together for thematic reasons, to show how deeply Jehoiakim and the men around him hated those who spoke the authentic word of YHWH.

27:1–28:17

The third text is narrated from the first person. Jeremiah tells how he made a yoke and put it on his neck as a sign that Babylon would conquer Judah and all the neighboring territory. He urged Zedekiah and representatives of other local states to submit peaceably to Babylon to avoid destruction, stating that YHWH had determined that Nebuchadnezzar's power could not be resisted (27:1–22). However, the prophet Hananiah son of Azzur purported to give an oracle from YHWH stating that Nebuchadnezzar's power was soon to be broken and that Jehoiachin and all who had been taken in the exile of 597 would soon return. To demonstrate his point, Hananiah took Jeremiah's wooden yoke and broke it. Jeremiah responded that God would give Nebuchadnezzar an iron yoke to put on the nations, and prophesied that Hananiah himself would die before the year was out; the prophecy came true (28:1–17).

29:1–32

The fourth text is chronologically out of sequence; it describes an event that took place some years before the yoke episode of 27:1–28:17. It concerns a letter that Jeremiah wrote to members of the Jehoiachin exile in Babylon, telling them that they would not quickly return to Jerusalem but should settle down for an extended stay in Babylon. In this, he was opposed by the false prophets Ahab son of Kolaiah and Zedekiah son of Maaseiah in Jerusalem and by Shemaiah the Nehelamite among the Babylonian exiles.[8] These men promised

---

8. We can assume that the prophets Ahab and Zedekiah were in Jerusalem because 29:21 predicts that they would be "given into the hands of Nebuchadnezzar" (that is, into his power). This implies that they were still in Jerusalem in the time of Zedekiah.

that the exile of Jehoiachin would speedily end. The contrast between true and false prophecy is the literary thread that binds this to the previous passages. In addition, Jeremiah's promises of restoration in 29:10–14 makes a segue to the promises of salvation for Judah and Israel in chapters 30–33.

Section V, Part 1 (34:1–35:19)

This contains three episodes that explore the significance of promises and covenants.

The Messages of Jeremiah 34:1–35:19	
A promise for Zedekiah	34:1–7
The broken covenant of the Jerusalem aristocracy	34:8–22
The example of the Rechabites	35:1–19

These three elements are chronologically far apart. The two episodes of chapter 34 took place late in the reign of Zedekiah, just before the fall of Jerusalem, but the episode of chapter 35 took place near the beginning of the reign of Jehoiakim, almost twenty years earlier. However, they are bound by the theme of demonstrating the consequences of keeping or violating a sacred vow, and they illustrate the greatness of Jerusalem's guilt.

34:1–7

The first episode, the promise to Zedekiah, is somewhat problematic in that it promises him a peaceful death (34:5), and this contradicts what we see of him elsewhere. Zedekiah tried to flee Jerusalem while it was under siege and after famine set in, but he was captured by the Babylonians. In the presence of Nebuchadnezzar, he saw his sons put to death and then his eyes were gouged out, and he died in prison in Babylon (52:6–11). This hardly constitutes dying "in peace." This is not, however, an insolvable problem. As described in chapter 4 above, 34:5 is not an irrevocable promise of an easy death. It is conditional, being tied to the encounter in 38:14–28, which required Zedekiah to accept YHWH's verdict and surrender to Babylon.[9] The implied message is that the benefits of being in covenant with YHWH are conditioned on obedience. Those who are unfaithful to God should not expect God's covenant kindness for themselves.

34:8–22

The second episode describes how the aristocrats of Jerusalem made a promise to free their Israelite slaves and even made a covenant with YHWH to that effect, but then reneged and clawed their erstwhile slaves back into servitude. This is thematically but not historically connected to 34:1–7. The

---

9.   See also Garrett and Pearson, *Jeremiah and Lamentations*, 320–21.

covenant-breaking was further indication of how thoroughly godless the ruling class had become, and the clawing back of their slaves showed how cavalier they were about their duties toward their fellow Israelites.

35:1–19

In the third episode, Jeremiah invites a group of itinerant shepherds, the Rechabites, to come to the temple precincts of Jerusalem. He offers them wine to drink, but they refuse, stating that they were under a vow imposed on them by their ancestor Jonadab that they would never drink wine. Jeremiah then contrasts the fidelity of the Rechabites to their vow with the infidelity of Jerusalem to its covenant with YHWH.

Section V, Part 2 (36:1–45:5)

This portion of Jeremiah contains four narratives, illustrating the extreme hostility of the people and leaders of Jerusalem to Jeremiah and his message.

The Messages of Jeremiah 36:1–45:5	
Jehoiakim burns the scroll of Jeremiah's prophecies	36:1–32
Two episodes in which Jeremiah was held as a captive	37:1–43:7
Jewish refugees in Egypt reject Jeremiah's prophecy	43:8–44:30
An oracle for the distraught Baruch	45:1–5

The episodes are chronologically out of sequence. Both the first and fourth narrative come from the fourth year of Jehoiakim, creating an *inclusio* structure that holds the whole of 36:1–45:5 together. Also, Baruch is a prominent figure in both chapters 36 and 45. But episodes two and three, found in 37:1–44:30, take place during the final days of Jerusalem and in the period after its fall.

36:1–32

This narrative, in which Jehoiakim burns the scroll, is of decisive importance for understanding the history of the composition of Jeremiah, as described below in chapter 7. But it also powerfully shows how disrespectful Jehoiakim was to YHWH's word, which he mutilated and burned, and to YHWH's prophet, whom he was determined to kill.

37:1–43:7

Jeremiah 37:1–43:7 further illustrates disdain the people had for YHWH's prophet. It has two episodes in which Jeremiah was held as a captive. First, he was a prisoner in Jerusalem until the city fell, when he was freed by the Babylonians (37:1–39:18). Second, he was kidnapped by a group of Judeans and taken to Egypt (40:1–43:7). In both cases, no respect is given to Jeremiah's person or prophecies. First, the aristocrats under Zedekiah were determined to silence and finally kill Jeremiah; and second, the refugees from Jerusalem blatantly disregarded his word from YHWH. In both cases, Jeremiah was forcibly seized and taken captive.

43:8–44:30

Jeremiah 43:8–44:30 contains two oracles given to the Jewish refugees in Egypt (43:8–13; 44:1–30). The Jews have not escaped Nebuchadnezzar's reach or God's wrath. They are unrepentantly defiant, just as Jehoiakim had been when he burned the scroll.

45:1–5

Jeremiah 45 is a private oracle for Baruch. It includes a sorrowful lament from Jeremiah's scribe over how badly his life had turned out due to his loyalty to Jeremiah. His willingness to write out the scroll and proclaim it in the temple (Jer. 36) had only made him, like his master, a hunted refugee.

Parallel Elements Between Sections III and V

The formal similarity between sections III and V is that both place Jeremiah's messages in specific historical contexts, in contrast to sections II and VI, which are consistently undated. In addition, section III, part 1 is in three sections and begins with Zedekiah's request for a favorable oracle; section V, part 1 is also in three sections and begins with a favorable but conditional oracle for Zedekiah. Section III, part 2 is in four sections and begins with one of the pivotal episodes of Jeremiah's prophetic ministry, the temple sermon. Section V, part 2 is also in four sections and begins with another pivotal moment, Jehoiakim's burning of the scroll.

However, the similarities between sections III and V are more extensive than these formal parallels. They also echo one another in theme and content.

Failed Appeals for Divine Intervention

First, there is the appeal of Zedekiah to Jeremiah to intercede for the city so that God would save it from the Babylonians (21:1–7). This was evidently done in hope that Jeremiah could repeat the miracle done in the time of Isaiah and Hezekiah, when God sent a plague among the Assyrian troops besieging Jerusalem (Isa. 36–37). But Jeremiah gave an oracular response declaring that this time YHWH would fight against Jerusalem. The verdict was extremely severe:

> And afterward, declares YHWH, I will give Zedekiah king of Judah, and his officials and the people in this city who survive the plague, sword, and famine, into the hands of Nebuchadnezzar king of Babylon and into the hands of their enemies and into the hands of those who seek their lives. And he will strike them with the sword. And he will not show them mercy or pity or compassion. (Jer. 21:7)

Zedekiah and his officials failed to bring about a divine rescue for Jerusalem.[10]

Something comparable to this happens in Jeremiah 34. After YHWH offered Zedekiah the opportunity of a peaceful death, the leaders of Jerusalem made a covenant before YHWH to release their Israelite slaves in an implied effort to get him to deliver them from the Babylonians. But they quickly changed their minds and nullified the manumission of the slaves. God's response to this treachery was as severe as in the oracle of Jeremiah 21, as recorded in Jeremiah 34:21:

> And I will give Zedekiah king of Judah and his officials into the hands of their enemies and into the hands of those who seek their lives, and into the hands of the army of the king of Babylon, which has withdrawn from you.

Once again, Zedekiah and his officials failed to bring about a divine rescue for Jerusalem.

YHWH's Wine

The prophecies of doom for Jerusalem and many other nations in Jeremiah 25 would seem to have no counterpart in the episode of the Rechabites of Jeremiah 35. But the Rechabites are trying to escape a region of international conflict—precisely the kind of thing Jeremiah 25 predicts. More specifically, the drinking of wine plays an important role in both chapters.

In Jeremiah 35, Jeremiah appears to call upon the Rechabites to drink wine with divine sanction and even as a command from God: He is a prophet of YHWH, and he takes them to the house of God and sets wine before them:

> And I brought them to the house of YHWH into the chamber of the sons of Hanan, the son of Igdaliah the man of God, which was by the chamber of the officials, above the chamber of Maaseiah, son of Shallum, keeper of the threshold. And I placed pitchers full of wine before the Rechabites, and cups, and I said to them, "Drink wine!" (Jer. 35:4–5)

The detailed account of where they were gathered, in a chamber associated with "Igdaliah the man of God" and near chambers of high officials of Judah, was meant to convey to these rustic shepherds that they were in a place where one must not give offense. And yet the Rechabites refused:

> And they said, "We will not drink wine, for Jonadab son of Rechab, our ancestor, commanded us, 'You shall not drink wine, neither you nor your children.'" (Jer. 35:6)

---

10. A second account of Zedekiah's request that Jeremiah intercede for Judah appears in 37:3.

They were allowed to refuse the wine and were commended for having done so.

In contrast to this, because they offended God with their many atrocities, Jerusalem and the other nations were given wine that they could not refuse:

> For this is what YHWH, the God of Israel, said to me: "Take from my hand this cup of the wine of my wrath from my hand and make all the nations drink it—all the nations to whom I send you. And they will drink it and stagger and go mad when facing the sword that I will send among them." And I took the cup from YHWH's hand and made all the nations to whom YHWH sent me drink it: Jerusalem and the towns of Judah, and its kings and officials, to make them a ruin, a horror, derided, and cursed (as they are today); Pharaoh king of Egypt, his servants, his officials, and all his people, and all the foreigners there; all the kings of Uz; all the kings of the Philistine lands, including Ashkelon, Gaza, Ekron, and what is left of Ashdod; Edom, Moab, and Ammon; and all the kings of Tyre and all the kings of Sidon; and the kings of the coastlands beyond the sea; Dedan, Tema, Buz and all who shave their temples; and all the kings of Arabia and all the kings of the foreigners who live in the wilderness; and all the kings of Zimri, and all the kings of Elam, and all the kings of Media; and all the kings of the north, near and far, one after the other—all the kingdoms on the face of the earth. And the king of Sheshak [Babylon] will drink last of all. (Jer. 25:15–26)

While this extensive and diverse collection of nations and their rulers were required to drink YHWH's wine, a humble group of shepherds known as the Rechabites were not.

True and False Prophets

Sections III and V contrast the true prophets with the false, and both demonstrate how deeply Jeremiah was hated for his messages and faced death by either mob action or execution.

The narrative account of the temple sermon (26:1–19) tells how both the people and leaders reacted to his message with threats of murder:

> And it came about as soon as Jeremiah had finished speaking all that YHWH had commanded him to speak to all the people, then the priests and the prophets and all the people seized him while saying, "You must die!" (Jer. 26:8)

The next passage, the account of the death of Uriah the prophet (26:20–24), shows that these were not idle threats.

In Jeremiah 36, after Baruch read the scroll containing Jeremiah's prophecies, the scroll was read before Jehoiakim, who cut it to pieces and burned it:

The king and all his ministers, as they heard all these words, neither showed fear nor tore their clothes. (Jer. 36:24)

In Zedekiah's reign, Jeremiah was arrested and detained. After a period of imprisonment, the high officials declared that they could no longer tolerate Jeremiah's continued existence:

Then the officials said to the king, "This man must be put to death. The reason is that he is destroying the morale of the military men who remain in this city and the morale of all the people by saying such things as he says. This man is not seeking the good of this community but its ruin." "He is in your hands," King Zedekiah answered. "The king is not able to do anything against you." (Jer. 38:4–5)

The people and their leaders would rather commit murder than have to listen to Jeremiah.

Yet another parallel is between Jeremiah's conflicts with false prophets in Jeremiah 28–29 and his conflict with the Jewish exiles in Jeremiah 43–44. After Hananiah broke Jeremiah's yoke and declared that Nebuchadnezzar would not take Jerusalem into exile, Jeremiah replied that YHWH did not send Hananiah, who made the people trust a lie (28:15). Similarly, when prophets living among the Jehoiachin exiles in Babylon predicted that they would all soon go home, Jeremiah responded:

For thus says YHWH Sabaoth, the God of Israel: Do not let your prophets among you and your diviners trick you! And do not listen to your dreamers who give dream oracles! For they are prophesying lies to you in my name; I did not send them, says YHWH. . . . Thus says YHWH Sabaoth, the God of Israel, concerning Ahab son of Kolaiah and Zedekiah son of Maaseiah, who prophesy a lie to you in my name: I am about to deliver them into the hand of King Nebuchadnezzar of Babylon, and he shall strike them down before your eyes. (Jer. 29:8–9, 21)

Jeremiah was vindicated in the course of events; the Jehoiachin exile did not end, and instead all of Jerusalem was destroyed.

In section V, however, it was Jeremiah who was accused of being a false prophet. After he told the remaining Jews in the land that God had commanded that they should not flee to Egypt and that the Babylonians would not punish them for Gedaliah's death, they flatly rejected his message, even though they had appealed to him for an oracle from YHWH and had promised to obey what Jeremiah said (42:1–6). When the message came, their response was:

You are telling a lie! YHWH our God has not sent you with the message, "You must not go to Egypt to settle there." But Baruch son of Neriah is inciting you against us to hand us over to the Babylonians, so they may kill us or carry us into exile to Babylon. (Jer. 43:2b–3)

When Jeremiah confronted the exiles in Egypt, particularly the women, with a message from YHWH condemning their continued devotion to the Queen of Heaven, they replied:

We are not about to listen to the message you give us in YHWH's name! Instead, we will do everything we said: Burn incense to the Queen of Heaven and pour out libations to her just as we, our ancestors, our kings, and our officials did in the towns of Judah and in the streets of Jerusalem. When we did that, we had plenty of food and were prosperous and suffered no harm. (44:16–17)

Even though Jeremiah's prophecies regarding the exile had proven true and his opponents Hananiah, Ahab, Zedekiah, and Shemaiah had been proven false, popular opinion continued to favor those men and to regard Jeremiah as a lying prophet.

Thus, the similarities between sections III and V go far beyond the formal parallel of both containing historically contextualized episodes. The two sections use similar language and develop parallel themes.

ESCHATOLOGICAL SALVATION

Section IV, a series of messages predicting salvation for Israel, stands at Jeremiah's structural center. Like the rest of the book, it contains both undated (30:1–31:40) and dated messages (32:1–44; 33:1–26).

The Messages of Salvation in Jeremiah 30:1–33:26	
Undated Messages	
The command to write the book of consolation	30:1–3
The pleasant dream	30:4–31:26
Two agricultural metaphors	31:27–30
The new covenant	31:31–37
The restoration of Jerusalem	31:38–40
Dated Messages	
The redeemed land, dated to the tenth year of Zedekiah	32:1–44
Jerusalem restored, dated to the tenth year of Zedekiah	33:1–26

The two dated messages come from the last days of Jerusalem and late in the ministry of Jeremiah; one would thus expect to find them near the end of the book. Indeed, it is common for most promises of restoration to be concentrated at the end of a prophetic book (as in Hosea, Amos, Isaiah, and Ezekiel). The fact that they do not implies that their placement is deliberate and according to a larger plan. The messages of salvation will be examined in chapter 8.

Conclusion

The data indicate that the book follows a deliberate and carefully constructed outline. It is by no means the chaotic, random collection of oracles and episodes that many scholars and readers have taken it to be. More specifically, it is a chiasmus in which the promises of salvation are in the central position.

A   Prologue: The beginning of Jeremiah's ministry (1:1–19)
    B   Two anthologies against Judah (2:1–20:18)
        C   Historically contextualized messages (21:1–29:32)
            D   Eschatological salvation (30:1–33:26)
        C′   Historically contextualized messages (34:1–45:5)
    B′   Two anthologies against the nations (46:1–51:64)
A′   Epilogue: The end of the house of David (52:1–34)

Although chiastic patterns are common in the Bible, no other book of prophecy has such a structure. This indicates that the book's layout is the product of careful thought and planning. It is unique. And despite all its words of condemnation, the book of Jeremiah has a message of salvation at its center.

CHAPTER 7

THE COMPOSITION OF JEREMIAH

The question of how the book of Jeremiah came to be written is argu-ably its most difficult feature. This problem is not obscure or created by some scholarly obsession with finding internal inconsistencies. It is right on the surface of the book's two most important primary sources, the Hebrew Masoretic Text and the Greek Septuagint. These texts differ from one other in such a profound way that it is hard to see how Septuagint Jeremiah can be called a translation of what we see in the Hebrew Bible.

THE PROBLEM AND PROPOSED SOLUTIONS

Early Critical Theories

Critical scholarship of Jeremiah has never enjoyed the kind of consensus that once prevailed for the Pentateuch (with the dominance of the Documen-tary Hypothesis) or Isaiah (with the theory of First, Second, and Third Isaiah). The first critical theory to attract significant attraction was that of Bernhard Duhm, who in 1901 proposed that in Jeremiah only the poetic oracles writ-ten in bicola (two-line strophes) were legitimately from the prophet; all other texts were secondary. In 1914, Sigmund Mowinckel divided the book among several sources, "A" (poetic oracles authentically from Jeremiah), "B" (biographical texts), "C" (secondary, Deuteronomistic sermons), and "D" (the optimistic oracles of Jer. 30–31). But these theories never gained a consensus. Today, virtually no one regards A, B, C, and D as distinct sources, although a few scholars still use the terms as formal categories, and some believe there was a Deuteronomistic revision of Jeremiah.[1]

---

1. For useful surveys of the history of source-critical scholarship in Jeremiah, see Holladay, *Jeremiah 2*, 11–14; and Robert P. Carroll, *Jeremiah: A Commentary*, OTL (Philadelphia: Westminster, 1986), 38–50.

I believe that the whole of the book comes from Jeremiah and his assistant, Baruch. Even so, the text is highly problematic, and the matter of its composition history is difficult. Two problems are apparent. First, the book appears to be an almost random collection of messages and episodes. Second, the Hebrew text of the book is strikingly different from the Old Greek version, the Septuagint (abbreviated as LXX). The previous chapter proposed a model for understanding Jeremiah's literary structure. In this chapter, we will examine the problem of the LXX.

The Problem of the LXX

The LXX Jeremiah is significantly shorter than the Hebrew Masoretic Text (abbreviated as MT). By one count, the LXX lacks the equivalent of 3,097 Hebrew words found in the MT, although it adds the equivalent of about 100 words.[2] Most strikingly, it moves all the oracles against the nations from their position near the end of the book (MT 46–51) to right after 25:13, near the middle of the book. In addition, the oracles against the nations are not in the same order in the LXX as in the MT, and the contents of the oracles are not precisely the same (the LXX lacks some verses found in the MT).

The differences in the oracles against the nations can be observed in the following table:

Hebrew (MT)			Greek (LXX)		
MT Order	**Nation**	**Location in MT**	**MT Order**	**Nation**	**Location in LXX**
1	Egypt	46:1–26	9	Elam	25:14–19
2	Israel	46:27–28	1	Egypt	26:2–25
3	Philistines	47:1–7	2	Israel	26:27–28
4	Moab	48:1–47	10	Babylon	27:1–28:64
5	Ammon	49:1–6	3	Philistines	29:1–7
6	Edom	49:7–22	6	Edom	30:1–16
7	Damascus	49:23–27	5	Ammon	30:17–21
8	Kedar	49:28–33	8	Kedar	30:23–28
9	Elam	49:34–39	7	Damascus	30:29–33
10	Babylon	50:1–51:64	4	Moab	31:1–44

The MT has other problems vis-à-vis the LXX. Frequently, a verse in the MT is longer than its equivalent in the LXX, implying either that the LXX has been deliberately abbreviated or that the MT has been embellished. For example, at 21:2, the LXX has only the "king of Babylon" while the MT has

---

2.   Lundbom, *Jeremiah 1–20*, 57–58.

"Nebuchadnezzar, the king of Babylon."[3] Sometimes, the differences between the two texts are more profound. For example, MT Jeremiah 36:32 says, "Jeremiah took a different scroll, and he gave it to Baruch the son of Neriah, the scribe, and he wrote." But the Greek equivalent (LXX 43:32) only says, "And Baruch took another scroll, and he wrote." When the MT has a text that the LXX lacks, one can call this text a "zero variant," or an "LXX minus," or an "MT plus." The term "MT plus" implies that the MT has expanded the original text, and "LXX minus" implies that the LXX has omitted words. The term "zero variant" is neutral, simply observing that one text (typically the LXX) lacks words that appear in the other (typically the MT).

Another issue is that the MT contains many "doublets," where the content of a passage in one location is repeated at another location. While the LXX sometimes has both doublets, at other times it has the text in only one place, whereas the MT has the same text in two locations. For example, a doublet occurs at MT 30:10–11 and MT 46:27–28; they both have substantially the same text. The LXX has the counterpart to MT 46:27–28 (at LXX 26:27–28), but it has no counterpart to MT 30:10–11.

A discovery at Qumran had a significant impact on this problem. Among the fragmentary Hebrew scrolls of Jeremiah found there was one designated 4Q71 (4QJer[b]). It is written in Hebrew, but in content it is closer to the LXX than to the MT.[4] This implies that the LXX translation is based on a Hebrew original; it is not simply an abridged translation based on the MT-type text. We thus must work with the assumption that the Hebrew *Vorlage* behind the LXX was in its contents similar to the LXX (a *Vorlage* is a text on which a translation is based). This, in turn, suggests that there were two separate and substantially different Hebrew text traditions for Jeremiah: one represented by the MT, and the other by the LXX translation. This obviously poses a problem: Which text tradition represents the more original or superior version?

Recent Interpretations of the Problem

For many in modern scholarship, J. Gerald Janzen's *Studies in the Text of Jeremiah* answered this question: The LXX *Vorlage* is closer to the original, authentic book of Jeremiah, and the MT is a secondary expansion of that text.[5] Janzen worked through the many doublets and zero variants in Jeremiah and argued that in case after case the evidence suggests that the LXX is an earlier, simpler text and that the MT is a secondary expansion. Today, many scholars take it as a given that the LXX represents a superior, more

---

3. For a discussion of the variants in proper names between the MT and LXX, see J. Gerald Janzen, *Studies in the Text of Jeremiah*, HSM 6 (Cambridge, MA: Harvard University Press, 1973), 69–86.
4. Karen H. Jobes and Moses Silva, *Invitation to the Septuagint* (Grand Rapids: Baker Academic, 2000), 173–77; Emanuel Tov, *Textual Criticism of the Hebrew Bible*, 3rd ed. (Minneapolis: Fortress, 2012), 289–92.
5. Janzen, *Studies in the Text of Jeremiah*, 128.

pristine version of Jeremiah.[6] Emanuel Tov has similarly concluded that the LXX is an earlier "Edition I," while the MT is a later "Edition II."[7] This is a significant and perhaps troubling conclusion, as it implies that the LXX is the "true" Jeremiah (or is at least closer to the true Jeremiah), while the MT has an enormous number of later, editorial additions. If correct, the MT additions to Jeremiah cannot be legitimately claimed to be from him; they are inauthentic. This suggests that our Bibles should contain a translation of the LXX Jeremiah and not of the MT.

But many scholars have concluded that the situation is much worse than that. They have concluded that in fact there were not just two versions. To the contrary, the book grew from an original kernel through many expansions and additions. The LXX represents an intermediate stage in that growth and the MT represents a later and possibly final stage. But in addition to the LXX and MT, there were many other versions of Jeremiah. These were different stages of the book's growth through the centuries.

William McKane argues that there was an original "kernel" to the book (which may or may not have had the actual words of the prophet). He also speaks of a "reservoir" of poetic texts in Jeremiah that served as a source for many other, later passages in the book. He asserts that there was a process of "generation" or "triggering," whereby a small text triggered exegesis or commentary by a later scribe. This commentary was then added to the text and became part of the canonical version. For example, he claims that the poetry of 3:1–5 triggered a prose expansion in 3:6–11. McKane further argues that Jeremiah grew as a "rolling corpus." The text through the centuries simply acquired more and more material, like a snowball rolling down a hill. From a small beginning, it grew to what became the Hebrew *Vorlage* of the LXX, and after that, the Hebrew text continued to grow until it became what we now see in the MT.[8]

Other Jeremiah scholars have reached similar conclusions. Leslie Allen compares Jeremiah to an English country house that, through the centuries, has had many wings and rooms added to it.[9] In this theory, it is meaningless to speak of an "original" or "superior" version of Jeremiah. Both the MT and the LXX are relatively late examples of a long process of growth; the kernel, the truly original book of Jeremiah, is long lost to us.

Robert Carroll traces the history of the book's composition as fully as possible. On the one hand, he is skeptical of finding anything that goes back to an original book of Jeremiah or to the man Jeremiah.[10] On the other hand,

6. E.g., Anneli Aejmelaeus, "Jeremiah at the Turning-point of History: The Function of Jer. XXV 1–14 in the Book of Jeremiah," *VT* 52, no. 4 (2002): 459–82, DOI:10.1163/156853302320764799.

7. Tov, *Textual Criticism of the Hebrew Bible*, 288.

8. William McKane, *A Critical and Exegetical Commentary on Jeremiah*, 2 vols., ICC (Edinburgh: T&T Clark, 1986, 1996), 1:xv–xcix.

9. Leslie Allen, *Jeremiah: A Commentary*, OTL (Louisville: Westminster John Knox, 2008), 11.

10. Other scholars are also doubtful about finding the "real" Jeremiah; see Peter R. Ackroyd, "The Book of Jeremiah: Some Recent Studies," *JSOT* 9, no. 28 (1984): 47–50, DOI:10.1177/030908928400902804;

he does believe that we can recover the historical situation or community that gave rise to many passages in Jeremiah. For him, the book is a kind of notebook containing competing texts inserted by diverse groups within postexilic Judaism. He claims, for example:

- The condemnation of Jehoiachin in 22:24–30 reflects the existence of an anti-Zerubbabel faction in the time of Haggai and Zechariah.
- Jeremiah 24:1–10 reflects a conflict between the Jerusalem Jews and those returning from exile during the time of Ezra and Nehemiah.
- The more optimistic prophecies of chapters 30–31 come from groups that sought to reconcile the communities and to rebuild the Jewish economy and state.
- The polemic against the Egyptian exiles (ch. 44) arose from a conflict between the postexilic Jewish community in Egypt and the community in Jerusalem.

The expanding book allowed different and sometimes mutually hostile Jewish groups of the postexilic period to insert their opinions in a book that ostensibly carried the authority of a prophet named "Jeremiah."[11]

Challenges to Janzen's Proposal

Against the above consensus, Robert Althann and Jack R. Lundbom have respectively argued that the LXX represents a deliberately shortened or corrupted text. Both explanations imply that the LXX translators had a Hebrew text that was close to our MT, and that the MT represents the earlier version of Jeremiah.

Althann says that the LXX translators did not appreciate the role of parallelism in Hebrew poetry and so cut out what seemed to them to be needless repetition.[12] If true, this means that the MT is indeed the earlier text and the LXX represents an abridgment of that text.

Lundbom, by contrast, argues that the LXX Hebrew *Vorlage* was a very bad copy, containing many scribal errors. He claims that this text was frequently cut short by accidents of haplography. This is an error in which the original text has the same word written twice fairly close to each other, but a copyist's eye jumps from the first occurrence to the second, skipping the words in between. Lundbom contends that the LXX *Vorlage* was riddled with such scribal errors and that the apparently more "expanded" version found in the MT is the earlier and accurate text. In his "Appendix III: Haplography

---

James L. Crenshaw, "A Living Tradition: The Book of Jeremiah in Current Research," *Int* 37, no. 2 (1983): 128–29, DOI:10.1177/002096438303700202.

11.   Carroll, *Jeremiah*, 65–82.

12.   E.g., Robert Althann, *A Philological Analysis of Jeremiah 4–6 in the Light of Northwest Semitic*, BibOr 38 (Rome: Biblical Institute Press, 1983), 29, 46–47, 69, 88–89, 305–7.

in Jeremiah 1–20," he lists fifty-two scribal errors behind the LXX for these chapters.[13] In "Appendix V: Haplography in Jeremiah 21–52," he catalogs the scribal errors that he thinks existed in the LXX *Vorlage* of these chapters, finding 263 in total.[14] If his findings are valid, we certainly cannot make the LXX out to be the earlier, more pristine version of Jeremiah. Unfortunately, these proposals do not save the MT of Jeremiah. Neither Althann's nor Lundbom's arguments bear close scrutiny.

The principal argument against Althann is this: Considering how much parallelism there is in the Hebrew Bible, it is surprising that of all the LXX, only Jeremiah has obliterated so much of it. Why, we might wonder, don't we see such hostility to parallelism in the LXX Psalms or Isaiah? Also, a large number of MT plus texts, although they are repetitive or expansive, do not involve poetic parallelism. As a solution, this is somewhat ad hoc and forced; it lacks any compelling evidence. We have no real basis for claiming that the LXX translators abridged the text they had received.

Lundbom's claim that the LXX *Vorlage* was rife with errors of haplography is equally forced. The shorter passages in the LXX are always clear, intelligible texts. Textual corruption by haplography would almost certainly create many garbled, untranslatable verses, since *haplography is by definition a random, accidental omission of a string of words*. For example, suppose we have an original text that reads, "This French sentence is incoherent, and we should not translate incoherent French into coherent English." But a copyist's eye skips from the first "incoherent" to the next and writes, "This French sentence is incoherent French into coherent English." Haplography has in this case produced a sentence that is itself incoherent! A similar example would be an original sentence that said, "The house that he built is a small house, but it is very cute." A copyist, however, by haplography jumps from the first instance of "house" to the second, and omits the words in between. The result would be the ungrammatical, "The house, but it is very cute."

A text of Jeremiah filled with errors of haplography would often be unreadable, but this is not what we see reflected in the LXX. For example, the first example in his "Appendix V: Haplography in Jeremiah 21–52" concerns the MT of 21:4, which has, "Look, I am turning aside the weapons of war *which are in your hand*, with which you are fighting *the king of Babylon and* the Chaldeans."[15] Because of the scribal errors, the words translated in italics were lost. But the supposedly corrupted *Vorlage*, lacking the words in italics, makes perfect sense: "Look, I am turning aside

---

13. Lundbom, *Jeremiah 1–20*, 885–87.

14. Lundbom, *Jeremiah 37–52*, 549–63.

15. Lundbom, *Jeremiah 37–52*, 549. Lundbom sees two cases of haplography here, the first caused by the repetition of אֲשֶׁר and the second by the repetition of אֵת. The first text lost by haplography was אֲשֶׁר בְּיֶדְכֶם and the second was אֶת־מֶלֶךְ בָּבֶל וְ.

the weapons of war with which you are fighting the Chaldeans." Also, the repeated Hebrew words that supposedly caused the haplography can be more reasonably explained without recourse to scribal error.[16] This makes for a much simpler, more persuasive explanation here than claiming a scribal error does.

A similar example is at 22:25. The MT translates to "and I will give you into the hands of those who seek your life, into the hands of those of whose faces you fear, even into the hands of King Nebuchadnezzar of Babylon and into the hands of the Chaldeans." The shorter LXX translates to "And I will give you into the hands of those who seek your life, of those whose faces you fear, into the hands of the Chaldeans." Lundbom argues that the loss of "even into the hands of King Nebuchadnezzar of Babylon," too, is a result of haplography, but once again the LXX is entirely coherent and shows no signs of having been corrupted.[17] The conclusion that the MT is an expansion is both plausible and simpler.

So it is in case after case: Lundbom's claims that the LXX translated a corrupted Hebrew manuscript do not withstand scrutiny. Indeed, to have made all the errors Lundbom suggests, the scribes behind the LXX *Vorlage* would have had to have been spectacularly incompetent while being extraordinarily lucky, in that their frequent errors almost never created a grammatically incoherent text. This is not to say that there are no possible examples of haplography in the Hebrew *Vorlage* to the LXX. Such cases, however, are more the exception than the rule.[18]

And of course, neither Lundbom's nor Althann's hypothesis explains why oracles against the nations are in a different place and in a different order in the LXX. Cumulative evidence strongly suggests that the text represented in the LXX is prior to the proto-MT. For example, the LXX often, but not always, gives titles for God that are shorter than those in the MT. An example is at 7:28, where the MT has "YHWH God," but the LXX only has "Lord" (= "YHWH") but not "God." In other places, however, the LXX

---

16. An MT plus in Jeremiah is frequently a grammatically matched expansion of the LXX, giving a fuller account but not really adding new information. In other words, the MT addition has the same grammatical pattern as the *Vorlage* behind the LXX, but it does little more than add a parallel phrase. Thus, where the LXX of 21:4 has "fighting the Chaldeans" (where "the Chaldeans" is a direct object), the MT has "fighting *the king of Babylon and* the Chaldeans" (where the MT adds an additional direct object, "the king of Babylon"). Because the MT plus phrase grammatically matches the apparent LXX *Vorlage*, it also has the word אֵת with both "the king of Babylon" and with "the Chaldeans." In other words, the repetition of אֵת is more reasonably explained as a grammatically matched expansion in the MT than as a scribal error in the LXX *Vorlage*.

17. Lundbom, *Jeremiah 37–52*, 549. Lundbom argues that וּבְיַד נְבוּכַדְרֶאצַּר מֶלֶךְ־בָּבֶל has been omitted due to the repetition of וּבְיַד in the received text being missed by the copyist or translator.

18. As noted by Holladay, *Jeremiah 1*, 484, a possible example can be found in Jeremiah 16:21–17:5, in which 17:1–4 is missing from the LXX due to haplography of יהוה at the end of 16:21 and beginning of 17:5. In my view, however, even this example is doubtful.

has the full "Lord God" for the MT "YHWH God" (e.g., 2:17).[19] This clear but inconsistent tendency for expanded divine names occurs throughout the MT Jeremiah as compared to the LXX. Furthermore, although the LXX at times has a shorter divine title, it never paraphrases but always translates literally, suggesting that the translator did not feel free to modify divine titles. Because the LXX translator never changes divine titles but only has shorter titles, the examples in the LXX imply that the translator had a *Vorlage* that often lacked the expanded divine titles we see in the MT.[20] We cannot deny that the LXX appears to be an earlier "Edition 1" of Jeremiah and that the MT is a later "Edition 2."

This is not to say, however, that Janzen has fully made his case. He sometimes forces the evidence. This can be demonstrated from his handling of MT 6:13–15, which MT 8:10b–12 substantially repeats. Thus, these two passages give us a doublet in the MT. The LXX has 6:13–15 but lacks 8:10b–12. Janzen says that this is an example of how the scribes behind the MT needlessly expanded the Hebrew original. But in the MT, 6:13–15 uses an orthography (a way of spelling words) that is characteristic of later Hebrew, but 8:10b–12 spells the words in a manner more characteristic of earlier Hebrew.[21] It is unlikely that a text written in an earlier orthography was a copy of a text written in a later orthography. But to sustain his larger hypothesis, Janzen insists 8:10b–12 was copied from 6:13–15.[22]

Much of Janzen's work is superficial, since he tried to handle the entire book of Jeremiah, comparing the MT to the LXX, in his relatively brief study. By contrast, Sven Soderlund has subjected the LXX 29:1–7 and 30:1–16 (in the MT, 47:1–7 and 49:7–22) to an intense and detailed analysis. Soderlund repeatedly shows that Janzen's conclusions are often based on a superficial review of the data. But Soderlund does not argue that the MT text was prior to the LXX *Vorlage*.[23] It still appears that the LXX *Vorlage* was prior to the MT text. Even so, one must use Janzen's analyses with caution. Soderlund demonstrates that the LXX Jeremiah we now possess is not a pristine, earlier version of Jeremiah. The standard LXX itself went through a process of development, and its final form was even influenced by the MT.

Janzen's work forces us to think through complex problems, and we cannot escape these problems by arguing that the LXX (which we can call "Edition 1") represents a deliberate or accidental abbreviation of the proto-MT (which we can call "Edition 2"). But saying that Edition 1 is "earlier"

---

19.   I.e., for the MT יהוה אֱלֹהִים, the LXX sometimes has κύριος and sometimes has κύριος ὁ θεός.

20.   I owe this insight to an unpublished paper written by my student Andrew Matthews.

21.   Jeremiah 6:13–15 uses the fuller orthography (employing many vowel letters), but 8:10b–12 lacks the extra vowel letters.

22.   For his explanation, see Janzen, *Studies in the Text of Jeremiah*, 95–96.

23.   Sven Soderlund, *The Greek Text of Jeremiah: A Revised Hypothesis*, JSOTSup 47 (Sheffield: JSOT Press, 1985), 203–46.

does not necessarily mean that it is "superior," if by that we mean a more accurate transmission of Jeremiah's words and intended meaning.

A Response to the Idea of the "Rolling Corpus"

Before proposing a solution, therefore, we must briefly reconsider the idea of the "rolling corpus" of McKane, Allen, and Carroll. This theory, that the book of Jeremiah was expanded from a small kernel by making numerous additions through the centuries, is highly implausible. The theory, in its various forms, works out as follows:

- An original kernel of texts made up a book that was much smaller than either the LXX or MT book of Jeremiah.
- This book grew through the years. Various scribes added new material by McKane's process of "triggering." Also, different groups within postexilic Judaism, each trying to use the authority of the book to further its own ideals, made additions to the book.
- Scribes sometimes duplicated material already in the book and moved the copied material to new locations, creating doublets.
- This created many separate editions of Jeremiah, but each new edition was longer than the previous one.
- At some point in the process, the LXX *Vorlage* became isolated and was translated into the Greek text we now have.
- Another edition continued to grow into the proto-MT. It became our standard Hebrew version of Jeremiah.
- All other editions were lost.

No aspect of this theory is persuasive. It treats the book as though it were an electronic text, a wiki, that different scribes could supplement or reshape at will. In reality, the book was handwritten onto a scroll of papyrus or vellum. The medium itself, the "paper," was extremely expensive. Every time a newly expanded version was created, it had to be entirely recopied (scribes could have made marginal notations, but later scribes would have had no reason to regard those notations as authoritative or to put them in the body of the text). Thus, we are to envision that a scroll was passed from one group of scribes to another group, so that the second group recopied the whole while adding new material of their own, creating a new and larger version of Jeremiah. This process was repeated countless times. And even though each group felt free to radically revise the text, they never deleted anything. When one sect received the book as altered by a rival sect, they accepted everything their rivals had inserted. They simply added new material of their own. Furthermore, every prior edition of Jeremiah was discarded except for the LXX *Vorlage*, which for some reason survived and was translated into Greek, and the final edition, the proto-MT. The theory can only exist in the world of scholarly hypothesis; it could not have happened in the real world of postexilic Judaism.

We may add to this that the proposed motivation for such an extended compilation history is unpersuasive. Carroll's proposals for a specific *Sitz im Leben* for each passage of Jeremiah are entirely speculative. It is true, for example, that Jeremiah 44 puts the Egyptian exiles in a bad light, and thus one can argue that it was written by some sect within Judaism that viewed the Egyptian Jewish community as rivals. But nothing within the chapter relates to a later generation of that community. Jeremiah 44 is focused on the adoration of the Queen of Heaven as practiced by the first generation of exiles (who were continuing to behave as they had when they lived in Jerusalem). The chapter does not imply that this form of idolatry was still practiced by Jews in Egypt centuries later (e.g., in the Alexandrian Jewish community). If the Alexandrian Jews did not worship the Queen of Heaven (and they did not), a polemic based on condemning that practice would have fallen flat. Similarly, Jeremiah never alludes to any practice that was identifiably carried out by a group of exiles of a later generation. Finally, it is hard to see why various texts in an earlier Jeremiah would "trigger" later, dramatic expansions of the book, contra McKane. This is not something we routinely see elsewhere in the prophets.

A PROPOSED SOLUTION

To summarize our conclusions thus far: The LXX should not be regarded as an abridgment of the proto-MT by the translators. Notwithstanding the excesses of Janzen's study, the evidence indicates that behind the LXX stands a Hebrew *Vorlage*. This is not to be construed as a badly corrupted copy of the proto-MT. To all appearances, the LXX is based on what we may call Hebrew Edition 1, a version of Jeremiah that is earlier than the proto-MT, or "Edition 2." This does not mean, however, that the editorial history of Jeremiah took place over a period of centuries or even of decades, nor does it imply that Edition 1 and Edition 2 were compiled by different editors. It is entirely reasonable to suggest that the same men who compiled Edition 1 also revised their first effort and created Edition 2.

The Source Texts in Jeremiah's Composition History
Within Jeremiah, we find significant evidence for a collection of source documents. These documents were written separately within the lifetime of Jeremiah but were not originally created as part of a single, unified book. These include but are not limited to:

- The account of Jeremiah's commission in the thirteenth year of Josiah (1:2)
- The scroll of Jeremiah's prophecies dictated to Baruch, dated to the fourth and fifth years Jehoiakim's reign (36:1, 9, with a replacement copy described at 36:27–28)

- The letters to and from the exiles taken away with Jehoiachin (29:1–32), dated to Zedekiah's reign (29:1)[24]
- Supplemental material—other texts that were added to the replacement copy of the scroll transcribed by Baruch (36:32)
- A scroll prophesying Babylon's collapse, dated to the fourth year of Zedekiah's reign (51:60)
- A scroll containing messages of hope and predicting final salvation for Israel. The existence of this scroll is indicated in 30:2, which contains the command, "Write all the pronouncements that I have spoken to you on a scroll." The extent of the original scroll is unknown, but it probably included at least 30:1–31:26, and perhaps included all the optimistic messages now found in 30–33.
- First-person accounts of episodes from Jeremiah's life (e.g., 28:1). Even these narratives have evidence for a somewhat complex history; the narrative of chapter 28 switches from first person to third person in 28:5, suggesting that there was at some point editorial modification.
- Much of chapters 37–44 may have been compiled as a single, biographical account of Jeremiah's life as a prisoner in Jerusalem and then as an exile in Egypt.

All the above sources were compiled and edited into the full book of Jeremiah, but this was a complex process. And of all these and other source documents, the most important is the Baruch scroll mentioned in chapter 36, because that was the first version of the book of Jeremiah we know of. It existed even before Edition 1, the LXX *Vorlage*.

The Baruch Scroll of Jeremiah 36

The place to begin, therefore, is with chapter 36, the account of Baruch's transcription of a message of Jeremiah into a scroll. This took place in the fourth year of the reign of Jehoiakim (604 BC). Lundbom argues that the sweeping messages of condemnation in chapters 1–20 are a single block of text, that they represent the scroll of Baruch, and that this was the original book of Jeremiah.[25] If this were true, all of Jeremiah 1–20 would have been written no later than in 604.

But this is not possible. For example, Jeremiah 10:17–25 indicates that a siege of the city is beginning, and the passage probably dates to around December of 598.[26] Even Lundbom acknowledges that it is from this time,

---

24. The contents of chapter 29 have been drawn together from at least three separate letters: Jeremiah's initial letter to the exiles (vv. 1–23), a letter sent from Babylon by Shemaiah the Nehelamite (vv. 24–28), and another letter from Jeremiah to Babylon (vv. 29–32). The chapter is thus a composite of extracts taken from copies of Jeremiah's correspondence

25. He states, "The earliest identifiable composition within the present book consists of chaps. 1–20," and he indicates that this is the scroll of Jeremiah 36 (Lundbom, *Jeremiah 1–20*, 93–94).

26. Holladay, *Jeremiah 1*, 340.

long after Jehoiakim's fourth year.[27] The message in 11:1–8, with its references to the breaking of a covenant and to the exodus, bears a conspicuous resemblance to the episode of 34:8–22, where the Jerusalem aristocracy break a covenant late in the reign of Zedekiah. The clause "when I brought them out of the land of Egypt" appears at 11:4 and 34:13, and both are in a context of covenant-breaking. The correspondence between 11:1–8 and 34:8–22 suggests that the former, like the latter, comes from the last days of Zedekiah's reign, around 587. Holladay dates 11:1–8 to the summer of 594, but even this is long after 604.[28] On the other hand, 17:19–25, where Jeremiah publicly goes to the city gates and encourages people to keep the Sabbath, probably dates from an earlier time in Jeremiah's ministry, before 604. The messages of 2–20 are thus a collection of excerpts from Jeremiah's messages from throughout his entire ministry. The whole body of texts cannot have been compiled in 604, relatively early in his ministry. It is thematically arranged, and came together at a late stage in the editorial process.

What did the Baruch scroll contain? Holladay believes that the Baruch scroll consisted of material now found in Jeremiah 1–7, because he thinks that the scroll offered the possibility of repentance and escape from judgment.[29] But this is unlikely. Both the dismay of all who heard the scroll and Jehoiakim's furious response to it—he cut up and burned the original scroll—imply it asserted that YHWH's judgment was final and that destruction was inescapable. It must have contained harsh condemnation and a specific prophecy of doom.

One passage was almost certainly part of the Baruch scroll: Jeremiah 25:3–13a. This text is dated to the year in which Jeremiah commissioned the scroll, Jehoiakim's fourth year (see 25:1 and compare 36:1–2). It declares that YHWH's patience was at an end, saying that he gave Jerusalem a chance to repent but they refused and must suffer the consequences (25:3–7). It predicts victory for "the tribes of the north" (that is, the Babylonians, 25:9). It also predicts a seventy-year exile (25:11–12; the specificity of the number implies that Jerusalem's destiny is fixed). It concludes with the words, "And I will bring upon that land all the things that I have spoken against it—everything written in this scroll" (25:13a). We therefore know that 25:1–13a dates to the year in which Baruch wrote the scroll of chapter 36, that it is a climactic judgment against Jerusalem (25:2–3), that it predicted victory for Babylon, and that it came to its audience in the form of a written scroll. Jehoiakim, when he heard the scroll read, asked, "Why did you write on it that the king of Babylon will certainly come and destroy this land and cause it to be without people or animals?" (compare this to 25:11, "This whole land will become a desolate ruin"). Jeremiah 25:3–13a is by far the best candidate to be a core text in Baruch's scroll.

---

27. Lundbom, *Jeremiah 1–20*, 602–3.
28. Holladay, *Jeremiah 1*, 351–52.
29. Holladay, *Jeremiah 1*, 2–4.

Even so, this does not mean that 25:3–13a was the whole of the Baruch scroll. The scroll had many columns of text (36:23). Indeed, 25:3–13a reads like the climactic ending of the scroll. On the other hand, the material that immediately precedes Jeremiah 25, the report about Jeremiah's vision of good and bad figs (24:1–10), is an entirely separate episode and is dated to after the exile of Jehoiachin, probably in Zedekiah's first year. It cannot have been part of the scroll of 25:1–13a. This suggests that during the editorial process that created the present book, 25:3–13a was detached from its original context at the end of the Baruch scroll. The rest of the Baruch scroll is probably found in various pieces scattered in chapters 2–20 (that is, not the whole of these chapters, but only parts). For example, 5:1–19, a severe condemnation of the people and an accompanying prediction that Jerusalem would soon be destroyed, may well have been included in the Baruch scroll. Therefore, one may propose that the present book of Jeremiah has not preserved the Baruch scroll intact but has broken up and relocated its contents.

Other Evidence for the Editorial Process

In the dated material, oracles and incidents from Jehoiakim's reign are mixed nonsequentially with those from Zedekiah's reign and with the exilic material, as shown below:

- Texts that date episodes and oracles to Jehoiakim: 22:18; 25:1; 26:1, 21; 35:1; 36:1, 9; 45:1
- Texts that date episodes and oracles to Zedekiah: 24:8; 27:1;[30] 28:1; 29:3; 32:1; 34:2, 6; 37:3, 17; 38:14; 49:34; 51:59
- Texts that date episodes and oracles to the exilic era: 40:1; 42:1–2, 7; 43:8; 44:1

Quite obviously, Jeremiah is not arranged in a chronological sequence. If this kind of chronological dislocation took place with the dated texts, we should assume it also took place with the undated texts of chapters 2–20, and we have already seen evidence pointing in this direction. Jeremiah 5:1–19 was likely to have been in the Baruch scroll and therefore to have been composed prior to the fourth year of Jehoiakim's reign (604 BC), but 10:17–25, written when the city was already under siege, probably around December of 598 BC, is a much later text. The data imply that Jeremiah's writings underwent a massive editorial process that included extensive rearrangement of material.

Putting Together a Hypothesis

The form that the book had in its earliest stages is almost entirely lost to us. Even so, we can create a plausible hypothesis for its composition history:

---

30. The MT of 27:1 has "Jehoiakim" here, but a few MSS have "Zedekiah," and this is certainly correct.

- The oracles and events of Jeremiah's ministry were at various times transcribed into diverse scrolls and letters. For some of these, we know the date of transcription (such as the Baruch scroll of chapter 36); for others, we do not (such as the book of consolation in chapters 30–31). We should not assume that from the beginning the goal was to produce a single "book of Jeremiah." Texts were produced at various occasions, were stored and preserved by Baruch, and initially were not arranged according to any master plan.
- The Baruch scroll mentioned in Jeremiah 36 was the most important of the early documents; it may be regarded as the first "book of Jeremiah." It contained some of the oracles and sermons now found within Jeremiah 2–20, as well as 25:3–13a. It did not contain all of chapters 2–20, and what it had was not necessarily in the present order. The scroll concluded with what is now 25:3–13a (ending with "all that are written in this scroll").
- LXX Jeremiah 25:1–13a illustrates the editorial process. The MT explicitly mentions either Nebuchadnezzar or Babylon in 25:1, 9, 11, and 12, but in every case, these names are missing in the LXX. It makes sense that Jeremiah, in his original prophecy, would have referred to Babylon in a somewhat oblique manner (the "tribes of the north" of 25:9). His purpose, when Baruch read out the scroll, was to focus on YHWH's condemnation of Jerusalem. Explicit reference to Babylon in the heated political atmosphere of Jerusalem in 604—when many in the "pro-Egyptian" party regarded Jeremiah as a "pro-Babylonian" traitor—would have been a distraction. But during the exile, when addressing a different audience and when speaking of Babylon indirectly served no purpose, Edition 2 made explicit what had been implicit (albeit obvious) in Edition 1.
- Therefore, the original Baruch scroll contained some of the oracles now found in chapters 2–20 and concluded with 25:1–13a. It obviously did not contain any messages that Jeremiah gave after Jehoiakim's fourth year, when the scroll was created.
- At some point, much of the material now found in the oracles against the nations was added to the Baruch scroll. This is indicated by the transition at the end of 25:13.
  - The MT of 25:13 reads, "I will bring upon that land all my words I have spoken against it, everything written in this scroll, which Jeremiah prophesied against all the nations." The last clause (25:13b), "which Jeremiah prophesied against all the nations," looks like an addition to a text that originally ended with "this scroll."
  - We can surmise that verse 13b was added as a bridge between the original Baruch scroll and a supplementary text, the oracles against the nations. These oracles appear next in the LXX. The

LXX versification reflects this. It transfers MT 25:13b to LXX 25:14, which reads, "What Jeremiah prophesied against the nations. The [oracle against] Elam."[31] We can therefore assert that MT 25:13b and some of the oracles against the nations were appended to the Baruch scroll (note that MT 36:32 says that "many other words like them were added" to the Baruch scroll).

- Most of the oracles against the nations are undated, and no doubt some of them come from before the year 604 and some are from a later date.[32] Thus, just as the original Baruch scroll contained some but not all of chapters 2–20, so also the original addition to the scroll contained some but not all of the present oracles against the nations.

- If the proto-LXX was Edition 1 and the proto-MT was Edition 2, the original Baruch scroll with the appended oracles against the nations can be considered "Edition 0." This expanded scroll was a decisive condemnation of both Judah and the nations.

- Jeremiah and Baruch eventually had a vision for a unified collection of material from throughout Jeremiah's ministry. They began to pull everything together into a single work. This was carried out in two parts:

  - First, other undated oracles against Judah and against the nations not originally in Edition 0 were added to it. But the new material was not simply appended to the end of Edition 0. All the messages against Judah, both from the original Edition 0 and from other sources, were reorganized, with 25:1–13a still serving as the conclusion to a more expansive judgment against Judah. As in Edition 0, this was followed by the (now enlarged) oracles against the nations. This material, containing what is now represented in LXX 2:2–31:44, was in effect an expanded Edition 0. It represented a full condemnation of Judah and the nations.

  - Second, Jeremiah and Baruch gathered and arranged other oracles as well as accounts of events from the life of Jeremiah into what became Edition 1, as represented by the LXX.

    - They placed LXX 32:15–38, a prophecy of the cup of God's wrath against the nations (= MT 25:15–38), directly after the oracles against the nations, which ends at LXX 31:44 (the LXX in the Rahlfs versification lacks 32:1–14). The common theme of God's wrath toward the nations governed this arrangement.

---

31. Greek: Ἃ ἐπροφήτευσεν Ιερεμιας ἐπὶ τὰ ἔθνη τὰ Αιλαμ.
32. E.g., the oracle against Elam is dated to the beginning of the reign of Zedekiah in MT 49:34, although it is undated in the LXX.

- ♦ They placed the oracles of salvation (LXX 37:1–40:13 = MT 30:1–33:13) immediately after the account of Jeremiah's letter to the Babylonian exiles (LXX 36:1–32). This makes sense, because the letter had assured the exiles that they would return, and that Israel had a future.
- ♦ Thus, all the material supplemental to Edition 0 was placed after the oracles against the nations, and this created the second half of the book. It is represented in LXX 32:15–51:30.[33]
  - They added Jeremiah's commission as a prologue to the expanded book (1:1–19). They also added two epilogues: the oracle to Baruch (LXX 51:31–35) and the account of the fall of Jerusalem (52:1–30, assuming that the account of the elevation of Jehoiachin, vv. 31–34, was added later).
  - The newly edited work was Edition 1, the *Vorlage* of the LXX.
- Edition 1 was not finished until after the last episode it records: the conflict with the exiles in Egypt (LXX 51:1–30 = MT 44:1–30). Since this took place in Egypt, and since Baruch was there with Jeremiah (LXX 50:6 = MT 43:6), we can conclude that they compiled Edition 1 in Egypt.
- Edition 0 had placed the oracles against the nations after 25:13, and Edition 1 preserved this order. This explains the placement of these oracles in the LXX.
- Some copies of Edition 1 (in Hebrew) survived in Egypt. This was the basis for LXX Jeremiah.
- During the first half of the sixth century, Baruch and possibly his brother Seraiah compiled a second edition of Jeremiah in Babylon.[34]
- The work moved to Babylon because Jeremiah had insisted that the future of Judaism lay with the exiles there (MT Jer. 24 and 29). It is not far-fetched to suggest that Baruch made his way from Egypt to Babylon. Jeremiah 45:5 (MT) implies that Baruch was destined to spend much of his life as a wanderer, going from place to place. Also, the apocryphal book of Baruch asserts that he ended up in Babylon (Bar. 1:1). This tradition is likely to be reliable, otherwise there is no other reason for the book to have claimed Baruch went to Babylon. It is not surprising that the book of Jeremiah says nothing about Baruch's moving to Babylon; it is concerned only with details of the life of Jeremiah, who probably died in Egypt.
- Baruch would have taken along all his source texts documenting the words and deeds of Jeremiah as well as a copy of Edition 1. The claim that Baruch possessed these texts is reasonable: MT 32:12 indicates

---

33. This follows Rahlfs versification.
34. See also Lundbom, *Jeremiah 1–20*, 100–101.

that Baruch was the trustee for Jeremiah's personal documents. As for his brother Seraiah, he had carried one of Jeremiah's oracles to Babylon and had personally performed a prophetic sign-act there (MT 51:59–64).

- Edition 1 served as a prototype, but Baruch and Seraiah, probably carrying out Jeremiah's instructions posthumously, took a fresh look at their source texts to create a thoroughly revised edition.

- Most significantly, they moved the oracles against the nations to the back of the book and gave Edition 2 the present structure of MT Jeremiah. They did this to create a chiastic framing, as described in the previous chapter:

    A   Prologue: The beginning of Jeremiah's ministry (1:1–19)
      B   Two anthologies against Judah (2:1–20:18)
         C   Historically contextualized messages (21:1–29:32)
           D   Eschatological salvation (30:1–33:26)
         C′ Historically contextualized messages (34:1–45:5)
      B′ Two anthologies against the nations (46:1–51:64)
    A′ Epilogue: The end of the house of David (52:1–34)

- In the new structure, a prologue was balanced with an epilogue, two anthologies of undated messages against Judah were balanced with two anthologies of undated messages against the nations, and two sets of dated messages and episodes were balanced against one another. Most importantly, the message of hope, 30:1–33:26, was framed as the centerpiece of the whole.

- In the interest of clarity and in order to create internal links, they reworked the material in a manner that made the new edition seem "expanded." For example, we have already seen that 25:1–13 has a number of "pluses" in the MT.[35] But this is explicable since, as noted above, the circumstances when the message was first given, in the Jerusalem of 604, were radically different from those of the exilic community in Babylon. Much of the material of Edition 1 was directly transcribed from sources composed in the middle of the Babylonian crisis, when the identity of various players did not need to be explicitly stated. Indeed, being overly explicit about the Babylonian threat would have needlessly gotten Jeremiah's message bogged down in political controversy, since one side was pro-Egyptian and favored rebellion and the other believed that submission to Babylon remained the wisest course of action. Although Jeremiah definitely

---

35. See also Anneli Aejmelaeus, "What Happened to the Text in Jer 25:1–7?," *TC* 22 (2017), https://jbtc.org/v22/TC-2017-Aejmelaeus.pdf; and Duane L. Christensen, "In Quest of the Autograph of the Book of Jeremiah: A Study of Jeremiah 25 in Relation to Jeremiah 46–51," *JETS* 33, no. 2 (1990): 145–53.

favored the latter group, his message was not a political tract. Edition 2, however, was reworked for future generations, and in it, expansions giving explicit references to Babylon were deemed useful to avoid confusion. The second edition more perfectly realized the goal of transmitting the message of the prophet.

- As the Babylonian exilic community thrived, it created Judaism. It gave attention to forming a competent scribal school, as would later be represented by Ezra. This school preserved and disseminated Edition 2 as the canonical version. Edition 1, however, remained the commonly accepted version in Egypt; the LXX was based on this text. However, the LXX we now have is not a perfect representation of the original Old Greek translation of its Hebrew *Vorlage*. Our current LXX Jeremiah is to some degree an amalgamation; it even shows evidence of having been influenced by the MT.

This does not imply that the present MT is a perfect representation of the text created in Babylon. It has textual corruptions. But one should not exaggerate this. Any corruptions were minor.

In summary, the composition history of Jeremiah can be described as follows:

- In an ongoing process, Jeremiah and Baruch preserved the prophet's sermons, letters, and other documents, but not as a single book.
- The original Baruch scroll, without any other oracles added to it, was from the fourth year of Jehoiakim. It included parts of chapters 2–20 and concluded with 25:1–13a.
- The Baruch scroll was then expanded to create Edition 0. That is, Edition 0 was the Baruch scroll with some additional material, including some of the oracles against the nations.
- The creation of Edition 1 involved several enlargements of Edition 0. Edition 1 came together in the following editorial process:
  - The original Edition 0 was expanded to include all of 2:1–25:13 and all the oracles against the nations. In the LXX, this is 2:2–31:44 (the LXX lacks 2:1).
  - Most of the remainder of the present LXX—including LXX 32:15–51:30, the prologue (LXX 1:1–19), and an epilogue concerning Baruch (LXX 51:31–35)—was added to the expanded Edition 0. This may have been the original Edition 1.
  - Eventually, various parts of LXX 52:1–34, the account of the fall of Jerusalem, were added to the original Edition 1, creating the complete Hebrew *Vorlage* of the LXX.
- Edition 1 became the *Vorlage* of the LXX.
- Edition 2 (preserved in the MT) was compiled in Babylon by Baruch after a reexamination of Edition 1 and all the original source material.

The four stages of the growth of Jeremiah are: the Baruch scroll (Jerusalem 604 BC), Edition 0 (Jerusalem in the reign of Zedekiah), Edition 1 (Egypt, under Jeremiah and Baruch), and Edition 2 (Babylon, under Baruch). A precise timeline is of course impossible, but the original Baruch scroll comes from 604. I would suggest that the initial version of Edition 0, which was primarily an addition of part of the oracles against nations to the Baruch scroll, was created within a few years, perhaps during the first exile of Jeremiah and Baruch, possibly in Moab. But 36:32 explicitly tells us that this version went through a long period of growth. Most of Edition 1 was completed, as described above, after Jeremiah and Baruch went to Egypt, probably no later than 570. The only text that could not have been written by this time is the account of Jehoiachin's release from prison in 52:31–34, which occurred in 562. This passage was probably not part of the original Edition 1. It was added to the text that became the LXX under the influence of the MT. As noted above, we have no pure or "uncontaminated" copy of the Old Greek Jeremiah. Our extant copies of the LXX show signs of having been modified by contact with the proto-MT. Edition 2 was completed in Babylon, probably no later than 550.

The above reconstruction is hypothetical, but it has great explanatory power and accounts for problems that render other interpretations implausible. It tells us when and how the split between the LXX and the MT occurred. It explains why Edition 1 was canonical in Egypt. It accounts for the isolation of Edition 1, since it would have been some time before Jews from the Egyptian exile encountered Edition 2, and by the time this happened, Edition 1 would have already had canonical status for the Egyptian Jews. This in turn explains why the Egyptian Diaspora in Alexandria translated Edition 1 instead of Edition 2 into Greek. On the other hand, the high prestige of the Babylonian exilic community (Jer. 24:1–10) explains why the MT version of Jeremiah became canonical for Jews everywhere else. The proto-MT was the Jeremiah of the Second Temple community, and it was the basis for the other versions, including the targum, the Peshitta, the Vulgate, and the later Greek versions (Aquila, Symmachus, and Theodotion). If the split between the first and second editions occurred early, with one edition in Egypt and one in Babylon, we can account for how each edition had its own constituency and thus explain how both persisted in the Jewish Diaspora.

The theory also explains the placement of the oracles against the nations in the LXX. Those oracles had been attached to the end of the Baruch scroll in Edition 0, and they naturally remained in that position in Edition 1. It is also possible that the placement of these oracles in Edition 1 imitates Isaiah, which places the oracles against the nations in chapters 13–23, directly after the initial series of prophetic messages against Judah. The chiastic structure of the revised MT text, however, explains why these oracles were moved to the end of the book in Edition 2: they create a balance to the undated oracles against Judah.

Apart from creating the chiastic structure described above, the placement of oracles of salvation at the center of the book in chapters 30–33 represents a great innovation. The experienced reader of the Old Testament is quite surprised at seeing them here. This structure contradicts what we often see in the prophets, where messages about God's eschatological salvation of Israel are often clustered at the conclusion of a book (e.g., in Amos, Ezekiel, and Isaiah). In Jeremiah, however, the salvation oracles are at the heart of the book. This suggests that Jeremiah, for all its diatribes and predictions of doom, is fundamentally a book of hope. The book revolves around, or hinges on, messages of salvation.

We can also posit an explanation for why the MT has a different order for the oracles against the nations compared to the LXX. It is difficult to determine why the LXX arranges the nations as it does, with Elam first (LXX 25:14–19) and Moab last (LXX 31:1–44). It may be that the LXX is in reality a random collection. Perhaps the LXX represents the original sequence in which the oracles were given over the years of Jeremiah's ministry. The MT arrangement, however, is more explicable. It begins and ends with the two nations competing for domination over Judah at the end of the seventh century, Egypt (46:1–26) and Babylon (50:1–51:64). Israel itself is in the second place (46:27–28). After that, nations are arranged in two groups according to their proximity to Judah: first are those closest to Judah (Philistines [47:1–7], Moab [48:1–47], Ammon [49:1–6], and Edom [49:7–22]), and then those farther away (Damascus [49:23–27], Kedar [49:28–33], and Elam [49:34–39]). Also, in retribution for its destruction of Jerusalem, Babylon receives the final and longest oracle of judgment. The movement from the random (and perhaps chronological) order of the LXX to the more logical structure of the MT order implies that the latter is a refinement of the former. But this too could have been carried out by Baruch and does not imply a composition history that spanned several centuries.

This hypothesis can provide a model for dealing with some of Jeremiah's thorny textual problems. The longest MT plus is at Jeremiah 33:14–26, which is entirely absent from the LXX. Some scholars regard this passage as a late and secondary addition and not authentically from Jeremiah.[36] Others prefer to treat it as authentic but offer no compelling explanation for why the LXX lacks it.[37] A complication is that Jeremiah 33:15–16 is almost a verbatim copy of 23:5–6; both speak of a "righteous sprout" that will spring up from the line of David and both mention a new name, "YHWH is our righteousness."

---

36. E.g., Allen, *Jeremiah*, 374; Holladay, *Jeremiah 2*, 228.

37. Both Goldingay and Smothers, Keown, and Scalise indicate a preference for treating the text as authentic but offer little argumentation in its favor (Goldingay, *Jeremiah*, 686; Smothers, Keown, and Scalise, *Jeremiah 26–52*, 169). Lundbom, as he commonly does, tries to save the MT by arguing that there was haplography in the LXX *Vorlage* (*Jeremiah 21–36*, 358). But this requires that the scribe's eye jumped from the last word of 33:13 (יהוה) to the first word of 34:1 (הדבר) and inadvertently omitted all the intervening text simply because of the repetition of ה. This is not plausible.

However, in 23:6, "YHWH is our righteousness" is the name of the future messianic king, but in 33:16 it is the name of redeemed Jerusalem as home to united Judah and Israel. It seems doubtful that a later scribe who created an expansion of chapter 33 would insert into it a copy of 23:5–6 that was nearly identical except for a dramatically changed meaning of "YHWH is our righteousness."

If we work with the hypothesis that 33:14–26 is an authentic oracle of Jeremiah, we can suggest a reason that it is missing in Edition 1. Jeremiah 23:1–4 concerns the corruption of the rulers of Jerusalem, and thus 23:5–6 predicts the coming of a messianic, Davidic king who will provide righteous leadership. Thus, 23:5–6 makes sense in its context. But Jeremiah 33 is given on the eve of the fall of Jerusalem and concerns the city's future. The two passages, therefore, address different problems, with the former dealing with the need for righteous leadership and the latter with whether Jerusalem will ever be restored. Of itself, 33:1–13 (= LXX 40:1–13) makes a sufficient and complete promise of restoration for Jerusalem. In Edition 1, where the oracle is solely concerned with the future of the city, nothing else was needed.

However, 33:14–26 (missing in the LXX) moves in a different direction and predicts a restoration of the line of David. This oracle was possibly originally given on a different occasion (as demonstrated, the book regularly groups oracles thematically rather than chronologically). Perhaps 33:14–26 was originally given on the same occasion as the parallel passage, 23:5–6. Indeed, 23:5–6 seems to be an unusually abbreviated account of something so momentous as the promise of a messianic David. It could be that in Edition 1, for the sake of being succinct, only the short version of the prophecy was given in 23:5–6. The prophecy now found in 33:14–26 was left free floating but for some reason failed to make it into Edition 1. If so, this was corrected when Baruch included it in Edition 2.

In its present context, 33:14–26 addresses a problem raised throughout Jeremiah, that Judah had a misplaced hope in the house of David, supposing that the city was impregnable because of the promises that David's dynasty would be eternal. Against that, Jeremiah asserted, Jerusalem would be destroyed and the last representative of the royal line, Jehoiachin, would be recorded as childless (Jer 22:30). But 33:14–26 promises that a messianic David will indeed be the salvation of the city, and it could have been given in the same historical context as 23:1–6. By giving the messianic title "YHWH is our righteousness" to restored Jerusalem (33:16), it indicates that the future of the city and of the house of David are intertwined. Baruch, having this oracle in his possession, realized that the best place to include it was after the promise of the city's restoration in 33:1–13.

In conclusion, the difficult history of the text of Jeremiah should not drive us to abandon our confidence that the MT is the canonical Old Testament for the church. Baruch was not an insignificant figure in the process, and we should not think of him as someone who did nothing but transcribe dictation.

He was closely involved in Jeremiah's ministry and in the documentation of his messages from the very beginning, and the prophet entrusted him and his brother with the oracles of God. Baruch knew Jeremiah's purposes and intentions, and he twice shared in his exile. The arrangement of material found in the MT of Jeremiah accurately conveys the message of the prophet and the meaning of his life.

PART 3

THE ENDURING

MESSAGE OF JEREMIAH

CHAPTER 8

THE THEOLOGY OF JEREMIAH

Aspects of Jeremiah's theology are self-evident even though the book does not necessarily spend much time on these topics specifically: YHWH is the one true God, and all the gods of the nations are lies. He is the maker of heaven and earth and the judge of all humanity. He has chosen Israel to be his people, but that does not exempt them from punishment. He is compassionate, willing to forgive, and patient, but his judgments can be severe. In all these things, Jeremiah agrees with the whole of the Old Testament.

The distinctive theological elements of the book are those things that came through the experiences of the prophet. Jeremiah's personal journey informs what is most distinctive and significant in the theology of his book.

THE NATURE OF SIN

Jeremiah is popularly regarded as the grimmest of all the prophets. It is with good reason that we call a harsh, denunciatory speech a "jeremiad." It is not surprising, therefore, that his book has a great deal to say about sin.

Depravity and the Human Heart

Although Jeremiah was himself a priest, he has almost nothing to say about priestly matters, sacrifices, and matters of ritual cleanness. Indeed, his principal message regarding matters of the "cult" is that it was folly to believe that the temple offered protection against enemies and catastrophes. Like Jesus, he did not associate corruption with failure to keep kosher (see Matt. 15:11). Instead, he said that evil and defilement proceeded from the heart.

You Are Fully Trained to Do Evil, and You Cannot Do Good

Perhaps the most straightforward statement in Jeremiah on the power sin holds over the human heart is 13:23:

Can the Ethiopian change his skin or the leopard his spots? If so, then also you who are trained to do evil would be able to do good.

Unfortunately, for the modern reader the question about whether an Ethiopian could change his skin color awakens concerns about racism. However, this is not an attack on people with black skin. The only point is that an Ethiopian cannot change his skin color. Jeremiah reports in chapter 38 how his life was saved by Ebed-Melech the Ethiopian, and in 39:16–18 he pronounces a special blessing from YHWH for this man. He clearly does not consider Ethiopians to be morally inferior. Furthermore, the point is not that black skin is aesthetically undesirable and that therefore an Ethiopian would want to change his skin color. If the ancient Israelites had any negative opinions about dark skin, this was not due to racial considerations but because it was common for peasants to work in the sun all day. That is, having dark skin may have had adverse cultural implications regarding a person's social status, but that does not mean that a person would be despised for his or her ethnicity. In Song 1:5–6, the woman sings,

I am dark yet lovely,
O daughters of Jerusalem,
Like the tents of Kedar, like the curtains of Solomon.
Do not stare at me, that I am swarthy,
And that the sun has gazed upon me.
It was my mother's sons! They burned with anger toward me.
They forced me to be a keeper of the vineyards,
While my vineyard—the one that was mine—I could not keep.

That is, she complains that she has been made to look like a common field worker by her brothers, who made her work in the sun. But what she says has no racial meaning, and in fact she asserts that, far from being something to hide, her dark skin is part of her beauty.[1]

The black skin of the Ethiopians was something of a novelty to the Israelites; being distinctive and memorable, it made for a convenient object lesson. Similarly, the verse does not imply that Israelites thought the spots of a leopard were unattractive. The spots were extraordinary to people who were more used to the bland coloring of their livestock and the tawny color of lions.

The issue for Jeremiah is not that dark skin or a spotted coat is undesirable; it is that they are impossible to change. In like manner, the people of Jerusalem could not change their ways and start behaving righteously.

Furthermore, Jeremiah 13:23 is more than an assertion of total depravity, although that may be implied as well. Significantly, the people are "trained" in

---

1.   For further discussion of this issue, see Duane A. Garrett, "Song of Songs," *Song of Songs/Lamentations*, by Duane A. Garrett and Paul R. House, WBC 23B (Nashville: Nelson, 2004), 131–34.

evil behavior.[2] It is something their culture has taught them. Doing evil is, so to speak, a skill they have acquired through practice. Their culture has taught them to embrace paganism, greed, violence, and lust, and they put forth the efforts to master these arts.

The passage thus teaches two things. First, sinful behavior can hold such a grip on a person's heart that it is unchangeable. Second, this is not entirely a matter of innate depravity. One's social environment can either encourage or discourage wrong practices. People further sink into vices when they put the immoral ideals of their culture into practice. When that happens, it is hard to break evil habits. People no long regard such actions as evil.

Your Idols Have Incised Evil on Your Hearts

As Jeremiah progressed in his understanding of the extent of the depravity of Judah, he came to focus upon the "heart" (a term encompassing the mind, will, and emotions of the individual). He realized that an externally enforced reformation, such as that promulgated by Josiah, would not change the nation. Indeed, he came to understand that the law itself was incapable of making such a change. People's hearts were impervious to ordinary persuasion and sound teaching (17:1–11). He did not assert, however, that this was purely a matter of innate disposition. A bad environment, poor choices, and destructive habits can shape the heart for the worse, making it ever more perverse. He explores this in 17:1–4:

> The sin of Judah is written with an iron pen,
> Engraved with a stylus of flint on the tablets of their hearts.
> And [the stylus] belongs to the horns of your altars.
> [The engraving happens] whenever their sons remember their altars,
> And [when they remember] their Asherim at every green tree,
> On every high hill, [and on] my mountain, [and] in the open country.
> Your wealth, all your treasures I will give as plunder
> [As a penalty] for your high places, for sin that is in your territories.
> And you will drop your hand from your inheritance, which I gave to you,
> And I will make you serve your enemies in a land that you do not know,
> Because you have kindled a fire in my anger, and it will burn forever.[3]

These lines demonstrate how Jerusalem's idolatry must lead to its destruction (16:10–17:4). Altars in Israel had horn-like protrusions on their four upper corners. In an elaborate metaphor, Jeremiah portrays the people of Judah going to their pagan altars on hills and in groves of trees. Every time

---

2. The adjective לִמֻּד means "taught" or "trained in" (*HALOT* s.v. "לָמַד*" 531). It does not specify the agent of the teaching, whether one is taught by another or self-taught.

3. For a defense and explanation of this translation, see Garrett and Pearson, *Jeremiah and Lamentations*, 195–96.

they participate in the rites of these shrines, hostility to YHWH and his covenant is engraved more deeply on their hearts, as though a horn on the altar were a flint stylus used to make an engraving on a tablet. Their hearts, already as hard as stone, had the precepts of paganism written into them. Paganism had so come to dominate their thinking that even remembering a day spent at the shrine provoked greater apostasy. For that reason, obliteration of the cult sites was necessary, as was the exile of the people. The metaphor of apostasy being engraved on the heart is a profound assertion of how sin enslaves people, making them incapable of turning from it and to God.

Jeremiah then proceeds to divide his audience, and indeed all humanity, into the two categories of those who put their faith in human power and those who put their faith in God:

> Thus says YHWH:
> Cursed is the man who trusts in people,
> And who makes flesh his strength,
> And whose heart turns away from YHWH.
> He is like the scrubby desert juniper.
> He does not experience anything good come his way.
> And he will inhabit the barren, stony places of the wilderness:
> A salty land that no one can inhabit.
> Blessed is the man who trusts in YHWH,
> So that YHWH is his source of confidence.
> He is like a tree planted by water.
> It sends out its roots to a stream.
> And does not experience any drought that comes,
> For its leaves remain green.
> And in a year of drought, it is not anxious,
> For it does not cease bearing fruit. (Jer. 17:5–8)

This poem provides a succinct and self-contained lesson on the two ways of going through life: without God, or with God. It may have been composed by Jeremiah at a time separate from the composition of its present literary context. The metaphor of a tree planted near water, representing the blessings that accrue to the one who fears YHWH, is conspicuously like Psalm 1. However, we should not assume that it is dependent on Psalm 1 (or that Ps. 1 is dependent on this text). The metaphor of a tree near water is common in the Bible (Num. 24:6; Job 14:9; 29:19; Ezek. 19:10; 31:1–17). However, Jeremiah's choice of this metaphor, with its focus on a plant in the harsh conditions of the desert as opposed to a tree by a flowing stream, suggests that it was written during the great drought early in Jehoiakim's reign.

In this context, the contrast between those who trust in human power and those who trust God follows upon Jeremiah's denunciation of those whose hearts were perverted by idolatry. The implication is that Judah is like the man who places confidence in man-made devices. Like that man, Judah is doomed to languish and waste away as in a drought. The nation cannot flourish. The text holds out the possibility of a devout and wholesome life, "the man who trusts in YHWH," but in Jeremiah's historical context that is almost an idealized hypothetical. It exists in contrast to the reality that Judah is abandoned, stunted, and dying.

In Jeremiah 17:9–10, the text returns to the theme of the dark and twisted heart:

> The heart is more crooked than anything, and it is incurably sick. Who can know it? I, YHWH, search the heart and test its inner workings so that I may give to every man according to his ways and according to the fruit manifest in his deeds.

In his painful pilgrimage toward awareness of how incorrigibly evil his people were, Jeremiah had many unhappy surprises. Josiah's reformation had not touched the hearts of the people. The men of Anathoth, Jeremiah's home city, wanted to kill him. He warned Jerusalem that the temple could not save them and almost got lynched. The educated elite and the priests turned out to be no less superstitious than the most ignorant peasant. He could only conclude that the human heart was a dark and devious maze and that no one, least of all himself, was able to see through the façade. Only YHWH, who had warned him repeatedly of how things really stood, could rightly judge the intents of the heart.

Jeremiah then offers another short poem, almost a proverb, on how evil leads to ruin:

> A partridge that broods [over its eggs] but bears no young:
> [So is] one who gains riches but not by justice.
> In the middle of his life, [his wealth] will abandon him.
> In the end, he is a fool. (Jer. 17:11)[4]

This, like 17:5–8, is a pithy, self-contained teaching, and may have been an independent teaching Jeremiah appropriated for this text. We thus have two texts that speak of the obstinance and darkness of the heart in 17:1–4 and 9–10, and these are placed with two didactic poems in 17:5–8 and 11. The poems describe how people descend into ruin when they turn from God. Also, 17:1–4 speak of trusting in idols, 17:5–6 describe placing one's faith in human power, and 17:11 speaks of faith in wealth. But all of it is predicated on the belief that the human heart is desperate, deceitful, and incurable.

---

4. For an explanation of this translation, see Garrett and Pearson, *Jeremiah and Lamentations*, 197–98.

Deceit and Zeal

Perhaps the most surprising thing about Jeremiah's theological and moral conflicts with Jerusalem is that the people did not consider themselves to have turned away from YHWH and the covenant. To the contrary, they thought that it was Jeremiah who was both a heretic and a traitor. Their view that he was a traitor is perhaps the easier of the two to demonstrate and understand. When he was seeking to get to Anathoth to deal with a matter of family property, he was accused of deserting to the enemy and was arrested (37:13). Later, a group of nobles accused him of discouraging the people in the face of the Babylonian enemy because he repeatedly claimed that Jerusalem could not win and needed to surrender (38:1–4). The complaints of Jeremiah's enemies are understandable in that one does not want a prominent man to discourage the nation in a time of war. Indeed, Jeremiah's predictions of defeat and appeals for surrender could be compared to the speech of Assyria's official propagandist, the Rabshakeh, when he tried to persuade Hezekiah's Jerusalem to give up the fight (Isa. 36:4–10).

But Jeremiah was no traitor. He called on Zedekiah to surrender out of a desire to preserve Judah, not because he wanted to destroy it. He lamented bitterly over Jerusalem's fall. A defiant resolution to keep on fighting in the face of impossible odds may be patriotic, but it is not always wise—particularly when God himself, as announced by his prophet, has announced that defeat is inevitable. But this was a lesson the Jews would again fail to learn when, against the warnings of Jesus (Luke 23:28–31), they chose to resist Rome to the bitter end and saw their city and temple again burned to the ground in AD 70.

It is more surprising for the modern Christian reader to learn that Jeremiah's foes considered themselves to be faithful to YHWH. We imagine them to be so depraved by their idolatry (which included even child sacrifice) that we suppose that they must have openly and explicitly despised YHWH and the covenant. But this is far from the truth. Although we think of them purely as apostates, their religious beliefs were a mixture of apostasy and fundamentalism. I here define "fundamentalism" as an intense and exclusive focus on a few biblical concepts resulting in a distortion of a more complete and wholesome understanding of biblical teaching. Their apostasy manifested itself in the worship of other gods, in the deployment of idols throughout their land, and in the depraved practices that often accompanied ancient paganism. Their fundamentalism, as already noted in this study, manifested itself in a fixation on the promises to David and on the special status of the temple; this gave them a blind certainty that no enemy could take Jerusalem.

The idea that the people of Jerusalem could worship other gods and yet still believe themselves to be loyal to YHWH is hard for us to comprehend because we are so far removed from their cultural and religious environment. The cult of Baal is so alien and frankly so bizarre that we cannot imagine that anyone would practice that religion and imagine it to be compatible with what God requires in the Bible. But every age has beliefs and practices that are entirely opposed to biblical teaching and yet so prevalent that they seem normal and, in the minds of some, valid expressions of an orthodox faith and perhaps even its spiritual center and true meaning. We may look with horror upon the attitudes and deeds in earlier ages of the Christian church (e.g., the burning of heretics or the practice of slavery). Earlier generations of Christians, if they could look upon us, would be dumbfounded that churches could endorse homosexuality and transgenderism. When the Jewish exiles in Egypt mingled the worship of the Queen of Heaven with the belief that they were YHWH's people, they were heavily influenced by their environment and were certain that they, not Jeremiah, represented the faithful remnant.

There were several reasons for their blind confidence that their city would endure against all enemies. First, there was the historical example of YHWH defeating the forces of Sennacherib and saving Jerusalem (Isa. 37). Second, and as an explanation for why God had saved Jerusalem from the Assyrians, the people had reasons to think that they were special. They were under the Davidic king, and God had promised that he would preserve the throne of David's sons forever (2 Sam. 7:13). They took this promise at face value to mean that the dynasty could not fall. This outlook was shared by many who were truly devout, such as the psalmist behind Psalm 89, who recited in full the promises made to the dynasty but then reacted in dismay and confusion upon seeing God reject the Davidic king and make his city desolate. Also, they had the temple of YHWH, God's very dwelling place on earth. Surely God could never allow his own house to be defiled by foreign invaders.

Careful consideration would have convinced the people that their reasoning was deficient. Moses had prophesied in his song that Israel was destined to disobey God and suffer destruction and scattering (Deut. 32). The promises to David did not abrogate that. As such, the hope of an eternal throne for the Davidic monarch had to have some other means of fulfillment. It was not to come about through a simple and unending prolongation of the earthly kingdom. And as for the temple, Jeremiah himself had pointed out that Shiloh had once housed the true dwelling place of YHWH's name, and yet it was destroyed (7:10–14). Even so, Jeremiah's audience fanatically held to the belief that their city was inviolable and considered the prophet to be a blasphemer for daring to say that it was not so.

The combined paganism and nationalistic fundamentalism of Jeremiah's Jerusalem serves as a warning to us. Those who are in some respects apostates or syncretists may be in other respects extreme conservatives who take a valid concept to an unbiblical extreme. The great danger is that we, like they, may fall into this trap and never recognize how we have managed to turn aside both to the left and the right at the same time.

The Universality of Sin

At the time of the French Revolution, society was divided into three groups: the first estate (the clergy), the second estate (the nobility), and the third estate (the commoners). Jeremiah, analogously, routinely attacks the corruption of three elements of Jerusalem society: the kings and nobles, the priests and prophets, and the common people. Unlike the factions of the French Revolution, Jeremiah did not regard any class as morally privileged over the others; all were equally corrupt.

Kings and Rulers

Jeremiah demonstrates that a superior education, social rank and prestige, religious training, and the leisure to study the law do not make a person more faithful to God. In fact, the kings, nobles, priests, and court prophets had greater guilt than the common people, and not just because much would be required of those who had been given much. The leaders were in fact often morally worse than the ordinary, uneducated people.

The response to the delegation from Zedekiah (21:1–23:40) summarizes the case against the royal house after the death of Josiah. A group from the king came to the prophet seeking deliverance from the Babylonians and evidently hoping for a repeat of the miracle against Sennacherib during the reign of Hezekiah (this episode is discussed above in ch. 4). In his response, Jeremiah laid out the case against the royal house and other elites in Jerusalem: They neglected their fundamental duty and yet remained confident that their position was unassailable:

> House of David, thus says YHWH: Execute justice in the morning, and deliver those who have been robbed from the hands of those who exploit them! Otherwise, my anger will go forth like fire, and burn with no one to quench it, because of your evil actions. See, I am against you, Inhabitant of the valley, Rock of the plain, says YHWH, although you say, "Who can descend against us, and who can enter our lairs?" (Jer. 21:12–13)

Instead of looking upon their authority as a stewardship from God that carried with it the obligation to protect the lives and rights of the people, they regarded Jerusalem (the "Rock of the plain") as their private fortress, allowing them to plunder the people on the inside and giving them protection from enemies on the outside.

Other episodes from Jeremiah's time, already discussed in the chapters above, further illustrate the corruption of the upper classes. Their breaking of their promise to release their Israelite slaves, despite having made a solemn covenant with YHWH (34:8–22), demonstrated that they regarded their fellow Israelites as beneath contempt. They could deceive and exploit the poor without any qualms of conscience. Of course, it also showed how they had disdain for any promises made before YHWH. For Jehoiakim, constructing a grand palace for himself was the surest proof of his greatness (22:13–19). His burning of the scroll of Jeremiah's prophecies demonstrated how devoid he was of any fear of God:

And it so happened that as Jehudi read three or four columns, the king would slice them off with a scribe's knife and throw them into the fire in the brazier, until the whole scroll was consumed in the fire that was in the brazier. The king and all his ministers, as they heard all these words, neither showed fear nor tore their clothes. And although Elnathan, Delaiah, and Gemariah urged the king not to burn the scroll, he did not listen to them. (Jer. 36:23–25)

But it was not as though Jeremiah showed nothing but contempt for the aristocracy. Early in his ministry, in his sermon at the People's Gate (17:19–27), he only asked that they enforce the rules concerning the Sabbath. Had they done so, he promised, "then kings who sit on the throne of David and officials shall enter by the gates of this city. They will be riding in chariots and on horses, they and their officials, along with the people of Judah and the inhabitants of Jerusalem. And this city shall be inhabited forever" (17:25). But even that was too much for Judah's elites. Their hostility continued until, when it was clear that his prophecies would come true, their hatred reached a fever pitch. Even as the Babylonians were at the gates, the Jerusalem aristocracy was determined to put Jeremiah to death.

Priests and Prophets

Jeremiah stood nearly alone against the entire religious establishment of Jerusalem. The prophets who opposed Jeremiah were not voices in the wilderness on the fringes of society; they were closely associated with the temple and priesthood. Thus, Jeremiah often grouped the priests and prophets together as a single company of greedy religious leaders who perverted the word of God and were destined for judgment:

> The prophets prophesy with lies, and the priests scoop out [what they want] with their own hands.[5] My people love to have it so, but what will you do when it all comes to an end? (Jer. 5:31)

These men had turned the temple into a criminal racket. The prophets peddled messages that kept the people firmly in their grasp (and the people, deluded as they were, "loved to have it so"). The priests used the sanctuary offerings to fatten themselves. The claim that they "scoop out" what they want may allude to the sin of the sons of Eli, who used their priestly authority to

---

5. This clause, וְהַכֹּהֲנִים יִרְדּוּ עַל־יְדֵיהֶם, is often translated either as "the priests rule as the prophets direct" (NRSV) or "the priests rule by their own authority" (NIV). See, e.g., Craigie, Kelley, and Drinkard, *Jeremiah 1–25*, 93, and Lundbom, *Jeremiah 1–20*, 410. However, the verb רדד here is probably not to "rule" but the homonym meaning to "scoop out," as in Judg. 14:9, "And he scooped out [the honey] with his hands." It refers to the greed of the priests. See Garrett and Pearson, *Jeremiah and Lamentations*, 123; Holladay, *Jeremiah 1*, 201.

choose the best cuts of meat for themselves (1 Sam. 2:22–36). But their enterprise would soon "come to an end," and they would have nothing. Even so, both groups continued to seek profits even while Judah collapsed around them:

> If I go out into the field, I see those slain by the sword! And if I enter the city, I see those who suffer the diseases of famine! But even so, both prophet and priest ply their trade through the land, and they have no knowledge [to offer]. (Jer. 14:18)[6]

Even though an authentic word from YHWH was what the people desperately needed, these priests and prophets could not provide it. They treated their religious work as a business and continued to use the crises of the time to justify their continued domination of the spiritual life Judah, turning it all to their own material advantage. Thus, he condemned the temple establishment in memorable language, later cited by Jesus:

> Do you regard this house, which is called by my Name, as a hideout for robbers? But I see [what you are doing there], says YHWH. (Jer. 7:11; see also Matt. 21:13)

The priests and prophets thought that they could cynically take advantage of their religious authority and hide what they were doing from the masses, but God saw it all.

Jeremiah gives other examples of the corruption of the religious establishment. As described above, the temple sermon enraged the city and especially the priests. Jeremiah soon found himself expelled from the temple district and even had to use Baruch as a spokesman to deliver his prophecy (Jer. 36).

A distinctive complaint concerns the religious scribes (who were probably all priests):

> How can you say, "We are wise, for we have the law of YHWH"? In reality, the lying pen of the scribes works it into a lie. The "wise" are disgraced, dismayed, and trapped. They have rejected the word of YHWH, so what wisdom do they have? Therefore, I will give their wives to other men and their fields to men who will claim them. From the least to the greatest, all are greedy for gain! Prophets and priests alike, all work the lie. (Jer. 8:8–10)

The "wise" here are not to be associated with wisdom literature; the word is used more generically and not as a technical designation for a class of sages or a genre of literature. The priestly scribes claimed to have a superior knowledge and therefore to be able to instruct the people because they

---

6.   On the translation of the last clause, וְלֹא יָדָעוּ, see Garrett and Pearson, *Jeremiah and Lamentations*, 183.

had the law, which they could expound for the masses. This is an evident allusion to the copy of the law discovered in Josiah's reign; the priests had co-opted the event and were using it for their own advantage. Jeremiah does not precisely explain how "the lying pen of the scribes" worked the law into a lie. We can surmise that they made midrashic or targum-like paraphrases of the law that were purported to be easier to understand but that in subtle but important ways changed its real meaning. They then taught this abridged version of the law to the people. But as always, their real motive was that they were "greedy for gain." But they would be humiliated when all that they had promised failed and when foreigners came in and took their women and property.

Jeremiah had several encounters with the self-styled prophets who opposed him. When he tried to warn Judah and the surrounding states that forming a coalition to resist Babylon was contrary to the will of God and doomed to bring on their own destruction, the prophet Hananiah contradicted him before the assembly and predicted that God was about to break the power of Nebuchadnezzar (28:2–4). Ahab son of Kolaiah and Zedekiah son of Maaseiah declared, in opposition to Jeremiah, that the Jehoiachin exile would be short-lived and that all the Jews would soon return home (29:21). Jeremiah mocked the theatrical performances of all such prophets, who often claimed to have received dream oracles:

> I hear what the prophets, who prophesy lies in my name, say: "I have had a dream! I have had a dream!" (Jer. 23:25)

Both priests and prophets put on a show of having secret knowledge before the people in order to maintain themselves in positions of wealth and power.

The Common People

Jeremiah gives more attention to the sins of the kings, nobles, priests, and prophets than he does to the sins of the ordinary people. This is perhaps because he initially had high regard for the elites of society but was disillusioned when he came to see how evil they were (5:3–5). One always reserves the strongest vitriol for those one once believed in but turned out to be frauds. Even so, there are places where he shows that even the ordinary citizens were deeply corrupted. This is especially the case in his account of the plot of the men of Anathoth to silence or kill him. As he felt betrayed by the corruption among the Jerusalem's secular and religious leaders, so also he was deeply shaken by the hostility that came from his own kin:

> But YHWH made it known to me, and then I knew. It was when you [YHWH] showed me their evil deeds. And I had been like a gentle lamb led to the slaughter. And I did not know that they were devising schemes against me, saying, "Let us destroy the tree with its fruit! Let us cut him

off from the land of the living, so that his name will no longer be remembered!" (Jer. 11:18–19)

When he gave the temple sermon, it was not just the religious establishment but also the common people who seethed with rage:

And as soon as Jeremiah finished relaying to all the people everything YHWH had commanded him to say, the priests, the prophets, and all the people seized him and said, "You must die!" (Jer. 26:8)

And even at the end of his ministry, when in exile in Egypt, he saw how defiantly pagan and apostate his people were, as they angrily insisted that they should have never ceased to make offerings to the Queen of Heaven (44:15–19).

Summary

Jeremiah's understanding of human nature grew out of his personal pilgrimage, which began in Josiah's reign with optimism about Judah's future. He was aware that many in Judah were apostate, but he initially believed that this was mostly confined to the lower classes. He still had some confidence that Jerusalem could be saved and prayed that God would be merciful to its people. In the course of time, he came to see that all his people—including the nobility, the clergy, and the common people—were hopelessly corrupt. He saw that the workings of the human heart were twisted and hidden by layers of deceit. He also saw that the practice of various sins, such as idolatry, trained a person to do evil so that such behavior became an automatic, conditioned response. He also saw that people were so self-deceived that they could justify themselves by combining contradictory ideas and holding to both with ferocious severity. They could be fundamentalist about some beliefs while at the same time being heretics who committed heinous sins. This is Jeremiah's message for his readers about sin. If this makes the mature Jeremiah seem cynical, one need only remember what was said of Jesus:

But Jesus on his part would not entrust himself to them, because he knew all about people and because he did not have any need for someone to give testimony about human nature. For he himself knew what was inside a person. (John 2:24–25)

Like Jeremiah, Jesus encountered sinners in every segment of society and was persecuted by people who were both fanatical and apostate.

ISRAEL AND THE NATIONS

Although the oracles against the nations (Jer. 46:1–51:64) speak specifically to many of the Gentile states of Jeremiah's time, his theology regarding the nations more succinctly appears in 27:1–11. This was the occasion when Zedekiah convened a group of representatives from the surrounding nations to form a coalition against Babylon, and Jeremiah appeared among the assembled delegates with a yoke on his neck. He warned them not to put any faith in the predictions of their prophets and diviners and declared that for the present time, God had decreed that all the nations of their world would be under the yoke of Babylon. When the time was right, God would break Babylon's power and bring it down, but until then Nebuchadnezzar was his chosen instrument to chastise them all for their sins. To resist Babylon would only increase their sin against God, and they would suffer even more.

The implication is that God manages and punishes states by allowing a single more powerful state, an empire, to dominate the others for a time. This notion anticipates the presentation of the four empires of Daniel, each of which in turn dominates the world during the "times of the Gentiles." It also implies that God controls the flow of human history, with individual nations rising to prominence and power before sinking into feebleness if not disappearing altogether. It does not necessarily mean that resistance to an empire is always sinful, and it does not lessen the guilt of the empire. In Hezekiah's time, it was right for Judah to refuse to surrender to Assyria. And while all the nations listed in Jeremiah's oracles in 46–51 face God's punishment for their sin, no nation has its guilt so thoroughly explored or its judgment more forcefully expressed than Babylon (50:1–51:64).

Finally, no nation but Israel is promised eschatological salvation, a new covenant, or a messianic king. Some of the nations are promised that they will endure and to some degree recover after having suffered under Babylon. For example, the oracle against Elam ends with "But at the end of the days [of trouble], I will restore the fortunes of Elam, says YHWH" (Jer. 49:39). This only implies that Elam will not be entirely obliterated by Babylon, and that in the days to come it will to some degree thrive again. It is not a promise of a messianic kingdom for Elam.

What, then, does Jeremiah say regarding the destiny of the nations? Although he does not speak of inclusion of the Gentiles in the kingdom of God as directly as Isaiah does, he implies that apart from adoption into Israel, there is no future for the nations. There is hope for them, but only under the identity of Israel and Israel's Messiah.

THE IMPORTANCE OF COVENANTS

It is something of a cliché in Old Testament studies to speak of the importance of the idea of "covenant." It is undeniable, however, that the word has a central place in the book of Jeremiah. The breaking of the covenant is the explanation for Judah's destruction. Jeremiah frequently uses the term in reference to the Sinai covenant, focusing on what the law requires. Flippant disregard for keeping the covenant illustrates the moral perversity of the aristocracy. Also, however, the concept of "covenant" is at the heart of Israel's hope for eschatological renewal.

Covenant Violation

Jeremiah deals with covenant violation first by expressing, in general terms, how little heed Judah paid to the demands of the Sinai covenant. Second, giving the concrete example of a quick and flagrant violation of a newly made covenant, the book shows that Jerusalem's leading citizens had no regard for any covenant made with God.

Judah's Principal Sin

A pivotal text describes how Judah's violations of the Sinai covenant explain YHWH's anger toward the nation:

> The word that Jeremiah received from YHWH: Listen to the words of this covenant, and then recite them to the men of Judah and the inhabitants of Jerusalem. And say to them, Thus says YHWH, the God of Israel: Cursed is the man who does not listen to the words of this covenant, which I decreed for your fathers when I brought them out of the land of Egypt, from the iron-smelter. I said, Obey my voice, and carry out all that I command you. And then you will be my people, and I will be your God, so that I may perform the oath that I swore to your fathers, to give them a land flowing with milk and honey, and this promise still holds true today.[7] And I [Jeremiah] responded, "Amen! So be it, YHWH!"[8]

> And YHWH said to me: Proclaim all these words in the cities of Judah, and in the streets of Jerusalem: Listen to the words of this covenant and do them! For I specifically gave a warning to your fathers when I brought them up out of the land of Egypt, and to this day I have persistently warned them, saying, Obey my voice! But they did not obey or incline their ear, but everyone walked in the stubbornness of their evil hearts. So, I brought upon them all the things prescribed in this covenant, since they did not do what I commanded them to do.

> And YHWH said to me: A common act of quiet treason [against the covenant] has been discovered among the people of Judah and the inhabitants of Jerusalem. They returned to the iniquities of their ancestors of old, who refused to listen to my words. They went after other gods to serve them. The house of Israel and the house of Judah broke the covenant that I made with their fathers. Therefore, thus says YHWH, Look, I am bring-

---

7.   "And this promise still holds true today" is literally "like this day" (כַּיּוֹם הַזֶּה).
8.   More literally, this is simply, "Amen, YHWH!" (אָמֵן יְהוָה).

ing disaster upon them that they cannot escape. And when they cry out to me, I will not listen to them.

And the cities of Judah and the inhabitants of Jerusalem will go and cry to the gods to whom they make offerings, but they will not in any manner save them in the time of their disaster. For you have as many gods as you have towns, Judah, and the altars you have set up to "Shame," that is, altars to make offerings to Baal, are as many as the streets found in Jerusalem. (Jer. 11:1–13)

This text does not give us its historical context, but two features suggest that it is from early in Jeremiah's ministry, probably from the reign of Josiah. First, God tells Jeremiah to "Listen to the words of this covenant, and then recite them to the men of Judah and the inhabitants of Jerusalem." This suggests that Jeremiah was a young man listening to the reading of the newly discovered law and that it was in this context that he received YHWH's message. That is, God is commanding Jeremiah to preach to the people the commands of the law, which he was in the process of hearing as they were read aloud. Also, Josiah had led the people in a great covenant-renewal ceremony, in which the king and "all the people" vowed to follow all the decrees and commands found in the Sinai legislation (2 Kings 23:3). Second, YHWH says that if the people keep his covenant, they will be his people and he will be their God, and he will provide them with all the blessings of a land of milk and honey. Jeremiah responds, "Amen! So be it, YHWH!" This suggests that he was still hopeful that a full revival would occur and that a golden era was ahead for Judah. We can imagine him standing in the temple courtyard, hearing the terms of the covenant and believing that the law's proclamation under the good king's ministers and prophets would gloriously renew the state. Unfortunately, the oracle Jeremiah received from God was very dark: Jerusalem was in rebellion against the covenant and would suffer the punishments prescribed in the law.

In the book's literary context, this passage stands at the head of the lengthy series of texts (11:1–20:18) that describe Jeremiah's progress from being a prophet who fervently prayed for Judah's peace and spiritual revival to his realization that his people were hopelessly corrupt. He came to see there was no alternative to Jerusalem's destruction and exile. At the end of the process, he prayed that their punishment would come. The very next passage after 11:1–13 leaps ahead several years to the moment when God commanded Jeremiah to stop praying for Jerusalem (11:14–17). In the space of a few verses, therefore, we move through a momentous transition: from a young prophet's optimism that Judah will keep the covenant and be saved to a wiser prophet's sad realization that the nation was so far gone in apostasy that even praying for them was counter to God's will.

At the opening of the oracle, "Cursed is the man who does not listen to the words of this covenant" (Jer. 11:3) loosely cites Deuteronomy 27:26, "Cursed be anyone who does not uphold the words of this law by observing them," a verse that concludes a series of maledictions for disobedience to the law. In Deuteronomy, this leads into a series of blessings Israel will receive if they uphold the covenant (Deut. 28:1–14) and a much longer series of curses that will fall upon them if they break it (Deut. 28:15–68). The latter text concludes with a harrowing account of Israel enduring invasion, siege, defeat, and exile:

> YHWH will bring against you a nation from far away, from the end of the earth, which will swoop down like an eagle. It will be a nation whose language you do not understand—a stern-faced nation that shows no respect to the old and gives no kindness to the young. . . . And it will besiege you in all your towns until your high and unassailable walls, in which you trusted, come down throughout your land. . . . YHWH will scatter you among all peoples, from one end of the earth to the other. (Deut. 28:49–50, 52a, 64a)

This was the biblical context in which YHWH spoke to Jeremiah of bringing upon Israel "all the things spoken of in this covenant" (Jer. 11:8).

At this point in the oracle, YHWH tells Jeremiah that the people do not support Josiah's efforts to reform the nation:

> And YHWH said to me: A common act of quiet treason [against the covenant] has been discovered among the people of Judah and the inhabitants of Jerusalem. (Jer. 11:9)

The translation "common act of quiet treason [against the covenant]" is an expansive paraphrase of the single word קֶשֶׁר (qesher). This is often translated as "conspiracy" (as in the NIV: "There is a conspiracy among the people of Judah"). But that is somewhat misleading because the English word suggests only a small group of people meeting secretly to plan a political coup or criminal act. The word literally means a "binding," but it generally implies an alliance of people for some common purpose (often for an act of treason). It can be done, at least initially, in secret (2 Sam. 15:12; 2 Kings 11:14). But it can grow until it includes a large part of the population and becomes public, and yet it is still called a *qesher*, a "binding" of people for a common political cause.

For example, Absalom's *qesher* grew as time went on and the hidden supporters of his treason became more and more numerous, until he was ready to act (2 Sam. 15:1–12). In Athaliah's reign, a quiet "conspiracy" gathered around the young Joash until they had acquired sufficient strength to act. When Athaliah saw that the whole nation had turned against her, she cried out, "*Qesher! Qesher!*" (2 Kings 11:14, and often translated "Treason! Treason!"). In Jeremiah 11:9, there is a quiet, growing sentiment against Josiah and the renewal of the covenant with YHWH. The people have an unspoken agreement among themselves to formally obey Josiah's decrees, but their hearts are not with him. By common tacit consent, they go along with the reforms while waiting for the day when they can openly resume their prior apostasy. The verse describes the apostasy of Judah in political terms, saying that "treason has been discovered." In the metaphor, YHWH is Judah's lawful but distant suzerain, and the people are under oath to maintain fealty to him. By analogy, King Hoshea was the vassal of the king of Assyria, but "treason [*qesher*] was discovered" in the Israelite king, so that the Assyrians came and destroyed Samaria (2 Kings 17:4).[9]

Thus, the meaning here in Jeremiah 11 is not that people are meeting in secret to lay plans for a coup. YHWH is telling his prophet that he has discovered a widespread practice of subverting the covenant. He says the people "returned to the iniquities of their ancestors of old" (Jer. 11:10). While this may be a historical and literary allusion to the apostasy recounted in, for example, the golden calf episode or the Judges narrative, it has a more immediate context here. Josiah had sought to turn the people back to YHWH and the covenant, but they were determined to remain in the paganism that had characterized their people for generations. Worship of Baal was too widespread in the community and too deeply embedded in the minds of the population to be eradicated. And throughout the whole of 11:1–13, Jeremiah focuses on the nation's attitude toward the "covenant" to characterize their apostasy. Quietly disregarding and subverting the covenant is their essential, fundamental sin. This oracle appears to have been crucial in the formation of Jeremiah's thinking as he came to understand how deeply corrupted his people had become (and thus it is placed at the head of the series in 11:1–20:18). Jeremiah would speak of the breaking of the Sinai covenant again at 22:9; 31:32; and 34:13–14.

The Covenant of Slave Manumission

The breaking of the covenant to free the slaves in Jeremiah 34:8–22 is another example of the importance this term plays in the book. As we have already looked at this text (see chapter 4), we will not examine it in detail again. However, the passage does vividly illustrate the primacy of covenant-breaking in Jeremiah's condemnation of Jerusalem. We have just observed how YHWH, near the beginning of Jeremiah's ministry, confronted him with Jerusalem's "treason" against the Sinai covenant. In chapter 34, near the end of Jeremiah's ministry and just before the fall of the city, the civic leaders again demonstrated how little regard they had for a covenant with God. Also, this account, like Jeremiah 11, refers to Israel's consistent disregard for the terms of the Sinai covenant:

> Thus says YHWH, the God of Israel: I made a covenant with your fathers when I brought them out of the land of Egypt and out of the house of slavery, saying that at the end of seven years each of you must set free his

---

9.   In both 2 Kings 17:4 and Jer. 11:9, the noun קֶשֶׁר is used with the verb מצא, to "find" or "discover."

Hebrew brother who was sold to you and worked for you for six years. You must release him from your service. But your fathers did not listen to me or incline their ears to me. (Jer. 34:13–14)

Both passages also speak of YHWH bringing an enemy upon Jerusalem to punish it for its covenant breaking. Jeremiah 11:11 states,

Therefore, thus says YHWH, Look, I am bringing disaster upon them that they cannot escape. And when they cry out to me, I will not listen to them.

Jeremiah 34:22 likewise states:

And look, I am issuing a command, says YHWH, and I will bring [the Babylonians] back to this city; and they will fight against it, and take it, and burn it with fire. I will make the towns of Judah into a desolation without inhabitant.

From the beginning of Jeremiah's ministry to the end, the Israelites had shown themselves to be incapable of keeping a covenant with YHWH.

The New Covenant

But if "covenant" is a key term in Jeremiah for describing the transgression of Israel, it is also a key term in describing its salvation. The concept of Israel's eschatological repentance and redemption from exile is introduced in Deuteronomy 30:1–10 and further developed in almost every prophetic book.[10] When Jeremiah speaks of eschatological redemption, however, he alone speaks of it as a "new covenant" (although Ezekiel, who is directly influenced by Jeremiah, does speak of a "covenant of peace" [Ezek 34:25]). No one else, including Ezekiel, uses the terms of a covenant to paint a portrait of Israel's glorious future.

The Text of the New Covenant

The crucial text is Jeremiah 31:31–34:

Look, days are coming, says YHWH, when I will make with the house of Israel and the house of Judah a new covenant. It will not be like the covenant that I made with their fathers on the day when I took them by the hand to bring them out of the land of Egypt. They broke my covenant although I was their husband, says YHWH. For this is the covenant that I will make with the house of Israel after those days, says YHWH: I will put

---

10.   E.g., Isa. 41:8–12; Ezek. 34:25–31; 36:16–38; Hos. 14:4–7; Joel 2:28–32; Amos 9:11–15; Obad. 20–21; Mic. 7:12–20; Zeph. 3:9–20; Zech. 12:10–13:2.

my law within them, and I will write it on their hearts. And I will be their God, and they will be my people. And no one of them will any longer teach his neighbor and each his brother, saying, "Know YHWH!" For all of them will know me, from the least of them to the greatest, says YHWH. For I will forgive their iniquity, and I will no longer remember their sin.

Here too, there is a callback to YHWH's initial complaint against Israel's covenant violation. Jeremiah 11:3b–4 speaks of "this covenant, which I decreed for your fathers when I brought them out of the land of Egypt, from the iron-smelter. I said, 'Obey my voice, and carry out all that I command you. And then you will be my people, and I will be your God.'" So too, Jeremiah 31 speaks of the exodus, when YHWH took them by the hand and brought them out from the land of Egypt, and it recalls the promise, "I will be their God, and they will be my people."

Jeremiah understands that Israel is unable to keep the commands in the Sinai covenant, and therefore he conceives of redemption for Israel as embodied in the issue of a new covenant. Importantly, this is not presented here as a grand work for all of humanity; YHWH will enact it "with house of Israel and the house of Judah." Other prophets, especially Isaiah, explored at length how eschatological salvation would reach out to the most distant Gentile nations (Isa. 2:1–4; 42:1–4). Later, Paul would explain how the Gentiles, who were "alienated from the common life of Israel and strangers to the covenants of promise, having no hope and without God in the world" (Eph. 2:12), are grafted into the olive tree that is Israel so that they could partake of the blessings of the new covenant (Rom. 11:17–20). But for Jeremiah, the issue was that Israel, in both its northern and southern kingdoms, had shown itself unable to meet the demands of the covenant, and therefore God needed to offer them an entirely different covenant if they were to have any future.

The Marriage Metaphor

For Jeremiah, the Sinai covenant was like a marriage in which YHWH had been "a husband to them," but both Israel and Judah had been adulteresses, and each had been given their divorce papers (Jer. 3:6–10). This metaphor implicitly asserts that the relationship is irrevocably broken, as is made clear in Jeremiah 3:1–5:

Consider: A man divorces his wife, and she goes from him and becomes another man's wife. Would he return to her? Wouldn't that terribly pollute this land? You have prostituted yourself with many lovers. Can you return to me? says YHWH. Lift your eyes to the bare heights and see! Where have you not been lain with? You have sat by the road waiting for lovers, like a nomad girl in the wilderness. You pollute the land with your prostitution and evil behavior. Therefore, the showers have been withheld, and the spring rain has not come. You have the forehead of a prostitute;

you refuse to be embarrassed. So do you now call to me, "My Father! You are the companion of my youth!" [And you say,] "Will he keep this up forever? Will he perpetually maintain this attitude?" This is how you speak, and you can say such things while you behave wickedly.[11]

The background to this text Is Deuteronomy 24:1–5, which sets up a situation in which a man divorces his wife, and she then marries another man. She then is divorced from the second husband. In such a case, the woman and her first husband are not allowed to remarry. "That would be detestable in the eyes of YHWH," and it would "defile the land with sin" (Deut. 24:4). But Judah has done far worse, Jeremiah says. She was not just married to one other man; she has been promiscuous with countless men (a metaphor for the idols Israel worshipped on the hill shrines). Although she had done this, she supposed she could just go back to YHWH, her covenant husband, at any time and renew the relationship. She addressed YHWH as her lord and appealed to him as her God while recklessly violating the covenant. Even worse, Judah was confused and irritated that YHWH continued to show displeasure toward the nation by withholding rain from them. "Will he keep this up forever?" they asked. The prostitute's "forehead" refers to her face being brazen and shameless; but beyond that, it implies that, like a prostitute who scorns traditional morality, she cannot comprehend that she has anything to be ashamed of. But the real lesson of the marriage and divorce analogy is that the relationship is forever broken. There can be no reconciliation and no remarriage because this is not simply a matter of the two parties having disagreements to work through. A marriage covenant that is annulled because of adultery cannot be repaired.

It is against this backdrop that we must understand the new covenant. It is not simply a renewal of the relationship with Israel. There was such a thing as a "covenant renewal." A famous example is Exodus 34:10–28, in which YHWH renewed the covenant after the golden calf incident. But now, Jeremiah says, that is not possible. Analogous to the law of Deuteronomy 24:1–5, the relationship is forever ended. If that is the case, however, how can there be any future relationship between God and Israel? But the new covenant that Jeremiah predicts is not simply a renewal of the marriage vows. The best analogy for Jeremiah's meaning is in Paul's explanation of how the new covenant works in the life of the individual:

Do you not know, brothers (for I am speaking to those who know the law) that the law has authority over a person only for as long as that person lives? After all, a married woman is bound by law to her husband as long as he lives. But if her husband dies, she is released from the power of the law concerning her husband. Accordingly, she will be designated an

---

11. "This is how you speak, and you can say such things while you behave wickedly" is literally, "Look, you speak, and you do wicked things, and you are able" (הִנֵּה דִבַּרְתְּ וַתַּעֲשִׂי הָרָעוֹת וַתּוּכָל).

adulteress if she gets with another man while her husband is alive. But
if her husband dies, she is free from that law, so that she is no adulteress
if she gets with another man. And so, my brothers, you too have died to
the law through the body of Christ, so that you may belong to another,
to him who was raised from the dead in order that we may bear fruit for
God. (Rom. 7:1–4)

Behind Jeremiah's declaration of a new covenant is a theology of death and
resurrection. Adulteress Israel could not remarry her husband, but there has
been a death that annulled the power of this law. In one sense, it was her death.
Israel is taken into exile, and the place chosen for YHWH's name, the Jerusalem
temple, is reduced to ashes. There would never be another Davidic king ruling
over Judah. The people who survived the ordeal were either carried off to Babylon or scattered across the world in diaspora. A new covenant with Israel was
therefore possible because she was not the same woman who had committed
adultery against her husband; that woman was dead. She would be a resurrected
Israel. In the New Testament, of course, there is an even deeper fulfillment. Not
only did Israel die in some metaphorical sense, but her Lord came and literally
died for her and in her place, allowing the new covenant to be enacted.

The Provisions of the New Covenant

The terms of the new covenant in Jeremiah are straightforward. God will
embed his law in their hearts. They will be changed from within, and obedience will no longer be a matter of external compulsion. "I will put my law
within them, and I will write it on their hearts." Besides self-evidently referring to an internal change in the people, this is a reversal of Jeremiah 17:1
discussed above:

The sin of Judah is written with an iron pen,
Engraved with a stylus of flint on the tablets of their hearts.
And [the stylus] belongs to the horns of your altars.

Idolatry had thoroughly hardened the hearts of the people, but in the
new covenant, God would reverse this, writing the law on their hearts as the
counterpart to how idolatry had engraved apostasy on their hearts. As they
had impulsively worshiped other gods, even so they would one day feel an
inner compulsion toward loyalty and love for YHWH.

In addition, everyone "from the least of them to the greatest" would know
and love YHWH. This is a reversal of Jeremiah 5:3–5:

YHWH, do not your eyes [look] for truth? You strike them, but they do
not care! You are finishing them off, but they refuse to take correction!
They make their faces harder than rock! They refuse to repent. Then I
thought, "These are just the poor. They are foolish, for they do not know

the way of YHWH [or] their God's way of justice. I will go to the great so that I may speak to them, for they know the way of YHWH [and] their God's way of justice." But all of them had alike broken the yoke. They had torn off their restraints.

The severe punishment prescribed in the law had no good effect on the people. Rather than abandon their idols and submit to God's requirements, they became ever more determined to seek help from Baal and other deities. And it was not just the peasants and the lower classes, the people with no real instruction in the law, who turned to pagan superstitions for help. Even the most sophisticated and religiously trained of them were wholly apostate.

The last provision of the new covenant is that YHWH will "forgive their iniquity, and . . . will no longer remember their sin." This, like the previous provision, looks back to and echoes the oracle of Jeremiah 5:

Roam through the streets of Jerusalem, and look around! And get to know it and search through its squares. If you can find someone who deals honestly and seeks [to practice] faithfulness. [If you can find one,] I will forgive this city. But if they say, "As YHWH lives," they are swearing falsely. (Jer. 5:1–2)

This text implicitly compares Jerusalem to Sodom, which fell because God could not find ten righteous people in the city (Gen. 18:32). In Jerusalem, however, God could not find even one. This is hyperbole, but it sets up an important contrast: Under the new covenant, everyone will know YHWH. Jeremiah 5 also speaks of the city's obstinate evil: God cannot forgive them because they are incapable of turning from evil. Under the new covenant, however, he will forgive.

The provision that God will no longer "remember" their sin looks back to Jeremiah 14:10. The prophet has just made a petition in Judah's behalf, confessing that they were a backsliding people but appealing to YHWH to remain with his people and save them (14:8–9). But he receives a stern answer in the next verse:

Thus says YHWH concerning this people: They love to wander so much! They do not restrain their feet! Therefore, YHWH does not accept them. He will now remember their iniquity and punish their sins. (Jer. 14:10)

In this verse, YHWH will "remember" their infidelity and punish them. The wandering of Judah is the desire of the people to find salvation in something other than YHWH. They might go to the Egyptians or to other nations seeking an alliance against the Babylonians. Or they might turn to the storm god Baal for help in time of drought. They are perpetually going in a futile search for help that leads them far from their God. In contrast to this, in what may be considered as part of the preamble to the new covenant, YHWH addresses his people as follows:

> Set up signposts! Put road marks in place!
> Focus your attention on the route—on the road you will travel!
> Come back, Virgin Israel, Come back to these your cities!
> How long will you wander afar, O Daughter who keeps turning about?
> YHWH is creating a new thing in the land,
> O Female [who] wanders around [like] a man in his prime!
> (Jer. 31:21–22)[12]

Here, Israel is portrayed as a woman who, contrary to custom and culture, wandered far away with the carelessness one would normally only see in a man who was in the prime of life and certain of his ability to deal with any threats. The young woman Israel wanders about, heedless of the danger she is in. Signs should be set up to point her back to her homeland. On one level, this speaks to the end of the Jewish Diaspora and the regathering of the people. But it more fundamentally addresses the spiritual wandering of Israel. They are looking for help everywhere except for where it can be found—with their own God, YHWH. But the salvation that Jeremiah 31:21–22 promises is eschatological; it is a fulfillment of the promise in Deuteronomy 30:1–10. Until that day, Israel is doomed to wander.

The consistent theme of the book of Jeremiah is that Judah is incurably evil and so cannot be saved or forgiven. The new covenant's grand reversal of this is a unilateral act of God. He will transform their hearts, making them pliant and obedient. It is not a matter of Judah suddenly recognizing the error of their ways and returning to God and his laws. It is rather God who acts to change them, to bring about their repentance, and thus to be able to forgive their earlier sins.

Jeremiah's presentation of the new covenant is notable for having no specific promise of salvation for the Gentiles. This is because the promise in Jeremiah is inextricably bound to its context in his life and ministry. He went through the experience of first praying for the nation and then, as YHWH showed him how perverse they had become, being commanded to cease making intercession. He conceived of Israel's apostasy as a rupture beyond healing. She was like a woman who broke the covenant of marriage and had taken many lovers, and no recovery of the old covenant relationship was possible. He therefore could present any future act of salvation only as a new and eschatological covenant "for the house of Israel and the house of Judah." Put simply, Jeremiah was focused on Israel's fallen condition and on what

---

12. The standard translation of this text, particularly at 31:22b (as in the ESV, "For the LORD has created a new thing on the earth: a woman encircles a man") is both incorrect and unintelligible. For a survey of how scholars have tried to make sense of it and for a defense of the above translation, see Garrett and Pearson, *Jeremiah and Lamentations*, 274–77.

God would have to do to bring Israel back. He does not deny that there is hope for the Gentiles, but it is not his immediate concern.

Jeremiah's New Covenant in Biblical Theology

Jeremiah's presentation of the new covenant is based upon earlier biblical texts, and in turn it leads into restatements and expansions in later texts. Although there are many passages one could consider, we will here pay particular attention to Deuteronomy 30:1–10; Ezekiel 34:25–31; 36:16–32; and Hebrews 7:11–8:13.

The New Covenant and Deuteronomy 30:1–10

Deuteronomy 30:1–10 is foundational for the theology of Israel's fall and restoration that is developed throughout the prophets. Jeremiah's prophecy of the new covenant is based upon it and advances beyond it. The Deuteronomy text is as follows:

> And this will happen: All these things that I have set before you, the blessings and the curses, will come upon you, and then you will bring them to mind in all the nations to which YHWH your God drives you. And you will return to YHWH your God and obey him, doing everything I command you today, and both you and your children will do so with all your heart and with all your soul. And YHWH your God will bring about your restoration and have compassion on you and gather you again from all the nations where YHWH your God scattered you. Even if some of you are banished to [a land under] the far end of the sky, from there YHWH your God will gather you and receive you. And YHWH your God will bring you to the land that belonged to your ancestors, and you will take possession of it. He will make you more prosperous and numerous than your ancestors. And YHWH your God will circumcise your hearts and the hearts of your offspring, so that you may love him with all your heart and with all your soul, and live. And YHWH your God will put all these curses on your enemies and on those who hate and persecute you. And you will again obey YHWH and carry out all his commands, which I am issuing to you today. And YHWH your God will make you prosperous in all the work of your hands, in the fruit of your womb, in the young of your livestock, and in the crops of your land for your happiness. YHWH will again delight in you and make you prosperous, just as he delighted in your ancestors, if you obey YHWH your God and keep his commands and decrees that are written in this book of the law and turn to YHWH your God with all your heart and with all your soul.

This passage anticipates that all the curses pronounced Deuteronomy 28, particularly the destruction of Israel and the exile from their land, will come about. After that, it says, there will be a great deliverance for the nation.

A difficult problem is that this text is ambiguous regarding the order of Israel's salvation. On the one hand, it seems to say that YHWH will respond with favor after the Jews scattered across the world repent and seriously commit themselves to obey his laws. On the other hand, it speaks of YHWH of his own accord regathering his people and circumcising their hearts. The latter implies that God first acts to bring about a change in the people, who then respond with repentance. The metaphor of circumcising the heart suggests that their hearts are pagan, like the bodies of male Gentiles, and that God must create in their minds a willingness to obey. One might argue, with some merit, that this is an artificial problem. Repentance is both a work of God and a human decision to turn toward God and away from evil. But this is not a fully satisfactory answer. The question of which comes first is valid, and Deuteronomy 30 is frustratingly ambiguous.

In addition, Deuteronomy 30:9b–10a seems to envision little more than a return to the law and the Sinai covenant, so that restored Israel is once again living under the old, preestablished covenant: "YHWH will again delight in you and make you prosperous, just as he delighted in your ancestors, if you obey YHWH your God and keep his commands and decrees that are written in this book of the law."

The answer to both problems is that the promises of Deuteronomy 30:1–10 are not purely eschatological. There are two restorations in view. The first is the postexilic return of the Jews to Jerusalem, the building of the second temple, and the establishment of a commonwealth that at least in its ideal form was dedicated to keeping the law. While this too involved the work of God on at least some human hearts among the Jews, it was more precisely a national or ethnic movement among the Jewish people to return to their land and rebuild their institutions. While a whole community can be moved to act, that is not the same as the circumcision of an individual person's heart. And the postexilic restoration involved a severe application of the law to enforce its rules. The people had to be forcibly driven to obey the law, as Nehemiah 13 attests. And even in their reconstituted state, they often found ways to skirt the law's requirements, as Malachi 1–2 attests. This was a community of persons, some pious and some not, that generally but not necessarily wholeheartedly followed the requirements of the Sinai covenant.

But Deuteronomy 30 also attests to an eschatological salvation of persons whose hearts have been changed by God. He will gather them to himself as a new community composed entirely of the redeemed. Deuteronomy 30 is at the same time the reconstitution of the Jewish commonwealth in a postexilic environment and a shadowy glimpse into God's intention to create for himself a people made up entirely of individuals whose hearts are pure in their devotion.

There is something of this double meaning in Jeremiah as well. In the promises of redemption found in chapters 30–31, there is the expectation both of a communal, postexilic restoration and of an eschatological redemption. For example, Jeremiah 30:10 speaks of bringing the Jews back from a distant place, which has at least a partial fulfillment in the postexilic return. However, in the new covenant of 31:31–34, there is no such ambiguity. It speaks exclusively of an eschatological salvation, where the new community is formed entirely of people who have had the law written on their hearts, and where there is no need even to encourage anyone to know God, "For all of them will know me, from the least of them to the greatest, says YHWH."

Jeremiah has not contradicted Deuteronomy 30 but has advanced beyond it. He did not deny that there could be a limited and voluntary return to the land. The postexilic community could be swept up in a movement, partly borne of religious zeal, to return to their land and reestablish Jerusalem as the place to worship YHWH. However, he had seen for himself that a people can become so perverse that they are incapable of repentance. If they are ever to have their hearts changed, God himself must it bring about. Furthermore, Jeremiah fully grasped the implication of the breaking of the Sinai covenant: It was a full annulment. Things could no more go back to the way they were than a divorced woman who had been with other men could remarry her first husband (Jer. 3:1–5). If Israel was ever again to be in covenant with God, it would have to be in an arrangement that "will not be like the covenant that I made with their fathers on the day when I took them by the hand to bring them out of the land of Egypt." Deuteronomy does not explicitly envision an annulment of the Sinai covenant; this is a new concept that first appears in Jeremiah.

The New Covenant and Ezekiel 34:25–31; 36:16–32

Ezekiel shows signs of having been influenced by Jeremiah. He sometimes expands upon brief sayings found in Jeremiah. The lengthy and graphic account of the sisters Oholah and Oholibah (Ezek. 23:1–49) expands Jeremiah's brief use of the metaphor of the two unfaithful sisters (Jer. 3:6–10). Where Jeremiah only briefly refutes the saying, "The fathers have eaten sour grapes, and the children's teeth are set on edge" (Jer. 31:29–30), Ezekiel answers it with a detailed examination of the issue of moral responsibility (Ezek. 18:1–32). Ezekiel also draws upon the idea of a new covenant between YHWH and Israel, but deals with it in two passages in a distinctive manner. He does not simply repeat Jeremiah's teachings.

The first text is in Ezekiel 34. This oracle is undated, denounces Israel's wicked shepherds (that is, their leaders), and declares that YHWH will himself become Israel's shepherd and will judge righteously over the sheep (that is, the people). He also declares that "David" will be their shepherd (34:1–24). He then describes the covenant under which this new Israel will live:

> I will make with them a covenant of peace and stop wild beasts from living in the land, so that [my sheep] may dwell in the wilderness securely and sleep in the woods. And I will make them and the places around my hill a blessing, and I will send down the showers in season. They will be showers of blessing. And the trees of the field will give their fruit, and the earth will

give its produce, and they shall be secure in their land. And they will know that I am YHWH when I break the bars of their yoke and deliver them from the hand of those who use them as slaves. They will no longer be a plunder for the nations, and the beasts of the land will not devour them. They will dwell securely, and no one will terrify them. And I will make them famous for their agricultural production, so that they will no longer be seized by hunger in the land, and they will no longer suffer the reproach of the nations. And they will know that I am YHWH their God with them, and that they, the house of Israel, are my people, says Lord YHWH. And your women will be my sheep! Your men will be the sheep of my pasture![13] And I will be your God, says Lord YHWH. (Ezek. 34:25–31)

For Ezekiel, the new covenant is a "covenant of peace," implying both that there will be no more conflict between YHWH and his people and that it will enact an era of well-being for the people.[14] In addition, Ezekiel describes the benefits of this covenant in highly metaphorical terms, speaking of the people as livestock that need to be protected from predators, require good pasturage, and must be freed from the yoke their enemies have set upon them. Where Jeremiah 31:34 speaks of social rank, saying, "For all of them will know me, from the least of them to the greatest," Ezekiel speaks of gender, saying that both men and women would be God's "sheep." Ezekiel declares that the land on which they graze will be lush because of "showers of blessing."[15]

Ezekiel adds a new dimension to this ideal of eschatological redemption in Ezekiel 36:16–32:

And I received a word from YHWH, as follows: Son of man, when the house of Israel was living in their own land, they defiled it by their way and their deeds. Their way was like menstrual uncleanness to me. And I poured out my anger upon them because of the blood they poured out in the land and because they defiled it with their idols. I scattered them among the nations, and they were strewn throughout [many] lands. I judged them for their way and their deeds. And they went to the nations. And where they went, they profaned my holy name, when [people] said of them, "These are YHWH's people, and they came from his land." And I felt badly for my holy name, which the people of Israel profaned among the nations where they went. Therefore, say to the house of Israel, Thus says Lord YHWH: What I am doing is not for your sake, house of Israel. Instead, it is for the

---

13. The translation "And your women will be my sheep! Your men will be the sheep of my pasture" reflects the fact that the Hebrew first uses the feminine plural form of "you" (וְאַתֵּן) and then the masculine plural form (אַתֶּם).

14. The term שָׁלוֹם implies freedom from both warfare and poverty, and both are promised in the "covenant of peace" (שָׁלוֹם).

15. Ezekiel had lived in Jerusalem during the drought of Jehoiakim's reign, and he therefore portrays redeemed Israel as enjoying nurturing rain showers.

sake of my holy name, which you profaned among the nations where you have gone. And I will sanctify my great name, which has been profaned among the nations, which you profaned among them. Then the nations will know that I am YHWH, says the Lord YHWH, when I am sanctified through you before their eyes. And I will take you from the nations, and I will gather you from all the lands, and I will bring you back into your land. And I will sprinkle clean water on you, and you will be clean. I will cleanse you from all your impurities and from all your idols. And I will give you a new heart and put a new spirit in you. And I will remove your heart of stone from you and give you a heart of flesh. And I will put my Spirit in you. And I will cause you to follow my decrees and to keep my rules and carry them out. And you will dwell in the land I gave your fathers. And you will be my people, and I will be your God. And I will save you from all your uncleanness. And I will call to the grain and make it abundant and will not bring famine upon you. And I will make the fruit of the trees and the crops of the field abundant, so that you will no longer suffer disgrace before the nations because of famine. And you will remember your evil ways and your deeds that were not good, and you will feel disgust at yourselves because of your iniquity and your abominations. I am not doing this for your sake, says Lord YHWH. That should be clear to you. Be ashamed and humbled about your conduct, house of Israel!

Although both Jeremiah and Ezekiel were priests, the priestly vocation is far more evident in Ezekiel. Thus, he portrays Judah's sin in terms of ritual uncleanness, describing it as like the impurity of menstrual blood, and he speaks of Judah's restoration as analogous to ritual cleansing.

Throughout the text, however, Ezekiel gives essentially the same message as Jeremiah, but he presents it in an entirely new manner, not slavishly copying Jeremiah. Where Jeremiah had spoken of Israel as a woman who had committed adultery with many lovers and whose marriage to YHWH was irrevocably broken, Ezekiel presented their slaughter of children for Baal under the metaphor of "menstrual uncleanness." Where Jeremiah had presented Israel as a woman wandering among the nations who needed to return to her land and her God, Ezekiel presents Israel in exile as a reproach to the name of YHWH among the nations; the Gentiles regarded God's people as outcast reprobates. Where Jeremiah had spoken of God on his own initiative doing a great work among his people, Ezekiel saw God acting for the sake of his name. Where Jeremiah spoke of God writing the law and their hearts so that all would know him, Ezekiel spoke of changing their hearts of stone into living hearts of flesh, of giving them a new heart enlightened by God's Spirit, and of so transforming their minds that they would themselves be appalled by their former behavior. If anything, Ezekiel is even more explicit about Israel's eventual redemption and transformation as entirely a work of God. It is not prompted by God seeing something good and praiseworthy in his wayward people.

The New Covenant and Hebrews 7:11–8:13

Hebrews 4:14–5:14 and 6:19–8:13, establishes that the priesthood of Jesus "after the order of Melchizedek" is superior to the Aaronic priesthood and cites Jeremiah 31:31–34 in full (Heb. 8:8–12). We cannot here examine the context of the citation in detail, and we will not deal with the use of the figure of Melchizedek in Hebrews. For our purposes, the crucial verses are Hebrews 7:11–12, 18–19, 25; 8:1–2, 6–7, 13:

> If perfection could have really come about through the Levitical priesthood (after all, the people were made subject to legislation [focused] upon [this priesthood]),[16] why was there still need for another priest to arise, one in the order of Melchizedek, not in the order of Aaron? For with the priesthood removed, of necessity a removal of [the enabling] law comes about. . . . For a removal of the former regulation came about because it was weak and useless. After all, the law did not perfect anything. But the enactment of a better hope came about, by which we draw near to God. . . . Therefore, [Jesus] can save entirely those who approach God through him, because he always lives to intercede for them. . . . Here is the main point of what we are saying: We have such a high priest, who sat down at the right hand of the throne of the Majesty in heaven. He is the minister of the sanctuary, the true tabernacle set up by the Lord, not by a human. . . . And now Jesus has attained a far superior ministry, equivalent to how he is mediator of a better covenant, which has been legislated for the sake of better promises.[17] For if the first covenant

---

16. The meaning of ὁ λαὸς γὰρ ἐπ' αὐτῆς νενομοθέτηται in 7:11 is disputed, as noted by William L. Lane, *Hebrews 1–8*, WBC 47A (Dallas: Word, 1991), 174. BDAG suggests, "on the basis of it (i.e. the Levit. priesthood) the people received the law" (BDAG s.v. "νομοθετέω" 676; cf. NRSV). But this is problematic because the law was the basis for the priesthood and not the reverse. The Aaronites and Levites had priestly functions because the law ordained it, and they ministered according to the rules of the law. Lane observes that Philo, *On the Special Laws* (1.235; 2.35) has analogous examples where the meaning is "concerning." This would mean that the law speaks "concerning" the priesthood. However, ἐπ' αὐτῆς is an unusual way to say "concerning it," and the examples from Philo represent rare usage. Furthermore, taking the text to mean that the law speaks "concerning" the priesthood would mean that the law spoke about this among many other things. While that is strictly true, it does not do justice to ἐπ' αὐτῆς, "upon it," which implies more strongly that the law is focused on the priesthood. The preposition ἐπί implies that the law is built upon or built around the priesthood. That is, the law has the Aaronite priestly religion at its heart, and the legislation is meant to enable the priesthood to function. The law is "on" the priesthood in the sense that the priesthood is its focal point.

17. This text (8:6) reads ἥτις ἐπὶ κρείττοσιν ἐπαγγελίαις νενομοθέτηται. It is similar to Heb. 7:11, the only other New Testament text having the verb νομοθετέω, and again used with ἐπί (albeit with a genitive object in 7:11 and a dative in 8:6). This can be translated "[the covenant] which is enacted on better promises" (ESV; other translations are similar). But this translation, like the similar translation for 7:11, is a problem. The new covenant *sets forth* the better promises; it is not enacted "on" them. A good analogy, having both a passive verb and ἐπί with a dative, is Gal. 5:13, Ὑμεῖς γὰρ ἐπ' ἐλευθερίᾳ ἐκλήθητε, literally "for you were called upon freedom." The meaning is, "You were called with the purpose that you experience freedom." That is, freedom is the goal of the calling. In the same way, "good promises" are the goal of the new covenant.

were faultless, there would have been no occasion for seeking another. . . . In calling [this covenant] "new," he made the first one obsolete. And that which is obsolete and outdated will soon disappear.

Hebrews develops the theology of the new covenant beyond anything in Jeremiah or Ezekiel, asserting that it implies the obsolescence of the Levitical priestly order. The purpose, it seems clear, was to dissuade Christians from turning to the ritual life of Second Temple Judaism for salvation. It states that "perfection," which here means forgiveness of sin and freedom from its power, is not found in the sacrifices and cultic practices of the temple. Furthermore, the religion of the priesthood is inextricably bound to the law, which authorized it and stipulated all its rituals of sacrifice, cleansing, holy days, and priestly investiture. Jeremiah asserted that the law had failed to change the hearts of the people and thus could not turn them away from apostasy, but he did not explicitly speak of the end of the Levitical system.

With remarkable insight, the writer of Hebrews asserts that the law is "[focused] upon" the Levitical priesthood. This means that the Levitical priesthood is the living heart of the law, or that the law is largely centered upon priestly matters. This is obviously true when one considers the sheer bulk of material that is given to these matters. Discussions of sanctuary, priesthood, sacrifice, ritual purity, and holy days take up Exodus 25–31 and 35–40, virtually all of Leviticus, and much of Numbers.

Theologically, moreover, matters of sanctuary and priesthood are the heart of the law. Modern Judaism and Christianity both tend to think of the law as essentially a list of rules to be kept, as though keeping rules was the whole point of Israel's religious life. For modern readers, therefore, the rules for the priesthood and sacrifice, especially as found in Leviticus, are a secondary and distracting matter (in other words, we think that the priestly rules are less important than the moral laws). *But the law's rules have no meaning or value unless there is a way for people to relate to God.* In the law, the avenue to God is the Aaronic priestly ministry at the temple. The rules exist so that priesthood and temple may function as the focal point of Israel's worship. Access to God is mediated by the priesthood, and the law governs the procedures by which this is to be done. These laws also define the infractions that defile the worshiper and the temple. But if the Levitical priesthood is replaced by another after the order of Melchizedek, there is now a new access to an encounter with God, and the rules of the Sinai covenant become obsolete. There must be a new covenant.

Hebrews established from Psalm 110:4 that Christ's priestly office is of the "order of Melchizedek" (Heb. 5:5–10). And because the Aaronic priesthood is removed, so too there must be a "a removal of [the enabling] law." In this framing of things, the priesthood, whether of the Aaronites or of Christ, is conceptually central to its associated covenant. Continuing to hold on to the terms of the Sinai covenant has no meaning if the priesthood of Aaron has been superseded, because the religious heart of the covenant has been removed. And, Hebrews asserts, this is precisely what the oracle of Psalm 110:4 does. It announced the coming of a new priesthood of a different order, thereby disestablishing the priestly function of the house of Aaron.

Hebrews focuses heavily on Christ's priestly work because that is what empowers the promises found in the new covenant. It implies that there is a reciprocal relationship between priesthood and covenant. The covenant terms authorize the priesthood and define its purpose, and the priestly ministry is the raison d'être for the covenants.

In the Sinai covenant, the law set up all the rules for the priesthood; the Aaronite clergy gave Israel's existence under the law its religious life. The cult was the domain of Israel's worship of God, and it also removed the people's guilt. But it was all a "shadow" (Heb. 8:5); that is, it was done in a ritualized and symbolic manner. The blood of bulls and goats could not take away sin (Heb. 10:4), and the priests were themselves sinners (Heb. 5:3; 7:23). Analogously, the "better promises" of the new covenant require a different priesthood. Instead of the rules of the law, the promises are that the people's sins would be forgiven and their hearts would be changed, enabling them to love God, and all of this would be carried out by the priest "after the order of Melchizedek." In that sense, Hebrews argues, the covenant of Jeremiah 31:31–34 authorizes the creation of a new priesthood in the same way the law authorized the Aaronic priesthood. Reciprocally, Jesus's priestly ministry as "mediator of a better covenant" empowers and enables the new covenant, so that its promises are realized. In contrast to the shadow ministry of the Aaronic priests, however, he "sat down at the right hand of the throne of the Majesty in heaven" (Heb. 8:1) and "can save entirely those who approach God through him, because he always lives to intercede for them" (Heb. 7:25)

Hebrews goes well beyond but does not contradict Jeremiah. Indeed, what Hebrews teaches is implicit in what came before. Jeremiah understood, in the metaphor of the divorced woman who takes multiple lovers, that Israel could not simply renew the Sinai covenant and go back to doing things the old way. A new covenant, "not like" the old one, was required. The logical corollary to Jeremiah's new covenant is that there had to be a new priesthood that opened a new way for Israel to worship God.

Summary: Jeremiah's New Covenant in the History of Salvation

Jeremiah's prophecy of the new covenant marks a major transition in salvation history. Deuteronomy had foreseen that Israel was destined to fail to keep the terms of the law and would be scattered. It predicts a great restoration, but does so in terms that are somewhat ambiguous. It is in part fulfilled in the postexilic era and arises in the determination of the people to try to keep the law and rebuild their homeland; and it is in part an eschatological act of God, circumcising the hearts of the people. Jeremiah's new covenant is entirely eschatological. It is a community whom God has transformed by writing his law on their hearts so that all know God, and all are redeemed and holy. Ezekiel poetically enlarges upon Jeremiah's vision with new and at times highly metaphorical language, still insisting that Israel will relate to God in a new way, through the "covenant of peace." Hebrews, citing Jeremiah's prophecy in full, demonstrates that priesthood is at the heart of the covenants, so that when God appointed a messianic priest after the order of Melchizedek, this did more than remove the house of Aaron from its traditional position. It meant that the whole of the Sinai covenant, which centered on the Levitical priesthood, had become obsolete.

THE HOPE OF ISRAEL

Living Water in a Time of Drought

The Hebrew of Jeremiah 17:12–13, as noted in chapter 3 above, is a prayer of Jeremiah voiced during the drought. The prayer calls YHWH the "Throne of glory," the "Lofty height [that has existed] from the beginning," and "The place of our sanctuary." All these titles allude to the majesty of God and imply that he is above and in control of any earthly calamity. The prayer uses wordplay, employing a single word that means both "hope" and "water reservoir"[18] to make the point that God is Israel's only hope during the crises that confront the nation (in this case, a severe drought). He employs another wordplay, making use of the close similarity between the verb meaning "be ashamed" and the verb meaning "dry up." The word in the text is *yēbōšû*, "They will be ashamed." With a minor change in pronunciation, it is *yibāšû*, "They will dry up." The prayer thus implies, "All who abandon you are put to shame (and dry up)."[19] Those who do not put their faith in YHWH are only "weeds," the worthless plants that spring up in dry and abandoned soil. YHWH, the prayer says, is the "spring of living water." Jeremiah uses the context of the drought to assert that YHWH controls all things and to assert that he alone is Israel's hope for salvation.

The Great Reversal

Jeremiah 30:1–4 introduces the series of promises of salvation that make up Jeremiah 30–33. In 30:2, we see that there was originally a separate scroll of salvation oracles:

> Thus says YHWH the God of Israel: Write all the pronouncements that I speak to you on a scroll.

This echoes and reverses the oracles of condemnation that were originally contained in the "Baruch scroll" mentioned in Jeremiah 36. That scroll

---

18. The Hebrew word is מִקְוֵה.
19. The verbs are בּוֹשׁ and יבשׁ.

contained a harsh condemnation and prediction of judgment for Jerusalem; Jehoiakim was so incensed that he burned it. As argued above in chapter 7, Jeremiah 25:1–13 should be understood to have been the conclusion to the original Baruch scroll, as 25:13 reads:

> And I will bring upon that land all the pronouncements that I have spoken against it, [that is,] all that is written in this scroll, which Jeremiah prophesied against all nations.

The similar language in 25:13 and 30:2 suggests that the scroll of salvation oracles was deliberately conceived to be a counterpart to the dreadful oracles of the Baruch scroll and a reversal of those predictions.

First and foremost, the scroll predicted a reversal of the exile and dispersion of Israel. This was contained in what can be called the "pleasant dream" oracle (30:4–31:26), so named because it ends with Jeremiah waking up and declaring that his sleep had been pleasant (31:26). This passage has a dual fulfillment, promising a restoration that is on one level the return from Babylon and the establishment of the postexilic community but on another level is a final, eschatological regathering of the eternal community of Israel. The text promises that Israel's previous military defeats will be reversed, and Israel will again live in its own land (30:5–11). Using the metaphor of an incurable wound, the passage asserts that although Israel has been given a fatal blow, has been abandoned by all, and has even deserved what it received, God will nevertheless heal them and drive away their foes (30:12–17). Their cities, which had been left as desolate ruins, will be rebuilt (30:18–31:1), and the refugees will return home from all the places to which they were scattered (31:2–14). Rachel's children, who had gone far from YHWH, will come back to him and stop seeking salvation in foreign places (31:15–25).[20]

These texts are tied to their temporal context but also timeless. They address Judah's destruction and captivity, declaring that Jerusalem will be rebuilt and inhabited. But they also declare that although Israel's status as God's people does not grant them immunity from punishment, God's election of Israel implies that they will never be abandoned. True salvation consists not just in a termination of punishment but in the recognition of one's guilt and need for repentance. A spiritual return to God is more meaningful than a physical return to the land. This can only come about by a great work of God that changes the hearts of Israel's spiritually lost sons and daughters (31:18–22). This leads into the eschatological promise of the new covenant, which has been explored above. For Gentile readers, this passage does point to Israel's status as God's chosen people and by implication that salvation for the nations of necessity involves their being grafted into Israel.

---

20. For a full exposition of these passages, see Garrett and Pearson, *Jeremiah and Lamentations*, 268–78.

A New Land

Jeremiah 32 continues the oracles of hope with a promise of a new land. This promise is fulfilled both eschatologically and historically.

The chapter begins with the account of Jeremiah purchasing land in Anathoth while he was imprisoned in Jerusalem as the city was under siege (32:1–15). This event was discussed above in chapter 4. After he completed the purchase, Jeremiah made a lengthy and eloquent prayer (32:16–25), which is discussed below in chapter 10. The main point of Jeremiah's prayer is only implied and not explicit. He observes that YHWH ordered him to buy a field, even though the land was overrun by the Babylonians and soon all would be left as a desolate wasteland (32:25). The implied question is, "Why did you have me buy the land?" God answers in 32:26–44.

YHWH's answer begins with a rhetorical question: "Look! I am YHWH, the God of every living thing. Is anything too hard for me?" (Jer. 32:27). The question alludes to Genesis 18:14, God's response to Sarah's laughter, when she supposed that she, an elderly woman who had always been barren and already experienced menopause, could not have a child. The implied message is that just as God could create a nation from the body of an old, barren woman, so also he could make Israel thrive again on its dead and barren land. YHWH further repeats to Jeremiah that Judah was being punished because of its apostasy, and especially because of its idolatry and child sacrifice (32:28–35). Even so, this was not the end of the Jews:

> Look, I will collect them from all the lands where I banished them in anger, fury, and great wrath. I will bring them back to this place and let them live securely. They will be my people, and I will be their God. I will set their hearts and actions to a single purpose, so that they will fear me for all the days to come, and so that all will then go well for them and for their children after them. I will make with them an eternal covenant, [promising] that I will never turn away from doing good to them. And I will put the fear of me in their hearts, so that they will never turn aside from [following] me. (Jer. 32:37–40)

We see in this text echoes of the new covenant of Jeremiah 31:31–34. God will restore his people and change their hearts. They will love and obey him. And this will be an "eternal covenant," implying that Israel would never again fall into apostasy and suffer as it had before. This promise is clearly eschatological; it was not fulfilled in the postexilic community. The Second Temple Jews, although they had many admirable qualities, were by no means unified in their love for God, as illustrated by the complaints of Ezra, Nehemiah, Malachi, and the preaching of Jesus. As a result of these failings, the Jews suffered another calamity in the Roman destruction of the city in AD 70.

Other aspects of Jeremiah's prophecy, moreover, are more historical in context and not necessarily eschatological:

I will rejoice in doing good for them, and I really will plant them in this land; [I promise this] with all my heart and soul. For thus says YHWH: As I have brought all this great disaster on this people, so I will give them all the good things I have spoken about. And property will be bought in this land, about which you say, "It is a desolation without people or animals! It has been given into the hands of the Babylonians!" (Jer. 32:41–43)

This merging of the historical and the eschatological answers Jeremiah's two great sources of despair. First, the land was being ravaged, making the buying and selling of property seem utterly pointless. Second, the people were hopelessly corrupt, such that the prophet became despondent over the layers of depravity in the human heart. But nothing was too hard for God. He would bring the people back from the exile so that once again houses would be built, land would be farmed, and fields would become valuable and be bought and sold. Even more wondrous, God would someday change the hearts of people so that they would forever be faithful to him and live under a new, eternal covenant.

A New David and a New Priesthood

Jeremiah 33 is the most explicitly messianic prophecy of the book and fits in its context as a second response to Jeremiah's prayer in 32:17–29. Unfortunately, standard translations of 33:2–6 take certain liberties with the Hebrew because, failing to see the connection between the two passages, most translators regard 33:2–6 as obscure and therefore either emend the text or give it a forced and paraphrastic interpretation. However, if one considers that it alludes back to Jeremiah's prayer, the meaning of 33:2–6 is clear:

Thus says YHWH who made [the earth], YHWH who formed it in order to establish it—YHWH is his name: Call to me and I will answer you, and I will tell you great and unassailable things that you did not know. For thus says YHWH the God of Israel: Concerning the houses of this city and concerning the houses of the kings of Judah that are to be demolished; concerning the siege ramps and concerning the sword, [the forces] coming with the Chaldeans to fight [the men of Jerusalem] and to fill [the Jerusalem houses] with human corpses, [men] whom I struck in my anger and my rage; And as for the fact that I have hidden my face from this city because of all their evil: I hereby announce that I will restore health and healing to her! And I will heal them, and I will show them an abundance of peace and security.[21]

---

21. For a full defense of this translation and explanation of its significance, see Garrett and Pearson, *Jeremiah and Lamentations*, 305–8.

Specific parallels demonstrate that 33:2–6 alludes back to the words of Jeremiah's prayer in 32:17–29 (words common to both passages are in italics). First, the opening to Jeremiah's prayer is echoed in God's response. In 32:17–18, Jeremiah prays:

> Ah Lord *YHWH*! You *made* heaven and the *earth* by your great power and by your outstretched arm. . . . *YHWH* Sabaoth *is his name*!

In 33:2, God responds:

> *YHWH* who *made* the *earth*,[22] YHWH who formed it in order to establish it—*YHWH is his name*!

Second, we have reference to siege-ramps, houses, and conflict in both the prayer and in God's answer. In 32:24, 29, Jeremiah prays:

> Now the *siege-ramps* are set up against the *city* to take it. And the city is being given into the hands of the *Chaldeans*, who *fight* against it with *sword*, famine, and pestilence. . . . The *Chaldeans* that *fight* against this *city* will come and they will set fire to this city and burn it and the *houses* upon whose roofs they offered incense to Baal.

In 33:4b–5a, God responds:

> Concerning the *houses* of this *city* and concerning the *houses* of the kings of Judah that are to be demolished; concerning the *siege-ramps* and the *sword*, [the forces] coming with the *Chaldeans* to *fight* [the men of Jerusalem] and to fill [the Jerusalem houses] with human corpses.

In Jeremiah 32, the prophet was bewildered that he had been told to buy land even though the country was under siege and Jerusalem would soon be left a burnt-out ruin. But 33:1–13 asserts that there is a future for the land. Jeremiah's prayer would be answered, and Jerusalem would again be home to a thriving Jewish community. It would contain "the voices of celebration and joy, the voices of bride and bridegroom, and the voices of those who say, 'Give thanks to YHWH Sabaoth, for YHWH is good!'" (33:11).

However, 33:15–26 speaks of an eschatological, messianic era (as described in chapter 7 above, this oracle may have given at the time of 23:1–6). Israel will have a new Davidic king and a new Levitical priesthood (33:15–18):

---

22. This is literally "who made her" (עָשָׂהּ), but in context this obviously refers to the creation of earth. Cf. NIV.

In those days and at that time I will cause a righteous sprout to emerge for David; and he shall enact justice and righteousness in the land. In those days Judah will be saved, and Jerusalem will abide securely. And this is what it will be called: "YHWH is our righteousness." For thus says YHWH: David will not be cut off from having a man to sit on the throne of the house of Israel, and the Levitical priests will not be cut off from having a man [who will stand] before me to offer whole offerings, to make grain offerings, and to make sacrifices, for all the days [to come].

This promise addresses the two things the people of Jerusalem had relied upon for their safety: that they had the Davidic king, the dynasty that God had promised would never end; and that they had the temple and priesthood that God had ordained. Jeremiah had many times warned that neither of these afforded the city the protection that his opponents had claimed. Even so, he now reaffirms the promise that the dynasty will not be cut off and that the priesthood will continue forever, and he even uses these promises to claim that "Judah will be saved, and Jerusalem will abide securely."

He speaks of the coming Davidic king as a "sprout" who will emerge from the soil from which the line of David had seemingly been cut off root-and-branch.[23] It springs up as an inconspicuous and seemingly tender young plant, but carries the promise of the eternal dominion of the house of David. Isaiah had spoken of an eschatological day of glory as the "sprout of YHWH" (Isa. 4:2) and as a time when Israel would be beautified as a garden that sends forth its "sprouts" (Isa. 61:11), but he did not speak of the "sprout" as a messianic king. In Jeremiah, however, the eschatological glorification of Israel focuses on a single man who fulfills the promises to David and saves the nation. He had first made this prophecy in Jeremiah 23:5:

Look! The days are coming, says YHWH, when I will raise up for David a righteous sprout, and he will reign as king and deal wisely, and will enact justice and righteousness in the land.

His reign would be a contrast to the corruption of the leaders of Jerusalem that Jeremiah knew (Jer. 23:1–3). Whereas Zedekiah's behavior and rule did not match the meaning of his name, "YHWH is righteousness," the Davidic king and his city would both rightly be called "YHWH is our righteousness" (23:6; 33:16).

In addition, Jeremiah promises that "the Levitical priests will not be deprived of a man [who will stand] before me to offer whole offerings, to make

---

23. The word צֶמַח is traditionally translated "branch," but this is misleading because in everyday English the word "branch" describes a small twig that grows out of a larger limb on a tree, but צֶמַח describes a young shoot just emerging from the soil. See *HALOT* s.v. "צֶמַח" 1034; and Garrett and Pearson, *Jeremiah and Lamentations*, 309.

grain offerings, and to make sacrifices, for all the days [to come]" (33:18). While Christians can easily see the Davidic sprout as fulfilled in Jesus, it is difficult to know what to do with this promise of a man who will forever fulfill the duties of the Levitical priests. Significantly, the promise of "a man," the eternal representative of the priests, parallels the promise of a singular, eternal Davidic king. For this reason, this is more than a prediction that the temple will be rebuilt or that sacrifices will again be offered. The eternal priest, like the eternal king, should be a single man and should carry out his ministry forever.

Neither the eternal king nor the eternal priest is exactly like his counterpart from the time of Jeremiah. The eternal king does not reestablish the Davidic dynasty as an earthly kingdom. The kingdom of Jesus is not of this world (John 18:36). Similarly, the eternal priest will not reestablish temple worship like that which took place in Jerusalem; the priesthood and sacrifices of the Second Temple are only a token fulfillment of the promise that a man would forever stand before God with his sacrificial offering. In the New Testament we see that the eternal king and the eternal priest are one and the same, the son of David who is also a priest after the order of Melchizedek.

CHAPTER 9

JEREMIAH THE TRUE PROPHET

J esus said, "A prophet is not without honor, except in his homeland and
among his relatives and in his own household" (Mark 6:4). If ever there
was an Old Testament prophet for whom these words held true, it was Jeremiah. We have already noted reasons for Judah's hostility. He was regarded as
a traitor for advising submission to Babylon and as an apostate for saying that
YHWH's temple did not make Jerusalem impregnable. Even after Jerusalem
fell, when it would have seemed that his prophecies had been decisively vali-
dated, his opponents turned this too on its head. They claimed that Jerusalem
had been destroyed because they had been prevented from worshipping the
Queen of Heaven. Jeremiah himself, although he never appears to have doubted
the legitimacy of his calling and message, was at times profoundly dismayed
by how his life had turned out, as a social outcast. He saw with sorrow that the
bulk of the populace, and especially the leading citizens in both political and
religious circles, were implacably hostile to him.

To a great extent, therefore, his book can be regarded as an apologetic
work. It defends the legitimacy of his prophetic call and message. He, not his
opponents, received and proclaimed the true word of God. The fall of Jerusalem was not through any fault of his. In the face of cruel opposition, he gave
the oracles of God that, if followed, would have saved the city.

Jeremiah Under Attack

Even on a superficial reading of the book, it is evident that Jeremiah was
constantly under attack. Because he did not believe that the presence of the
temple ensured that the city would never fall, he was considered a blasphemer
(Jer. 26:4–9). In 29:24–27, we read that Shemaiah the Nehelamite, a reputed
prophet living in Babylon among the Jehoiachin exiles, wrote to Zephaniah
the son of Maaseiah, a priest in Jerusalem, demanding that Jeremiah be
arrested and put in stocks for having predicted that the exile would last a long
time. He called Jeremiah a "madman who goes about spouting off prophecies"

(29:26). On another occasion, when Jeremiah sought to go to Anathoth on family business, a military officer named Irijah son of Shelemiah accused him of treason, claiming he was going over to the Babylonians (37:13).

A particularly important passage in this regard is 17:14–16:

> Heal me, YHWH, so that I may be healed.
> Save me so that I may be saved.
> For you are my object of praise.
> See how they say to me,
> "Where is YHWH's word? Let it come about!"
> I have not, out of an evil motive, been pushing behind you [to get Judah punished]![1]
> I had no desire for the day of utter disaster! You know that!
> Everything that has come from my mouth [was said] right in front of you!

Jeremiah's pain was deep, and he yearned for God's deliverance because the people blamed him for all their troubles. He never desired the destruction of his nation, and did not try to push God into punishing Jerusalem. He only ceased interceding for Judah because God commanded him to give it up, and the bitterness of his task of voicing condemnation and imprecation made him curse the day of his birth.

The challenge, "Where is YHWH's word? Let it come about!" might be taken to be pure scoffing: Jeremiah has made prophecies, but the people do not think they will ever come true. They have no fear of his predictions of disaster. But there may well be more here than a cynical sneer. Considering the implication of its context, that Judah was experiencing drought, their exclamation may express a desire for a powerful prophetic word calling down rains from the heavens, as Elijah did. They know that things are bad, and they cannot understand why Jeremiah, if truly he is God's prophet and has the same authority as Elijah, does not do anything about it.

The implication in all of this is that Jeremiah received criticism because he did not use his prophetic authority to save the nation. In their view, if he did intercede with God in their behalf, he was not a great enough prophet before God to bring about salvation. The two great crises confronting Jere-

---

1. Jeremiah 17:16a is often translated like the NIV's "I have not run away from being your shepherd," but this is unlikely to be the meaning. The verb אוץ does not mean "run away." It means to hurry some process to move forward, and often it involves trying to bring about something bad (Josh. 10:13; Prov. 19:2; 21:5; 28:20; 29:2; Isa. 22:40). Used with a person, it describes trying to hasten or push someone toward doing something (Gen. 19:15; Exod. 5:13). Also, the term מֵרֹעֶה does not mean "from being a shepherd" (it means either "from a shepherd" or "from a grazing animal"). As such, one can hardly make sense of the MT for this line. Against this, Aquila, Symmachus, and the Syriac all read רָעָה ("evil") instead of רֹעֶה ("shepherd" or "grazing animal"). This is the better reading. Jeremiah has "not pushed" (לֹא־אַצְתִּי) "because of evil" (מֵרָעָה, i.e., "from an evil motive") "behind YHWH" (אַחֲרֶיךָ) to get him to punish Israel.

miah's Jerusalem were the drought and the military aggression of the Babylonian Empire. Seeking to understand something of the real-world situation of this era, we can make a reasonable postulation that Jeremiah was compared unfavorably to the great men of the past. Specifically, he would have been considered a failure in comparison to Moses, Samuel, Elijah, and Isaiah.

Moses interceded before God at the golden calf incident and managed to persuade God—first, not to destroy Israel, and second, not abandon them in the desert but to accompany them to the land. In the process, Moses had a series of dramatic meetings with God that were so immediate and profound that his face glowed because of the glory he encountered (Exod. 32–34). Samuel was the prophet who anointed David to initiate the Davidic dynasty (1 Sam. 16), a dynasty that Jeremiah proclaimed to be at its end (Jer. 22:24–30). Also, Samuel's farewell words to the Israelites were, "As for me, far be it from me that I should sin against YHWH by failing to pray for you" (1 Sam. 12:23). What a contrast to Jeremiah, who finally stopped making intercession for them! Elijah, as noted above, prophesied at a time of terrible drought, but in response to his prayers, the drought ended and a great thunderstorm came (1 Kings 18:41–46). But even though Jeremiah prayed for God's help during the drought (Jer. 7:12–14), none was forthcoming.

Worst of all was the case of Isaiah. In his time Jerusalem was besieged by the Assyrian army, and its propaganda officer could rightly boast that Assyria had humbled many nations and their gods. But in response to Hezekiah's prayer, Isaiah declared that YHWH would destroy the invading Assyrians. That night, the angel of YHWH slew their army (Isa. 36–37). By contrast, when King Zedekiah sought Jeremiah to pray for deliverance from the Babylonians, his only response was to tell Zedekiah that the enemy would burn Jerusalem to the ground (Jer. 37:1–10)! This was hardly likely to boost Jeremiah's popularity before the king and people.

The book of Jeremiah directly refutes any charge that he was an inferior prophet, or not a prophet at all, or that he had no love for his land and people. In his commission narrative in chapter 1, God declares that he chose him and sanctified him before he was even born (1:5), making a powerful assertion the Jeremiah was his sanctioned spokesman. More than that, the text directly alludes to Moses. Jeremiah declared that he could not serve as a prophet because he did not know how to speak (1:6)—a plea that echoed Moses's request to be excused from duty because of his inability to speak well (Exod. 4:10). God's response to Jeremiah, "Do not fear them, for I am with you" (Jer. 1:8), recalls the assurance given to Moses, "I will be with you" (Exod. 3:12).

In addition, Jeremiah's protest that he could not serve as a prophet because he was a "boy" recalls that Samuel received his first prophecy—a prediction of impending disaster—when he was but a boy (in both cases, the prophet is called a "boy"; see Jer. 1:6 and 1 Sam. 3:1).[2] Jeremiah was from Anathoth, a town in Benjamin close to Samuel's city of Ramah, and repeatedly spoke of an event from Samuel's time: the destruction of Shiloh, the site of the tent of meeting (Jer. 7:12, 14; 26:6, 9). The Shiloh shrine was evidently destroyed when Israel suffered a crushing defeat at the hands of the Philistines. This event was the topic of Samuel's first prophecy (1 Sam. 3:11–14).

In response to Jeremiah's plea that he could not speak, God also "touched" his mouth (Jer. 1:9), an action that recalls Isaiah's commission to be a prophet. This occurred in Isaiah 6, in "the year King Uzziah died." Isaiah's reason for thinking he could not speak for God was not that he lacked eloquence like Moses, or that he was a boy like Samuel, but that he "was a man of unclean lips." In this case, an angel took a live coal from the altar and touched Isaiah's mouth, purging his impurity and enabling him to take up the prophetic task (Isa. 6:5–7). The parallel between Jeremiah 1 and Isaiah 6 here is quite strong: "and he touched my mouth." The Hebrew in the two cases is identical.[3] And if Isaiah's mouth was touched by a purifying coal, Jeremiah's was touched by the hand of God himself.

Allusion to Elijah in Jeremiah is indirect in that both ministered in a time of severe drought. In this case, however, Jeremiah seemingly fell far short of the man who was the prototype and ideal of the biblical prophet. When Israel was scorched by drought, Elijah called down rain. Jeremiah did not.

But the entire book demonstrates that he was the authentic bearer of God's message to his generation. He was the counterpart and worthy successor to the great prophets of earlier times. Against all opposition, he steadfastly preached that the two institutions that Jerusalem pinned its hopes on, the Davidic dynasty and the temple, were no safeguards against the city's imminent and complete destruction. In the end, he was vindicated by events. And in one sense, he was Elijah's true successor. Like that prophet, he was in his time regarded as the "troubler of Israel" (1 Kings 18:17).

THE EVIDENCE OF JEREMIAH'S COMMISSION

We have already noted that Jeremiah's calling included allusions to Moses, Samuel, and Isaiah. One other element in his commissioning specifically relates to his prophetic authority. In Jeremiah 1:10, YHWH states: "Look! I appoint you today over nations and kingdoms to uproot, and to demolish, and to kill, and to destroy, [as well as] to build and to plant." The main import of this is that God has given Jeremiah authority both to do good and to do harm to many nations, including of course Judah. That is, God says he will

---

2.   In both, the Hebrew is נַעַר.
3.   In both, the Hebrew is וַיַּגַּע עַל־פִּי.

listen when Jeremiah speaks either for or against a people. This is analogous to the authority Jesus gave to the assembled apostles after his resurrection:

> If you forgive the sins of any, they are forgiven them. If you hold back forgiveness from any, it is held back. (John 20:23)

In both cases, God's representative holds the authority to influence how God will treat a given party. Jeremiah's authority was illustrated by Jeremiah 28:15–17, in which he declared that Hananiah would die before the year was out, and Hananiah did die in that year. Simon Peter, analogously, pronounced judgment against Ananias and Sapphira, and they fell dead at his feet (Acts 5:1–10; curiously, Ananias is the hellenized spelling of Hananiah). In addition, Jeremiah was authorized to speak of the rise or fall of nations. With that authority, he spoke of the coming military success of Babylon and the imminent defeat and failure of many other nations such as Judah and Egypt. We are apt to think of this simply as a matter of Jeremiah relaying what YHWH had revealed to him, and that is certainly a critical aspect of the prophetic office. But the true prophet or apostle also carried intrinsic authority. When Moses appealed to YHWH not to destroy Israel, God listened to him as he would not have listened to another (Exod. 32:9–14). There is no indication that either Jeremiah or Simon Peter was simply relaying a message from God when they pronounced judgment respectively over Hananiah and over Ananias and Sapphira. They pronounced a verdict, and God carried it out.

The importance of Jeremiah 1:10 as a conferral of prophetic authority is illustrated by how often the book of Jeremiah alludes to the six verbs of the verse (uproot, demolish, kill, destroy, build, and plant), as shown in the chart below:[4]

Verb	Meaning	Usage Elsewhere in Jeremiah
נתשׁ (*ntš*)	To uproot	12:14, 15, 17; 18:7, 14; 24:6; 31:28, 40; 42:10; 45:4
נתץ (*ntṣ*)	To demolish	4:26; 18:7; 31:28; 33:4; 39:8; 52:14
אבד (*'bd*)	To kill	18:7; 25:10; 31:28; 46:8; 49:38
הרס (*hrs*)	To destroy	24:6; 31:28, 40; 42:10; 45:4; 50:15
בנה (*bnh*)	To build	7:31; 12:16; 18:9; 19:5; 22:13, 14; 24:6; 29:5, 28; 30:18; 31:4, 28, 38; 32:31, 35; 33:7; 35:7, 9; 42:10; 45:4; 52:4
נטע (*nt'*)	To plant	2:21; 11:17; 12:2; 18:9; 24:6; 29:5, 28; 31:5, 28; 32:41; 35:7; 42:10; 45:4

---

4.   This chart is drawn from Garrett and Pearson, *Jeremiah and Lamentations*, 74.

Jeremiah alludes to 1:10 to make the point that whenever he speaks of a nation's fate, he does so with divine authorization. The people may not have liked what he said, but that did not lessen his prophetic status.

Jeremiah's high authority also explains the amount of attention the book gives to his movement from interceding on Judah's behalf to his abandonment of making such prayers, and finally to praying against his people (see the discussion of 11:1–20:18 in ch. 6 above). Because of the high authority YHWH had given Jeremiah, he had to command and even persuade the prophet to stop praying for the nation. Indeed, this illustrates well both the reality and limits of Jeremiah's authority. On the one hand, God did not proceed to bring judgment down on Jerusalem until Jeremiah stopped praying for the city. On the other hand, God had the right to prohibit Jeremiah from continuing to intercede for them. This also answers the implied attack on Jeremiah—that if he had possessed both the willingness and the prophetic mantle, he could have stopped the drought and the Babylonian invasion. He did have the prophetic mantle and initially tried very hard to turn aside God's wrath. But the nation was too far gone for him to continue such an effort.

THE EVIDENCE OF JEREMIAH'S PRAYER LIFE

The book of Jeremiah records a remarkably large number of prayers voiced by the prophet. These are honest prayers. They come from a devout soul; they contain no shallow expressions of religious sentiment meant to paper over what Jeremiah really thought and felt. As the psalms do for the psalmists, Jeremiah's prayers open a window directly upon his inner life. In them, we see his piety, his pain, and his love.

One of his first prayers demonstrates both his honest appraisal of Judah's condition and his desire to show them how they should address it. Jeremiah 3:22 opens with a word from YHWH, calling the people to repentance: "Return, my apostate children! I will heal you of your apostasy!" This is immediately answered with a prayer of repentance:

> Look, we are coming back to you! For you are YHWH our God! It's true; what we got from the hills—the boisterous mountain worship—was just a lie. It's true that the salvation of Israel is in YHWH our God. And "The Shame" has consumed the labor of our fathers ever since our youthful days. It consumed their flocks and their herds and their sons and their daughters. We must lie down in our shame, and our disgrace must cover us. For both we and our fathers sinned against YHWH our God. From our youth until this very day, we have not obeyed the voice of YHWH our God. (Jer. 3:22b–25)

Despite the plural "we" of this prayer, it was not uttered by the people at large. It was Jeremiah's prayer, spoken on behalf of Judah and as a model prayer for them to follow if they would. The people expressed what they really believed in 2:31: "We will wander as we please! We won't come back to you [YHWH]!"

Jeremiah reverses this with, "Look, we are coming back to you!" He speaks of their devotion to Baal. He calls this god "The Shame," analogous to how Saul's son, Eshbaal, "Man of Baal," was remembered under the name Ishbosheth, "Man of Shame" (cf. 2 Sam. 2:8 and 1 Chron. 8:33; see also Jer. 11:13). The mountain shrines to the god were places of loud, unruly, and at times orgiastic rituals meant to get the god's attention and ensure fertility for the people, animals, and crops of Israel. But it was all a lie. It only consumed their livestock and children as sacrifices, leaving the people both destitute and disgraced for their folly and faithlessness. Jeremiah gives the prayer of 3:22b–25 as their representative and as an example for them to imitate. It illustrates how well he understood the gravity of their condition and their need for genuine repentance. It also speaks of the hope he harbored that his people would listen.

We have already observed how the drought and the Babylonian onslaught would have provoked against Jeremiah unfavorable comparisons to Elijah and Isaiah, and how people would have believed either that he did not pray for Jerusalem because he was unpatriotic or that if he did pray, he lacked the authority to move God to save the city. Jeremiah's prayers refute these claims. An example of one of his early prayers for his nation illustrates his patriotism:

> I know, YHWH, that a man's way is not his own.
> No man can go and choose his every step.
> Rebuke me, YHWH, but do so fairly.
> Do not do it in your anger, or you will bring me to nothing.
> Pour out your wrath on the nations that do not know you
> And on the clans that do not call on your name!
> For they devour Jacob!
> They devour him and finish him off!
> And they make his dwelling place into a desolation! (Jer. 10:23–25)

Jeremiah's request that God rebuke him fairly is not primarily for himself. The enemies mentioned in the prayer are nations and not individuals, implying that he is speaking for Judah. He acknowledges that the fate of Jerusalem is in God's hands ("No man can go and choose his every step") and that his nation deserves punishment, but he insists that the foreign nations are far worse and more deserving of God's punishment. This prayer answers the criticism that he lacked love for his country.

The book also addresses the implied claim that he lacked authority with God, so that even if he did pray for the nation it would have no effect. After reporting how Jeremiah made an impassioned plea for relief from the drought (Jer. 14:19–22), it records YHWH's harsh response:

But YHWH said to me: Even if Moses and Samuel were to stand before me, my heart would not be moved for this people. Send them away from my presence and let them depart! (Jer. 15:1)

It was through no fault of Jeremiah that God's anger had not abated. Moses himself, the champion who assuaged God's anger at the golden calf episode, could not have done anything for these people!

Another response the book gives to the critique that Jeremiah was an ineffective prophet is that his prayers were in fact answered—but they were prayers of imprecation against Jerusalem, not intercessions for it. We have already seen how, in 18:19–23, Jeremiah voiced a particularly harsh prayer against the city, which includes the following:

Well then, give their children over to famine!
Cast them out to the power of the sword!
Let their wives become childless and widowed!
Let their men die by pestilence!
Let their young men be slain by the sword in war!
Let a cry be heard from their houses when you bring plunderers swiftly upon them! (Jer. 15:21–22a)

YHWH most definitely did all that Jeremiah asked.

THE EVIDENCE AGAINST THE FALSE PROPHETS

Jeremiah spent much of his career in conflict with people who were self-styled as prophets but consistently contradicted his message. They predicted what the people wanted to hear: that Jerusalem would not fall, that Nebuchadnezzar and Babylon would soon collapse, and that the exile of Jehoiachin would soon end and he would return in triumph. Jeremiah knew early on that many prophets disputed his message, and even he was confused about how to resolve this contradiction. But YHWH responded that he should not let himself be duped; there was no ambiguity about the true word of God:

Then I said: Ah, Lord YHWH! Look, the prophets are saying to them, "You will not see the sword, and you will have no famine, but I will give you true peace in this place." And YHWH said to me: The prophets are prophesying lies in my name. I did not send them, and I did not command them, and I did not speak to them. They are prophesying to you a lying vision, divination, idolatry, and the deceit of their own minds. (Jer. 14:13–14)

Jeremiah did come to see how phony and dangerous the false prophets were, and in 23:9–40 delivers a major oracle against them. He declares that responsibility for the destruction of both Samaria and Jerusalem lay primarily with the prophets who promised peace and security without demanding that their audience repent or make any moral and spiritual changes:

> Among the prophets of Samaria, I saw something profoundly offensive: They prophesied in Baal's name and led my people Israel into error. And among the prophets of Jerusalem, I saw something horrifying: adultery and following lies. They encourage evildoers, so that not one of them turns from their wickedness. Every one of them is like Sodom to me, and the people of Jerusalem are like Gomorrah. . . . Do not listen to what the prophets are prophesying to you; they are deluding you. They speak of visions that come from their own minds and not from the mouth of YHWH. They repeatedly say to those who despise me, "YHWH has spoken: You will have peace." And they say to all who follow their stubborn hearts, "No disaster will befall you." (Jer. 23:13–14, 16–17)

The book provides specific examples of such prophets. Jeremiah 29 gives the account of the letter to the Jehoiachin exiles, which told them to abandon any hope of a return to Jerusalem in their lifetimes. They should build their lives in Babylonia, raise families, and understand that they would die before there was any return from exile. There were, however, prophets among the Jewish exiles who were promising a quick return, and Jeremiah warned his addressees to disregard such men entirely:

> For thus says YHWH Sabaoth, the God of Israel: Do not let the prophets among you, or any of your diviners, fool you. Do not listen to the dreams [of restoration bandied about among] you, which your people dream up.[5] They are prophesying lies to you in my name. I did not send them, says YHWH. (Jer. 29:8–9)

The passage even names the false prophets promising a quick return to Jerusalem: Ahab the son of Kolaiah, Zedekiah the son of Maaseiah, and Shemaiah the Nehelamite. The narrative reveals that these men were aware of what he had written in his letter and were trying to have him silenced. But the naming of his opponents makes an important point: There was an active debate in Jerusalem and among the exiles over who truly spoke the word of God. By pointing to this, the book addresses the crucial questions of whether

---

5.   The Hebrew here is somewhat obscure. It reads וְאַל־תִּשְׁמְעוּ אֶל־חֲלֹמֹתֵיכֶם אֲשֶׁר אַתֶּם מַחְלְמִים, which could mean either "And do not listen to your dreams that you dream" or "And do not listen to your dreams that you prompt to be dreamed." The idea seems to be that the people encouraged their prophets to issue promises of a speedy return home.

Jeremiah was a real prophet and, for the reader, of whether his words should be considered canonical.

The second specific example of a false prophet was provided by Hananiah son of Azzur in the episode of Jeremiah's yoke (Jer. 27–28). Jeremiah put on a yoke as a sign and, against the prognostications of many prophets and omen-takers from Judah and the surrounding nations, he declared that Nebuchadnezzar's power was growing and not diminishing. Every people in the Levant would have to go under his yoke. In response, Hananiah gave an oracle that contradicted Jeremiah's, and the book fully cites his message:

> Thus says YHWH Sabaoth, the God of Israel: I will break the yoke of the king of Babylon. Within two years I will bring back to this place all the vessels of the house of YHWH that Nebuchadnezzar king of Babylon took from this place and carried off to Babylon. I will also bring back to this place Jehoiachin son of Jehoiakim king of Judah and all the other exiles from Judah who went to Babylon, says YHWH, for I will break the yoke of the king of Babylon. (Jer. 28:2–4)

Hananiah framed his prophecy in the same formulaic language that Jeremiah had employed, such as the opening, "Thus says YHWH Sabaoth, the God of Israel." As Jeremiah had worn a yoke as a sign to the people, Hananiah broke the yoke before the assembled congregation and said that Nebuchadnezzar's demise was imminent; he would no longer have the power to subdue people. Once again, the question this posed was whether Jeremiah was a prophet or a fraud.

The book, of course, sets out to show that Jeremiah was the genuine prophet. The first piece of evidence came very quickly, when Hananiah died before the year was out in fulfillment of a curse laid on him by Jeremiah (Jer. 28:16–17). And as the months and years of Zedekiah's reign dragged on, it became evident to everyone that the exiles with Jehoiachin were not coming back within the two years Hananiah had predicted. Nebuchadnezzar's power was only growing, and the yoke he laid on his foes would not be broken.

The great but tragic vindication of Jeremiah was the fall of Jerusalem at the end of Zedekiah's reign in 587/586. And the book ensures that the reader understands this. There is a full account of the city's capture and destruction in Jeremiah 39:1–14, but in Jeremiah 52 there is an even larger account, describing the fall of the city, the plundering of the temple, the removal of the captives, and the many years Jehoiachin languished in a Babylonian prison until he was at last, as an old man, allowed to have a place among the nobles in the royal court of Babylon. This last part of the account shows that Jehoiachin, even if he was allowed to regain his dignity at the end of his life, was no longer a threat to Babylon. He was now harmless. Jeremiah's prophecy that

Jehoiachin would die in exile and be the last of the Davidic line to sit on the throne (Jer. 22:24–27) had been fulfilled.[6]

This extended account of the catastrophe of the fall of Jerusalem in Jeremiah 52 duplicates 2 Kings 24:18–25:30. Apart from serving as an epilogue, providing structural balance to the prologue in Jeremiah 1, the account in Jeremiah 52 seems unnecessary. The essential details of Jerusalem's destruction and the capture of Zedekiah are adequately presented in Jeremiah 39. However, by appending Jeremiah 52 as its epilogue, the book ends by forcibly reminding us that everything Jeremiah had said about the end of Jerusalem, of the Davidic kingdom, and of the temple had been thoroughly vindicated. This saved the reputation of Jeremiah the man and communicated to later generations that Jeremiah the book was the true and canonical word of God.

THE EVIDENCE OF THE JEWISH REFUGEES IN EGYPT

We have already seen how Jeremiah and Baruch were carried off to Egypt by the Jews who fled after the murder of Gedaliah. In Egypt, he encountered an even more ferocious apostasy among the Jewish refugees. They considered the syncretistic and paganized Yahwism of preexilic Judah to be the true faith, and they even blamed the exile and all their other troubles on how Josiah's reforms had prevented them from giving the Queen of Heaven the honor she was due. In response, Jeremiah declared those refugees to be accursed and destined to die out. They would have no place in the construction of postexilic Judaism, and their colonies would disappear.

This development was itself a fulfillment of the message given to Jeremiah early in the reign of Zedekiah of the good and bad figs. The oracle reads as follows:

> Thus says YHWH, the God of Israel: Like these good figs, I regard as good the exiles of Judah that I sent away from this place to the land of the Babylonians. I will set my eyes on them for their good, and I will bring them back to this land. And I will build them up and not tear them down, and I will plant them and not uproot them. And I will give them a heart to know me, that I am YHWH. They will be my people, and I will be their God, for they will return to me with all their heart. But like the bad figs, which are so bad they are inedible, says YHWH, so will I deal with Zedekiah king of Judah, his officials, and the survivors from Jerusalem, both those who remain in this land and those who live in Egypt. I will make them a horrible sign of evil to all the kingdoms of the earth: a reproach, a byword, a taunt, and curse, wherever I drive them. I will send

---

6. As stated in ch. 1 above, Jehoiachin probably died soon after Amel-Marduk elevated him. Zedekiah was Jehoiachin's uncle and a son of Josiah; Jehoiachin was Josiah's grandson. Therefore, Jehoiachin was the last generation to sit on the throne, although he was not chronologically the last king.

sword, famine, and plague against them until they are eliminated from the land that I gave to them and their fathers. (Jer. 24:5–10)

The future of Judaism lay with the Babylonian exiles and not with those who stayed in the land or those who fled to Egypt. Everything he prophesied came to pass. The Jews of the Mizpah community gave way to fear and unbelief and so fled the land. The Egyptian Jews at Elephantine were annihilated. They had no place in shaping postexilic Judaism. Everything that formed the Jewish faith in the aftermath of the fall of Jerusalem came from members of the Babylonian exilic community. Ezekiel, Daniel, the postexilic prophets, and administrators such as Ezra and Nehemiah all came from this body of exiles. This is the final evidence of Jeremiah's foresight into the future of his people. He was the true prophet of his time.

CHAPTER 10

JEREMIAH IN THE CHRISTIAN PULPIT

No matter how deeply one studies the historical and literary context of Jeremiah, it can still be a challenge to bring its message into the modern context and the Christian church. In the companion commentary to this book, my colleague Calvin Pearson provides guidance to the Christian minister in constructing sermons from Jeremiah.[1] As a supplement to his work, I want to point out below how Jeremiah is a model for the minister living through a time of great upheaval, polarization, and even calamity. The controversies he faced have parallels in our time; like him, we are in a world gone mad. Also, the way he carried himself is an example for us.

IN A WORLD GONE MAD

Orthodoxy and Patriotism

To understand how Jeremiah is applicable to us, we must first briefly reflect upon the extremism of our own time. In the present context, throughout Western civilization, there are broadly two kinds of extremism. The one is the aberration of the left. It is characterized by despising one's own country as particularly evil. Theologically, it has little regard for the authority of the Bible. It supports transgressive behavior, especially in the areas of sexual morality and in matters concerning children. That is, it supports unbiblical sexual behavior and abortion. It dismisses the Bible as violent, racist, and patriarchal. Many on the left despise the church, as they believe that Christianity is the handmaid of systemic oppression. Both, they say, are intertwined in the metanarrative that sustains racism, classism, and sexism.

Although they may scorn many aspects of their national culture, they are not at all adverse to using the power of the state to enforce their agenda. Simi-

---

1. Garrett and Pearson, *Jeremiah and Lamentations*.

larly, they are obsessively fixated on issues of race. As I write this, the leftist aberration is the dominant cultural force in the West, especially in academia. It has massive influence in finance and the arts, and it has given rise to numerous political movements. It is prevalent throughout the upper echelons of American society, including its government and military.

The other is the aberration of the right. This is generally hyperpatriotic. It is in some respects the mirror image of the leftist aberration. That is, like the left, it regards the Christian faith and patriotism as intertwined and mutually supporting, but against the left, it regards this as a good thing. For the right, the flag and the cross always go together. Like the left, it tends toward authoritarianism, as it frequently looks for a strong man who will set everything right. The right wing often takes the same positions on social and moral questions as do traditional Christians. That is, many hyperpatriots, like conservatives generally, also regard homosexuality, abortion, and transgenderism as immoral or at least not as something to celebrate. In these respects, what we can call "traditional Christianity" and "hyperpatriotism" are on the same page. Distinguishing them from one another, therefore, can be a difficult task. But doing so is essential if the church is to be true to itself.

Traditional Christians understand that they are to be subject to the whole of the Bible and must listen closely especially to those biblical teachings that make them uncomfortable. Biblical Christians do not despise patriotism. They understand that love for one's own family, people, and country is natural and healthy. They do not regard despising one's own culture as a virtue. Christians reject racism and all forms of class-based oppression, but they regard the left's fixation on race, gender, and equity as fanatical and dangerous. And they can simultaneously love their culture while appreciating the wisdom and beauty found in other cultures. The hyperpatriots, to the contrary, have an almost reflexive need to belittle the cultural practices of foreign nations. In their own way, they are as fixated on issues of race and culture as the leftists are. Most importantly, biblical Christians do not regard their own nation as the vessel of God's work on earth. Hyperpatriots look upon their nation as the new chosen people. In the mind of the hyperpatriot, if there is any hope for this world, it is that the other nations will submit culturally and politically to the new chosen people. Christianity, when it is true to biblical ideals, preaches the gospel of Jesus and his kingdom, a kingdom not of this world, without mixing it with nationalistic and cultural ideals.

We should note that the hyperpatriotism defined here is by no means confined to nations that have a Christian heritage. To be sure, one does see it the history of European states, which operated under an ideology of "God and king," and it exists in American politics and culture. As I write this, one of the best nominally Christian examples is the Russian Federation, which espouses the ideal of "Russian World" (Русский мир [*Russkiy mir*], which can also be translated as "Russian Peace" and is the Russian version of the ancient ideal of the *Pax Romana*). This espouses Russia to be the guardian of peace and morality in a unified domain under the political rule of the Kremlin and the religious rule of the Russian Orthodox Church. It is a domain that must be protected and extended (for this reason, the Russian Orthodox hierarchy encourages militarism). Russia also has distinguished itself for being hostile to the fluid sexual morality of the west and has recently taken a more anti-abortion stance. Although these positions agree with standard Christian teaching, this ideology is mixed in with Russia's aggressive imperialism and a personality cult centered on Mr. Putin.

There are also examples of hyperpatriotism in states that are violently anti-Christian, as in China under the Chinese Communist Party. This entity, by military, economic, and diplomatic aggression, seeks to establish the cultural, political, and financial preeminence of China, exporting "socialism with Chinese characteristics." Militant Islam provides another example of messianic states seeking to forcibly impose their version of the kingdom of God on the rest of us. It is possible that a new version of hyperpatriotism could emerge in the west, but as of the writing of this book, it is not clear what form it may take.

This brings us back to Jeremiah, who faced hostility that was, in our terms, both from the left and the right. The "leftist" opposition was characterized by abandonment of YHWH, by admiration for the Egyptian state and religion, and by various forms of gross immorality.[2] For example, the prophet complains against their paganism in Jeremiah 11:12–13:

> And the cities of Judah and the inhabitants of Jerusalem will go and cry to the gods to whom they make offerings, but they will not in any manner save them in the time of their disaster. For you have as many gods as you have towns, Judah, and the altars you have set up to "Shame," that is, altars to make offerings to Baal, are as many as the streets found in Jerusalem.

The worship of the gods of Canaan included child sacrifice, and their paganized religion naturally allowed for immoral behavior, as in Jeremiah 13:27:

> I see your abominations on the hills in the field: your adulteries, your lustful panting, and your disgraceful whoring. Woe to you, Jerusalem! When will you ever become clean?

---

2.   In Ezek. 8:7–11, Ezekiel is shown a secret chamber in the temple precinct in which leading members of Jerusalem's aristocracy are worshipping before a wall filled with images of "crawling things and unclean animals," obviously referring to images of Egyptian gods on a wall filled with hieroglyphs. This took place in the last days of Jerusalem, during the ministry of Jeremiah.

Judah's immorality and apostasy brought about a horrible abuse of their own children, whom they offered in sacrifice at the Ben Hinnom Valley:

> And they build Topheth, which is in the Ben Hinnom Valley, to burn their sons and their daughters in the fire. I never commanded such a thing, and the idea did not come into my mind. Therefore, days are coming, says YHWH, when it will no more be called Topheth, or the Ben Hinnom Valley, but the Killing Valley. And they will bury [their dead] in Topheth until there is no more room. (Jer. 7:31–32)

Jeremiah preaches against the folly and self-humiliation of going to Egypt for help in 2:16–18:

> Indeed, the men of Memphis and Tahpanhes have broken the crown of your head.[3] Did you not do this to yourself by forsaking YHWH your God when he was leading you in the way? And now, what do you gain from the way of Egypt, drinking the water of the Nile? Or what did you gain from the way of Assyria, drinking the waters of the Euphrates?

Memphis and Tahpanhes are here simply representative cities of Egypt. The breaking of Judah's crown refers to Necho's defeat of Josiah and indicates that this message comes from early in Jehoiakim's reign. Going to drink from the Nile refers to seeking military aid from Egypt; Judah is humiliating itself by pleading for help from a nation that had killed their king. The allusion to Assyria is historical and looks back to earlier kings who sought assistance from a previous terrible enemy of Israel, the Assyrian Empire, as Ahaz did in 2 Kings 16:7. In short, Israel's infatuation with foreign military power was another form of their apostasy. Jeremiah confronted all the elements of what we have called left-wing apostasy.

But he also experienced right-wing apostasy. The most obvious example was at his arrest while going take care of a land transaction in his home city of Anathoth:

> When he reached the Benjamin Gate, a sentry there named Irijah son of Shelemiah son of Hananiah arrested the prophet Jeremiah saying, "You are deserting to the Chaldeans!" (Jer. 37:13)

Jeremiah had long warned that the Babylonians would come and that their power would be irresistible, and he was proven right in both cases. But that did not stop people from regarding him as a traitor. He urged Jerusalem

---

3.   On the translation "have broken the crown of your head," see Garrett and Pearson, *Jeremiah and Lamentations*, 89.

to surrender, and this was proof enough to his enemies that he had no love for his country. But their zeal was not merely nationalistic. It was also theological.

The heresy of the right is to take a valid biblical concept and to distort and exaggerate, using it to justify ideas the Bible never teaches. They understood that the temple was YHWH's house, the place where he would make his name dwell (Deut. 16:11). They knew that YHWH "chose the tribe of Judah, Mount Zion, which he loves" (Ps. 78:68) and that "YHWH loves the gates of Zion more than all the dwellings of Jacob" (Ps. 87:2). The people of Jerusalem could give a hearty amen to all these verses. God would never allow Zion to fall under the boot of a foreign enemy! And yet Jeremiah, knowing they had distorted the true meaning of the words, mocked their faith:

Do not trust these deceitful words: "This is the temple of YHWH! The temple of YHWH! The temple of YHWH!" (Jer. 7:4)

Jeremiah was, in their eyes, a blasphemer. When he declared in his temple sermon that God would repudiate and obliterate this sacred structure, it was more than they could endure:

And [YHWH says,] "I will make this house like Shiloh and this city a curse among all the nations of the earth." And the priests, the prophets, and all the people heard Jeremiah speak these words in the house of YHWH. And as soon as Jeremiah finished declaring what YHWH commanded him to declare to all the people, they—the priests, the prophets and all the people—grabbed him and said, "You must die!" (Jer. 26:6–8)

More than that, they believed he had also belittled their faith in the Davidic covenant. However syncretistic they had become in other areas, they were fundamentalist on this point of their creed—that God had chosen the house of David to reign forever from Jerusalem: "[YHWH said,] I have made a covenant with my chosen one; I have sworn to David my servant: I will establish your offspring forever, and build up your throne from generation to generation" (Ps. 89:3–4). And yet Jeremiah had shown no respect for this element of their creed. Of their beloved King Jehoiachin, whom they hoped would have a speedy return from his deportation to Babylon, Jeremiah had prophesied:

As I live, says YHWH, even if [you,] Jehoiachin the son of Jehoiakim, the king of Judah, were a signet ring on my right hand, I would tear you off from it. (Jer. 22:24)

The people of Judah had seen proof that YHWH loved their city, their temple, and their Davidic king more than he loved all the places in Israel. The Assyrians had destroyed Samaria, the capital of the larger, Northern Kingdom of Israel, had brought down its temples, and had ended its royal house. But God had miraculously preserved Jerusalem against those same Assyrians! As Isaiah 37:36 says,

> And the angel of YHWH went out and struck the army of the Assyrians, which had 185,000 men. And so, when [the people of Jerusalem] got up in the morning, all those troops were dead bodies.

Those heretical ten tribes of Israel could perish, but Judah, guardian of YHWH's house under the Davidic king, could not. For Jeremiah, however, this was just another misapplied and distorted article of faith. Far from being better than Samaria, Jerusalem was much worse:

> And [Israel's sister Judah] saw that it was entirely because apostate Israel had committed adultery that I had sent her away and gave divorce papers to her. Yet her conniving sister Judah did not fear, and she went and behaved promiscuously as well. And through her casual promiscuity, she polluted the land. And she committed adultery with [idols of] stone and wood. And in all this, her conniving sister Judah did not return to me with her whole heart, but did so falsely, says YHWH. And YHWH said to me, "Apostate Israel behaved more righteously than conniving Judah." (Jer. 3:8–11)

What Jeremiah had to deal with, therefore, was in our terms a strange combination of left-wing and right-wing apostasy. They could worship other gods and engage in the most flagrant immorality and still hold to a fanatical confidence that the promises of God would forever keep them safe. In their minds, to believe that the temple and the house of David could fall was unpatriotic, heretical, and deserving of death. For us, the important lesson is that both forms of apostasy were equally abhorrent to YHWH. Indeed, in some ways their warped orthodoxy was worse. They threatened Jeremiah with death after he declared that the temple of YHWH could not save them. As far as we can see, they did not make such threats against him for his condemnation of their paganism. We should remember, moreover, that Israel and Judah in fact were the chosen people of God. If their faith in their status was exaggerated or misplaced, how much worse is it for a Gentile nation to behave as though it were the chosen people?

To further consider how the book of Jeremiah relates to the two varieties of apostasy, we can consider what the prophet says to the nations. Two short oracles against foreign nations serve as examples. The first is directed against Damascus:

> Concerning Damascus:
> Hamath and Arpad are dismayed, for they have heard bad news.

They melt away. There is turmoil in the sea; it cannot be quiet.
Damascus is weak. She turns to flee, and panic seizes her.
Distress and labor pains seize her, like a woman in labor.
Why don't they just abandon her?
She is renowned! She is the city of my joy!
Well then, her young men will fall in her streets,
And all her soldiers will perish in that day, says YHWH Sabaoth.
And I will kindle a fire in the wall of Damascus,
And it will consume the citadel of Ben-Hadad. (Jer. 49:23–27)

Damascus, Hamath, and Arpad had been significant and powerful cities, but Syria had been ravaged by the Assyrians and then thoroughly subdued by Babylon. They no longer held sway in world affairs. The world around them was in chaos ("There is turmoil in the sea; it cannot be quiet" is metaphorical for the upheaval of the late seventh century, when great armies swept through Syria). The local inhabitants should have taken flight from Damascus and escaped the warfare ("Why don't they just abandon her?"). But they did not leave because they continued to be enchanted by the grandeur that still lingered in the city gained long before, when Damascus was the hub of an empire ("She is renowned! She is the city of my joy!").

Jeremiah's oracle against Kedar occurs in 49:28–33:

Concerning Kedar and the Unwalled [kingdoms][4] that King Nebuchadnezzar of Babylon struck. Thus says YHWH:
Rise up, advance against Kedar!
Destroy the people of the east!
[The Babylonians] will take away their tents and their flocks.
They will carry away their curtains, all their goods, and their camels for themselves.
And they will shout over them, "Terror is all around!"
Flee, get away, go deep [into the desert], inhabitants of Unwalled! says YHWH.
For King Nebuchadnezzar of Babylon has worked out a plan against you
And has created a strategy against you.
Rise up, move against a nation at ease, says YHWH.
They live securely without gates or bars; they dwell in isolation.
Their camels will be plunder and their herds will be spoil.

---

4.   This is often translated as a proper name, "Hazor," but there is no evidence that any city of that name existed in that region. It is more likely that the term, though used as if it were a proper name, means "unwalled" and is a reference to how the Arab inhabitants of the region depended on the remoteness of their location and their ability to move quickly out of an area, rather than on walls, for their security. For further discussion, see Garrett and Pearson, *Jeremiah and Lamentations*, 401.

I will scatter to every wind the Arab tribes,[5]
And I will bring ruin against them from every side, says YHWH.
The Unwalled [kingdoms] will be a domain of jackals and an eternal
wasteland.
No one will live there, and no human will sojourn in it.

The distant Arabian tribes of Kedar had little to do with Israel, and no
specific offense against Israel is implied. Even so, they are about to face the
same judgment that God brought on Judah: the fury of the Babylonian Empire.
Kedar had carried out raiding parties into Mesopotamia, and Nebuchadnezzar retaliated in 599 with a major incursion into their territory. The Kedarites
had relied upon distance and the desert to keep them safe from retribution,
and thus they did not build great fortifications. But Jeremiah says that they
will have to flee deep into the desert if they want to escape the Babylonians.

What can we draw from these two oracles? First, God is judge of every
nation. God was using Babylon as his tool of judgment, and used it as readily
against these Gentiles as he did against Judah. Importantly, both the people
in great cities and the desert dwellers are judged. Neither the culture of high
civilization nor the culture of traditional pastoral agrarianism held a privileged
position in God's eyes. Every nation has the right to be proud of its own culture,
but none can rightfully claim to be the culture that God himself favors.

Second, we observe that no nation is addressed in the same manner as
Judah. Only the Israelites were in covenant with God, and only they are liable
for keeping the terms of that covenant. On the other hand, no other nation
was God's instrument for the redemption of humanity. Only Israel receives
the promise of eschatological salvation (Jer. 30–33). God's "new covenant"
is made only with "with the house of Israel and the house of Judah" (Jer.
31:31). The house of David alone will have the "righteous sprout" that God
will raise up to "execute justice" (Jer. 33:15). No nation except Israel has the
divine burden of leading humanity out of the wilderness, and no man from
any other nation is anointed by God to bring about the world's salvation. Only
Israel can provide a messiah. Hyperpatriotism treats one's own nation as the
chosen, messianic people, and it often indulges in a personality cult, whereby
a single person (usually a dictator) is praised as a savior.

A Community of Exiles

More positively, Jeremiah includes material that helps us to understand
how we can avoid turning aside from God's way either to the right or to the
left. This is found in the letter to the exiles in Jeremiah 29. As discussed in
chapter 4 above, early in the reign of Zedekiah there was optimism both in
Judah and among the exiles in Babylon that Jehoiachin and the other deport-

---

5. "The Arab tribes" is literally "[men with] shaved temples" (קְצוּצֵי פֵאָה), but it is a designation for
Arabs. See *HALOT* s.v. "פֵאָה I" 1.ii 908.

ees would soon return to Jerusalem. This optimism was prompted by false prophets, who assured the people that God would soon break the power of Babylon. Jeremiah wrote to the exiles to refute this. The instructions he gave them are of great significance to us:

> Thus says YHWH Sabaoth, the God of Israel, to all the exiles whom I have sent into exile from Jerusalem to Babylon: Build houses and live in them. Plant gardens and eat their produce. Take wives and father sons and daughters. Get wives for your sons. And give your daughters to husbands so that they may bear sons and daughters. Multiply there, and do not become fewer. And seek the prosperity of the city to which I have exiled you and pray to YHWH on its behalf! For its prosperity will be prosperity for you. (Jer. 29:4–7)

This passage tells us what it means to be an exile. The Jews in Babylon were not to despair of the normal blessings of life, including children. They were instead to set about building their lives. Marrying and having children means laying down roots and establishing businesses to provide for those families. Building houses and planting gardens means accepting that this place is now your home; you don't live in a tent, and you cannot quickly and easily depart (even if the Babylonians allowed that). Seeking the peace and prosperity of Babylon means not living a subversive existence against the land in which you reside. Besides praying for the city, as Jeremiah explicitly instructs, it implies living lawfully and seeking to contribute to the well-being of the larger community. This can even involve a certain level of patriotism toward the city. But the Jews were to never forget who they were and who their God was. They were Jews and not Chaldeans. They worshipped YHWH and not Marduk, Sîn, or any of the other gods of Babylon. They were in effect to have a dual citizenship: an earthly one, as residents of Babylon; and a heavenly one, as the people of YHWH.

This pattern of living, and the whole experience of the Jews in diaspora throughout their history, is a model for the Christian experience of being citizens of both a heavenly kingdom and an earthly nation. The Jews have lived in many places and have wonderfully benefited the countries that received them. They have made contributions in every area, including science, finance, the arts, and government. They have patriotically served the nations in which they resided. And yet they have never forgotten that they are Jews.

In the same manner, Christians are a community of "exiles" (1 Peter 1:1). They can build homes, raise children, start businesses, live lawfully, strive to be at peace with their neighbors, and serve patriotically in the land in which they reside. They can identify proudly with the race or nationality to which they belong. But they must never forget that they have a higher citizenship and an identity that is more fundamental. They must never think of their nation as having a messianic role in the world, and they must never look to any national, political, or activist leader as their guide or hope. Hopefully, these two realms will not come into conflict, but if they do, their identity as Christians must come first:

> [The Sanhedrin] said, "We strictly ordered you not to teach in this name, but you have filled Jerusalem with your teaching and are wanting to bring this man's blood on us." But Peter and the apostles answered, "One must obey God rather than people." (Acts 5:28–29)

A Christian's deepest ties are not with fellow citizens of any nation but with brothers and sisters in Christ, a community of "ransomed people for God from every tribe and language and people and nation" (Rev. 5:9). Maintaining this identity as exiles will prevent the church from falling into the transgressive militancy of the left as well as the extreme nationalism of the right. If one turns from God's way off toward either side, one is soon walking down the road toward embracing antichrist and worshipping his image.

Between Hope and Despair

Jeremiah ministered to a people whose apostasy had reached its nadir. If he had hated them, his life would have been in one sense psychologically easier. He could have simply looked on and cheered as the Babylonians slaughtered the people he despised. Against the accusations of his enemies, however, Jeremiah was no traitor. He loved his people, and he took no pleasure in issuing oracle after oracle denouncing them and promising that their destruction was nigh. But Jeremiah's experience illustrates a fundamental truth: Sometimes one must admit that the people are sinking into evil and that calamity is coming. In such a time, one does not give up hope but must admit that, for the time being, there is "terror on every side."

As described above, Jeremiah 11:1–20:18 thematically relates how Jeremiah moved away from making intercession for Jerusalem. Little by little, the scales fell from his eyes. He learned how hostile and corrupt his people were, and he realized the inevitability of their destruction. Jeremiah 20:7–18 concludes the account of this process with an outcry from the prophet. In this bitter prayer, we see what an emotional toll being God's prophet at such a time had taken on him. The prayer is in three parts.[6] The first is 20:7–9:

> You deceived me, YHWH, and I was deceived.
> You were too strong for me, and you prevailed.
> I have become a laughingstock. Everyone mocks me all day.
> For whenever I speak, I must cry out, "Violence!"

---

6.   It is possible that the parts of this prayer were originally given separately and stitched together here for literary purposes. Regardless, the prayer in its canonical form is a unity, and its unified form conveys the message the text intends.

And I must shout, "Destruction!"
For the word of YHWH has become my reproach and derision all day.
If I say, "I will not remind them of him,
And I will not speak in his name anymore,"
Then there is something within me like a burning fire caught in my bones!
I am exhausted from holding it in, and I cannot do it.

Jeremiah's protest that YHWH "deceived" him is rhetorical and hyperbolic, but it conveys an important message. The divine calling to be a prophet, placing him in the company of Moses and Elijah, was a high honor. And Jeremiah had assumed that role during Josiah's reformation, when he thought he would join the king in bringing Jerusalem into a glorious new era in which a faithful Judah lived under YHWH's blessing. But his youthful optimism was soon shattered. Although he rhetorically blames YHWH, the real meaning of his words is, "Things have not gone as I expected." Furthermore, he did not seek his office; in 1:6 he tried to avoid YHWH's prophetic commission on the grounds that he was only a boy. But YHWH forced him into it: "You were too strong for me, and you prevailed."

Readers of Jeremiah may be surprised at how grim and even monotonous the book seems; it is chapter after chapter of condemnation and predictions of doom. But such readers can be encouraged: Even Jeremiah was tired of this message! His every sermon, he says, could be summarized as "violence" and "destruction." But if he was tired of repeating it, his audience absolutely despised him for it. Thus, he tried to give up and just stop preaching. But YHWH had overpowered him, and the word God had implanted in his bones forced its way out. However reluctant he may have been to keep voicing grim warnings, he was unable to stop.

The second part is 20:10–13:

For I hear the slander of the crowd:
"Just tell him, 'Terror on every side!' Let's tell him that!"
Everyone who was at peace with me is watching for my fall.
"Perhaps he is deceived, and we will prevail over him,
And then we can take our vengeance on him."[7]
But YHWH is with me like a ruthless warrior.
Therefore, my persecutors will stumble and not prevail.
They will be thoroughly humiliated, for they will not succeed.
It will be an eternal dishonor, never forgotten.
YHWH Sabaoth, you test the righteous, you see the heart and the mind.
I will see your vengeance upon them, for I have committed my cause to you.

---

7.   For an explanation of the translation of Jer. 20:10, see Garrett and Pearson, *Jeremiah and Lamentations*, 221.

Sing to YHWH! Praise YHWH!
For he delivers the life of the needy from the hands of evildoers.

The hostility of the people was more than an irritant. They wanted to break him psychologically—and then kill him. Jeremiah alludes to Psalm 31:13, "For I hear what many are saying, 'Terror on every side!' as they scheme together against me, planning to take my life." Jeremiah uses "Terror on every side" with a double meaning. The people were mocking him as "Terror on every side," meaning that this was his only message, but they were also threatening to surround and terrify him, as in the psalm.[8] They hope that his dire predictions prove wrong, that "he is deceived," and not just for the obvious reason that they hope to avoid the calamities he forecast. They wanted his prophecies to prove false so that they could punish him as an imposter. But Jeremiah takes comfort in God, who will save him and bring down terror on his enemies.

The third part is 20:14–18:

Cursed be the day on which I was born!
The day when my mother gave me birth, let it not be blessed!
Cursed be the man who brought my father the good news,
"A son is born to you! It's a boy," making him very glad.
Let that man be like the cities that YHWH relentlessly overthrew!
Let that man hear an outcry in the morning and an alarm at noon!
For he did not kill me in the womb.
Then my mother would have been my grave,
And her womb would have been pregnant forever.
Why did I come forth from the womb to see trouble and sorrow,
And then come to the end of my days in disgrace?

The prayer shifts dramatically from the doxological conclusion of part two to the bleak despair of part three. Jeremiah curses the day of his birth.[9] The text implies that the custom at childbirth was that while midwives attended the woman in labor, a friend of the father was nearby, perhaps in an adjoining room, waiting for news of the delivery. He would then go to the father, who would be in a more removed location, to tell him what had transpired. This was evidently done to give the father a buffer between himself and events if something had gone terribly wrong, such as a stillbirth or the death of the mother. In the case of Jeremiah's birth, however, things could not have gone better. Mother and child were fine, and the child was a boy!

---

8.   The people were perhaps making a mocking allusion to Jeremiah's confrontation with Pashhur, whom he had called "Terror on every side" (Jer. 20:3). To them this name summarized Jeremiah's entire message.

9.   Job also curses the day of his birth in Job 3, a text analogous to Jer. 20:14–18. For a comparison of the two passages, see Garrett and Pearson, *Jeremiah and Lamentations*, 223–24.

But for Jeremiah, this was only the beginning of a life filled with disappointment, hostility, and isolation. He expresses his grief with two hyperboles. First, he curses the man who brought the news to his father, and second, he wishes his mother's womb could have been his tomb. Obviously, neither is meant literally. A curse laid on the bearer of news would not change anything, and he could not have remained in his mother's womb perpetually. But they forcefully make the point that Jeremiah's life was one of unceasing pain.

Jeremiah's prayer speaks powerfully to the Christian minister during a time of decadence and apostasy. Many young people enter training for the clergy filled with the optimistic sense that they are going to make a difference and that the call of God gives them a special purpose in life. As years go by, this happy zeal is often buffeted by hostility from the world, their own flock, and other ministers. Even the most successful of preachers can fall into despair, wondering if they are making the same exhortations repeatedly to diminishing results. But this is especially so when the cultural tide has turned and society has entered a "post-Christian" phase. The church, its teachings, and its faithful ministers are treated as abhorrent aberrations from social norms. Christian morality, and especially sexual morality, is treated not just as quaint and outdated but as positively hateful, perverse, and deserving of scorn. Within the church, many give way to the prevailing winds and subvert those who try to remain faithful, while others embrace an angry, extremist, conservative agenda. This is especially likely to occur in a culture that once had a sizable, vibrant, and influential church.

What, then, does Jeremiah's prayer say to Christians today? Like those who labor in a post-Christian environment, Jeremiah worked among Israelites who, whether they realized it or not, had abandoned the covenant with YHWH. They had lost their faith and jettisoned its moral restrictions.

Jeremiah's prayer reminds us, first, that we should not be surprised at such hostility, "for so they persecuted the prophets who were before you" (Matt. 5:12). When a bold and faithful minister speaks to a perverse generation, persecution is as natural as the reaction one gets when combining fire with gasoline.

Second, ministers should understand that such discouragement may cause them to wish they had never entered the clergy, to regret the path their lives have taken, and even to blame God, as though he had tricked them into taking up the mantle of the preacher. But Jeremiah did not remain forever in this despair and regret. The call of God on his life was too strong, and he persevered. Even if he suffered opposition to the very end, he was vindicated in the eyes of God and in the pages of the Bible.

Third, one can take comfort in the ultimate justice of God. We should not gleefully look for the suffering of our enemies. Even Jeremiah, although he issued imprecations against his opponents, did no such thing. He pleaded with them to the very end, telling them that they could avoid the worst suffering if they would only surrender to Nebuchadnezzar. However, the knowledge that those who despise God's ministers will face his justice should encourage us. Like Jeremiah, ministers who suffer such abuse can proclaim, "Sing to YHWH! Praise YHWH! For he delivers the life of the needy from the hands of evildoers" (Jer. 20:13).

Fourth, we should speak of our sadness and pain clearly before God, as Jeremiah did. We probably will not use the same idiom as he used, cursing the day of our birth, but we should pray forthrightly of our fear, disappointment, loneliness, and sorrow. It was through such prayers that Jeremiah endured his enemies. We certainly should not put up a false front of joy and fearlessness before God.

THE EXAMPLE OF JEREMIAH

Courageous Proclamation
Jeremiah had the courage of his convictions. Early in his career he may have been surprised by the ferocity of the opposition. He was not expecting the violent reception his temple sermon received (26:8–9). But as the years went by, he came to understand that the people's hostility to him and to his message was implacable. Even so, he never modified or held back his words of condemnation and warning, even when he knew that many were determined to kill him. But he was not a fearless man, and he did not court suffering and martyrdom. When Zedekiah sought an oracle of YHWH, Jeremiah first demanded to know if his answer would lead to his death (38:15). Their threats had clearly shaken him. And Jeremiah took no perverse pleasure in being an outsider or in making predictions of doom. These are the qualities that make him worthy of imitation. It is hard for us to imitate a man who is like a bronze statue, incapable of feeling fear and pain. He was afraid of the people around him and hurt by the ostracism he experienced, and yet he never wavered. His strength was not in being fearless but in pushing past his fear.

Personal Deprivation
Jeremiah is the only Israelite prophet we know of who was commanded by God to remain celibate (Jer. 16:2). Indeed, this is unprecedented in the Old Testament, where the rule and common practice for all people, including priests and prophets, was to marry and have children. Marriage and sexuality are a basic pleasure for mortals under the sun (Eccl. 9:9), and Jeremiah understood marrying and raising a family to be normative even for people in exile (Jer. 29:6). Jeremiah's celibacy was exceptional but necessary because of the times in which he lived and the nature of his ministry (Jer. 16:3–4). In this, he was an example and confirmation of Paul's exhortation that sometimes, because of imminent catastrophe, it is better not to marry but to devote one's life to the urgency of God's work (1 Cor. 7:26–27). More broadly, his experience is a reminder that ministers may need to endure deprivation of various kinds for the sake of their calling.

A Life of Prayer

The previous chapter argued that Jeremiah's prayers provided evidence that he was a true prophet, a man who conversed with God. Jeremiah's prayers also provide models for contemporary readers. This book has argued that a significant portion of the book of Jeremiah (11:1–20:18) concerns the prophet's spiritual journey, at the behest of God, from praying for Judah to abandoning that task and even to calling on God to punish his people. What we should not miss is that he in fact spent a great deal of time in prayer. Except for David's psalms, we have more examples of prayers from Jeremiah than we do for any Israelite.

His prayers, especially his intercessions, could praise God in the manner of the Psalms and other biblical texts. During the drought, he made use of familiar motifs as he called on God to save the nation:

Have you really, completely rejected Judah? Or do you loathe Zion? Why have you struck us beyond any hope of healing? If we hope for peace, nothing good comes. If we hope for a time of healing, we have only terror. We know about our wickedness, YHWH, and the guilt of our ancestors. For we have sinned against you. For the sake of your name, do not despise, do not have contempt for [Zion,] your glorious throne. Remember your covenant with us and do not break it. Are the useless idols of the nations able to bring rain? Or do the skies give their showers? Are you not YHWH our God? And so, we should hope in you, for you are the one who controls all these things. (Jer. 14:19–22)

This prayer is a helpful model for the Christian reader. It contains many elements found elsewhere in biblical prayers. Such prayers can be blunt about asking God to hurry up and send help (Pss. 22:1–2; 89:46–48). An appeal for God's help during crisis often contains confession of guilt (Neh. 9:16–17; Dan. 9:7–8). It acknowledges that God saves for the sake of his name and not because of our merit (Ps. 25:11; Ezek. 20:9, 14). It is founded on God's faithfulness to the covenant (Exod. 2:24; Lev. 26:44). In the Old Testament context, such prayers contrast the power of YHWH to save with the uselessness of idols (Ps. 31:6; Jonah 2:8–9). Jeremiah's prayer also reminds us that intercession for sinners is not a matter of praying for "them" but for "us."

Another thoroughly biblical prayer appears in 32:17–25, when Jeremiah responded to YHWH's command to buy the field in Anathoth:

Ah Lord YHWH! You made heaven and the earth by your great power and by your outstretched arm! Nothing is too hard for you. The one who shows grace to thousands but repays the guilt of parents into the laps of their children after them! The great and mighty God! YHWH Sabaoth is his name! Great in counsel and mighty in deeds, your eyes are open to all the ways of mortals, as you repay all according to their ways and according to the fruit of their actions! You showed signs and wonders in the land of Egypt, and [continue to do so] to this day in Israel and among all humanity. And you made yourself a name that [is renowned] to this very day. And you brought your people Israel from the land of Egypt with signs and wonders, with a strong hand and outstretched arm, and with great dread. And you gave them this land, that you swore to their fathers to give them, a land flowing with milk and honey. And they came and took possession of it. But they did not obey your voice or follow your law. They did not do all you commanded them to do. And you made them face this disaster in its entirety. Now the siege-ramps are set up against the city to take it. And the city is being given into the hands of the Chaldeans, who fight against it with sword, famine, and pestilence. What you spoke has happened as you look upon it. But you, Lord YHWH, said to me, "Buy the field for money and have witnesses certify it," even though the city is being given into the hands of the Chaldeans.

This prayer looks back to the creation narrative (Gen. 1), the Decalogue (Exod. 20:5–6), the miracles of Exodus (Exod. 7–14), and the conquest of Canaan and subsequent apostasy of Israel (Joshua–Judges). And Jeremiah connects all of this to the current crisis, noting that he bought the field of Anathoth even though this was an absurd act, considering how the Babylonians were in the process of devouring the land. God's mighty works of the past encouraged him to obey and do what would seem pointless. Out of this came a message of future salvation for Israel (Jer. 32:26–44). Out of death would come imperishable life. For us, moreover, Jeremiah's prayer models how to use the great narrative of the Bible as a template for prayer in a time of crisis.

Jeremiah did not see salvation for Israel in his lifetime. But as he grew discouraged, he continued to pray. As noted above in the discussion of 20:7–9, even when distressed with God he did not withdraw from him but spoke openly of his anguish. He poured out his heart in grief, as in his dialogue with YHWH at 9:1–6:

If only my head were filled with water and my eyes a cascade of tears! Then I would weep day and night for the slain of my dear people! If only I had a traveler's lodging place out in the desert! Then I would leave my people and get away from them! For they are all adulterers; they are an assembly of treacherous people. They arm their tongues like bows, to shoot lies. They are not valiant for truth in the land. "They go from evil to evil. They do not know me," says YHWH. "Be careful about your friends! Do not trust a family member. For every brother cheats constantly, and every associate goes about spreading slander. Each one of them deceives everyone he associates with, and they do not speak the truth. They train their tongues to speak lies! They work hard at committing iniquity! You dwell in a place filled with deception! In that deception they refuse to know me," says YHWH.[10]

This speaks especially to Christians who are living among a generation that is both perverse and headed toward disaster. The prayer speaks forthrightly of his distress and anger at the animosity and twisted logic of his opponents, but it has no *schadenfreude*. Even as Jeremiah affirms the rightness of YHWH's judgment, he also wishes that his body could produce a sufficient volume of tears to express the depths of his sorrow. Besides being active in prayer himself, he also recommended it for others. As noted above, he urged that his people who faced the frightening and disorienting experience of exile deal with it by praying for their new home:

> And seek the prosperity of the city to which I have exiled you and pray to YHWH on its behalf! For its prosperity will be prosperity for you. (Jer. 29:7)

Keeping Hope at the Center

This study has argued that the promise of Israel's eschatological salvation is at the structural center of the book of Jeremiah. This is unlike what we see in other prophetic books, where the message of hope usually appears at the end and reverses the book's earlier messages of condemnation. The order we see in the other books is more logical: Israel and the nations are sinful, and God will punish them, but at the end of days he will establish an everlasting kingdom of righteousness and peace. Jeremiah's structure, although subtle, carries an important, implied message: Hope and salvation are at the heart of the Word of God. Words of condemnation and destruction are authentic, but they are the outer husk. The Christian minister, even when confronting evil, must keep the gospel at the center of the message.

---

10. The correct text of 9:5c–6a is disputed, with the MT (at 9:4c–5a) being somewhat different from the LXX (also at 9:4c–5a). This translation follows the MT. There are good arguments for either reading; see Garrett and Pearson, *Jeremiah and Lamentations*, 145.

APPENDIX 1:
THE FULL STRUCTURE OF JEREMIAH

I. Prologue: The beginning of Jeremiah's ministry (1:1–19)
   A. Superscript (1:1–3)
   B. Jeremiah's commission (1:4–19)
II. Messages against Judah (2:1–20:18)
   A. First anthology: Illusions and reality (2:1–10:25)
      1. Introductory summary (2:1–4:4)
         a. Astonishing evil (2:1–3:5)
         b. An appeal to repent and promise of salvation (3:6–4:4)
      2. Deluded people and their coming destruction (4:5–6:30)
         a. Invasion: Sound the alarm! (4:5–8)
         b. Deceit: Bewildered and corrupt leaders (4:9–12)
         c. Invasion: The Babylonian storm (4:13)
         d. Deceit: Jerusalem, home of evil schemes (4:14)
         e. Invasion: The enemy approaches (4:15–18)
         f. Deceit: Senseless people and the earth in upheaval (4:19–28)
         g. Invasion: The towns deserted (4:29)
         h. Deceit: A cosmetic solution (4:30)
         i. Invasion: The helpless woman (4:31)
         j. Deceit: A city of liars (5:1–5)
         k. Invasion: Lion, wolf, and leopard (5:6)
         l. Deceit: Faithless to God and to marriage (5:7–9)
         m. Invasion: Ravaged vineyards (5:10)
         n. Deceit: Lying versus true prophets (5:11–14)
         o. Invasion: The all-devouring enemy (5:15–19)
         p. Deceit: Houses full of deceit (5:20–31)
         q. Invasion: Zion in flight; Jerusalem under siege (6:1–9)
         r. Deceit: Incapable of hearing the truth (6:10–11a)
         s. Invasion: The enemy takes all people and all property (6:11b–12)

      t.   Deceit: Saying "Peace" when there is no peace (6:13–21)
      u.   Invasion: The cruel army from the north (6:22–26)
      v.   Conclusion (6:27–30)
3.   Deceitful religion and real lamentation (7:1–10:25)
    a.   Deceit: Jerusalem's perverse religious culture (7:1–8:12)
       1) The temple sermon (7:1–15)
       2) The Queen of Heaven (7:16–20)
       3) Orthodox sacrifices and disobedient behavior (7:21–28)
       4) Abominable sacrifices (7:29–8:3)
       5) A nation in denial (8:4–12)
    b.   Lamentation over a godless land (8:13–9:26 [MT 9:25])
       1) Lamentation over the calamity (8:13–22)
       2) Lamentation over deceit (9:1–9 [MT 8:23–9:8])
       3) Lamentation over the calamity (9:10–11 [MT 9–10])
       4) Lamentation explained (9:12–16 [MT 11–15])
       5) Lamentation over the calamity (9:17–22 [MT 16–21])
       6) True and false exultation (9:23–26 [MT 22–25])
    c.   Deceit: Idolatry versus YHWH (10:1–16)
       1) YHWH exhorts Israel about idolatry (10:1–5)
       2) Praise for YHWH and disdain for idols (10:6–10)
       3) YHWH exhorts the nations about idolatry (10:11–16)
    d.   Lamentation over exile (10:17–22)
       1) Prepare for exile (10:17–18)
       2) Jerusalem's lament (10:19–21)
       3) A report of disaster (10:22)
    e.   Jeremiah's confession and imprecation (10:23–25)
B. Second anthology: From intercession to imprecation (11:1–20:18)
   1.   Introductory summary (11:1–23)
    a.   The covenant and its violation (11:1–13)
    b.   Intercession for Israel prohibited (11:14–17)
    c.   The treacherous men of Anathoth (11:18–23)
   2.   The end of prophetic intercession (12:1–15:9)
    a.   Jeremiah's first intercession (12:1–17)
       1) A complaint over wicked leaders (12:1–4)
       2) YHWH's response (12:5–17)
    b.   Two object lessons (13:1–14)
       1) The ruined loincloth (13:1–11)
       2) The jars filled with wine (13:12–14)

       c. Jerusalem cannot repent (13:15–27)
- 1) The appeal to repent (13:15–21)
- 2) An answer for bewildered Jerusalem (13:22a)
- 3) Jerusalem is incorrigible (13:22b–27)

       d. Jeremiah's second intercession (14:1–12)
- 1) Confession and appeal for mercy (14:1–9)
- 2) YHWH's response (14:10–12)

       e. Jeremiah's third intercession (14:13–18)
- 1) A complaint over false prophets (14:13)
- 2) YHWH's response (14:14–18)

       f. Jeremiah's fourth intercession (14:19–15:9)
- 1) Confession and appeal for mercy (14:19–22)
- 2) YHWH's response (15:1–9)

3. The beginning of prophetic imprecations (15:10–20:18)

       a. Jeremiah's complaints (15:10–21)
- 1) Jeremiah laments his situation (15:10)
- 2) YHWH reassures Jeremiah (15:11–14)
- 3) Jeremiah angrily complains to YHWH (15:15–18)
- 4) YHWH rebukes and reassures Jeremiah (15:19–21)

       b. Two object lessons (16:1–9)
- 1) Jeremiah not to marry (16:1–4)
- 2) Jeremiah not to attend funerals or weddings (16:5–9)

       c. Jerusalem cannot repent (16:10–17:4)
- 1) The answer to bewildered Jerusalem (16:10–18)
- 2) Jeremiah affirms YHWH's answer (16:19–21)
- 3) Jerusalem is incorrigible (17:1–4)

       d. The human heart (17:5–11)

       e. YHWH, Zion's fountain of living water (17:12–13)

       f. Jeremiah prays an imprecation (17:14–18)

       g. Messages at a gate and a house (17:19–18:17)
- 1) The sermon at the People's Gate (17:19–27)
- 2) The sermon at the potter's house (18:1–17)

       h. Jeremiah prays a second imprecation (18:18–23)

       i. Messages at two gates (19:1–20:6)
- 1) The sermon at the Potsherd Gate (19:1–15)
- 2) Jeremiah curses Pashhur at the Benjamin Gate (20:1–6)

       j. Jeremiah curses the day of his birth (20:7–18)

III. Historically contextualized messages (21:1–29:32)

  A. A failed intercession, figs, and cups of wine (21:1–25:38)

    1. Message (in 588) to the delegation from Zedekiah (21:1–23:40)

    2. Message (in 597) after the exile of Jehoiachin (24:1–10)

        3.   Message (in 605) during the fourth year of Jehoiakim (25:1–38)

    B. True prophets rejected and false prophets celebrated (26:1–29:32)

        1.   Jeremiah nearly lynched: The temple sermon (26:1–19)

        2.   The martyrdom of the prophet Uriah of Kiriath-jearim (26:20–24)

        3.   The false prophet Hananiah and the yoke bars (27:1–28:17)

        4.   The false prophet Shemaiah and letters to the exiles (29:1–32)

IV. Eschatological salvation (30:1–33:26)

    A. An undated message: The new covenant (30:1–31:40)

        1.   The command to write the book of consolation (30:1–3)

        2.   The pleasant dream (30:4–31:26)

        3.   Two agricultural metaphors (31:27–30)

        4.   The new covenant (31:31–37)

        5.   The restoration of Jerusalem (31:38–40)

    B. Two messages from the tenth year of Zedekiah (32:1–33:26)

        1.   The redeemed land (32:1–44)

        2.   Jerusalem restored under the new David (33:1–26)

V. Historically contextualized messages (34:1–45:5)

    A. A failed covenant and cups of wine (34:1–35:19)

        1.   Zedekiah's broken covenant (34:1–22)

        2.   The example of Rechabites (35:1–19)

    B. Jeremiah the true prophet rejected (36:1–45:5)

        1.   Jehoiakim burns the scroll (36:1–32)

        2.   Jeremiah the captive (37:1–43:7)

            a. Jeremiah's first captivity (37:1–39:18)

               1) Introductory summation (37:1–5)

               2) A prophecy for Zedekiah (37:6–10)

               3) The officials disbelieve and imprison Jeremiah (37:11–16)

               4) A second prophecy for Zedekiah (37:17–21)

               5) The officials disbelieve and leave Jeremiah to die (38:1–6)

               6) Ebed-melek saves Jeremiah (38:7–13)

               7) A third prophecy for Zedekiah (38:14–28a)

               8) The fall of Jerusalem; Jeremiah freed (38:28b–39:14)

               9) A prophecy for Ebed-melek (39:15–18)

            b. Jeremiah's second captivity (40:1–43:7)

               1) The oracle announcement and its background (40:1–6)

               2) Gedaliah's murder (40:7–41:18)

               3) An oracle, unbelief, and a flight to Egypt (42:1–43:7)

      3.   Jeremiah's two Egyptian oracles rejected (43:8–44:30)
         a.   A second Babylonian conquest (43:8–13)
         b.   The Queen of Heaven (44:1–30)
      4.   A message for Baruch (45:1–5)

VI. Two anthologies against the nations (46:1–51:64)
    A. Against many nations (46:1–49:39)
      1.   Superscript: Concerning the nations (46:1)
      2.   Concerning Egypt (46:2–26)
      3.   Concerning Israel (46:27–28)
      4.   Concerning the Philistines (47:1–7)
      5.   Concerning Moab (48:1–47)
      6.   Concerning Ammon (49:1–6)
      7.   Concerning Edom (49:7–22)
      8.   Concerning Damascus (49:23–27)
      9.   Concerning Kedar (49:28–33)
    10.   Concerning Elam (49:34–39)
    B. Against Babylon (50:1–51:64)
      1.   The oracles concerning Babylon (50:1–51:58)
      2.   The mission of Seraiah to Babylon (51:59–64)

VII. Epilogue: The end of the house of David (52:1–34)

APPENDIX 2:
THE LIFE AND TIMES OF JEREMIAH

All dates below should be regarded as approximations.

Date	Event
722	Assyria destroys Samaria
701 or 688	Sennacherib fails to take Jerusalem under Hezekiah
664	Ashurbanipal of Assyria places Psammetichus I on Egyptian throne, creating Twenty-sixth Dynasty
640	Josiah begins to reign; Jeremiah born
628–627	Josiah begins to purge the land of pagan shrines; Jeremiah receives initial prophetic call
622	Book of the law discovered in temple
618–610	Jeremiah begins to preach and is commanded to remain celibate; sermon at People's Gate is given during this time
612	Nineveh falls to Medes and to Babylonians under Nabopolassar
611–606	Drought in Judah
610–609	Necho II succeeds Psammetichus I; he heads toward Syria to assist Assyria at Harran and kills Josiah along the way; Jehoahaz named king in Jerusalem
610–609	Harran, last stronghold of Assyrians, falls to Medes and Babylonians; Necho returns south and replaces Jehoahaz with Jehoiakim
607–606	Nabopolassar campaigns in Syria but falls ill and leaves the command to Nebuchadnezzar
605	Necho returns to Syria to confront the Babylonians
605	Nebuchadnezzar defeats Necho at Carchemish, returns to Babylon, and is crowned king of Babylon; Jehoiakim submits to Nebuchadnezzar
605	Jeremiah calls Rechabites to the temple; later, he preaches the temple sermon and is subsequently forbidden to enter the temple grounds
604	Baruch reads scroll of Jeremiah's prophecies in the temple court; Jehoiakim burns scroll; Jeremiah and Baruch flee, possibly to Moab; Jeremiah gives a private oracle to Baruch

Date	Event
604	Nebuchadnezzar campaigns in Levant; sacks Ashkelon
602–601	Nebuchadnezzar campaigns again in the Levant; he tries to invade Egypt but is repulsed; Jehoiakim in Jerusalem is convinced that rebellion against Babylon can succeed
597	Jerusalem surrenders to Nebuchadnezzar; Jehoiakim dies; Jehoiachin briefly reigns but is taken into exile; Zedekiah named king in Jerusalem
597	Jeremiah and Baruch return to Jerusalem
597–596	Jeremiah receives oracle of two baskets of figs and sends letter to exiles in Babylon
595	Psammetichus II succeeds Necho as pharaoh
594	Zedekiah attempts to form anti-Babylonian coalition; Jeremiah interrupts the meeting wearing a yoke and warns against fighting Babylon; he has a confrontation with Hananiah
589	Hophra succeeds Psammetichus II as pharaoh
588	Zedekiah rebels against Babylon; Nebuchadnezzar lays siege to Jerusalem; Jerusalem nobility makes covenant with YHWH promising to free their slaves
588 or 587	Hophra attempts to relieve siege of Jerusalem and causes Babylonians to temporarily lift siege; Zedekiah appeals to Jeremiah for a favorable oracle but is rebuffed; Jeremiah breaks decanter as sign of coming obliteration of Jerusalem; Jerusalem nobility renege on their covenant and enslave those whom they had freed
587	Jeremiah arrested while trying to go to Anathoth; while in prison, Jeremiah issues major prophecies about future salvation of Israel
587 or 586	Hophra retreats into Egypt and siege of Jerusalem resumes; Jerusalem nobility tries to kill Jeremiah in a cistern, but he is rescued by Ebed-Melech; Zedekiah pleads to Jeremiah on behalf of his family at a secret meeting near the temple; Jeremiah tells him to surrender, but he is too afraid to act; Jerusalem destroyed by Nebuchadnezzar; Zedekiah is tortured and taken to Babylon; Jeremiah is set free by the Babylonians
586–585	Gedaliah named as governor over Jewish territory but is murdered by Ishmael; Jews flee to Egypt and take Jeremiah and Baruch with them
585–575	Jeremiah issues final oracles to apostate Jews in Egypt and dies there
570	Hophra overthrown by Amasis II in Egypt
568	Sortie by Nebuchadnezzar into the eastern borderland of Egypt, perhaps intended to restore Hophra; attempt fails, and Hophra slain
562	Nebuchadnezzar dies; succeeded by Amel-Marduk; Jehoiachin released from confinement
560	Neriglissar murders and succeeds Amel-Marduk
556	Neriglissar dies and is succeeded by Labashi-Marduk, who in turn is deposed by Nabonidus and his son Belshazzar
539–538	Babylon conquered by Cyrus II of Persia

BIBLIOGRAPHY

Ackroyd, Peter R. "The Book of Jeremiah: Some Recent Studies." *JSOT* 9, no. 28 (1984): 47–59. DOI:10.1177/030908928400902804.

Aejmelaeus, Anneli. "Jeremiah at the Turning-point of History: The Function of Jer. XXV 1–14 in the Book of Jeremiah." *VT* 52, no. 4 (2002): 459–82. DOI:10.1163/156853302320764799.

_____. "What Happened to the Text in Jer 25:1–7?" *TC* 22 (2017): 1–10. https://jbtc.org/v22/TC-2017-Aejmelaeus.pdf.

Ahmed, Sami Said. "The Jewish Colony at Elephantine." *Iliff Review* 22, no. 2 (1965): 11–19.

Allen, Leslie C. *Jeremiah: A Commentary*. OTL. Louisville: Westminster John Knox, 2008.

Althann, Robert. "Gedaliah (Person)." *ABD* 2:923–24.

_____. *A Philological Analysis of Jeremiah 4–6 in the Light of Northwest Semitic*. BibOr 38. Rome: Biblical Institute Press, 1983.

Avigad, Nahman. "Baruch the Scribe and Jerahmeel the King's Son." *IEJ* 28, nos. 1/2 (1978): 52–56.

Berridge, John M. "Jehoiachin (Person)." *ABD* 3:661–63.

Bright, John. *Jeremiah: With Introduction, Translation and Notes*. AB 21. Garden City, NY: Doubleday, 1965.

Bunimovitz, Shlomo, and Zvi Lederman. "Beth-Shemesh." *NEAEHL* 1:249–53.

Carroll, Robert P. *Jeremiah: A Commentary*. OTL. Philadelphia: Westminster, 1986.

Christensen, Duane L. "In Quest of the Autograph of the Book of Jeremiah: A Study of Jeremiah 25 in Relation to Jeremiah 46–51." *JETS* 33, no. 2 (1990): 145–53.

Cogan, Mordechai. "Chronology, Hebrew Bible." *ABD* 1:1002–11.

Cotterell, Arthur. *The First Great Powers: Babylon and Assyria*. London: Hurst & Company, 2019.

Craigie, Peter C., Page H. Kelley, and Joel F. Drinkard Jr. *Jeremiah 1–25*. WBC 26. Dallas: Word, 1991.

Crenshaw, James L. "A Living Tradition: The Book of Jeremiah in Current Research." *Int* 37, no. 2 (1983): 117–29. DOI:10.1177/002096438303700202.

Di Vito, Robert A. "Lachish Letters." *ABD* 4:126–28.

Finkelstein, Israel. "Shiloh." *NEAEHL* 4:1364–70.

Frahm, Eckart. *Assyria: The Rise and Fall of the World's First Empire.* New York: Basic Books, 2023.

Frick, Frank S. "Rechab (Person)." *ABD* 5:630–32.

Garrett, Duane A. *The Problem of the Old Testament: Hermeneutical, Schematic, and Theological Approaches.* Downers Grove, IL: IVP Academic, 2020.

_____. "Song of Songs." Pages 3–266 in *Song of Songs/Lamentations.* By Duane Garrett and Paul R. House. WBC 23B. Nashville: Nelson, 2004.

Garrett, Duane A., and Calvin F. Pearson. *Jeremiah and Lamentations.* Kerux. Grand Rapids: Kregel, 2022.

Goldingay, John. *The Book of Jeremiah.* NICOT. Grand Rapids: Eerdmans, 2021.

Granerød, Gard. *Dimensions of Yahwism in the Persian Period: Studies in the Religion and Society of the Judaean Community at Elephantine.* BZAW 488. Berlin: de Gruyter, 2016.

Greenberg, Moshe. *Ezekiel 1–20: A New Translation with Introduction and Commentary.* AB 22. Garden City, NY: Doubleday, 1983.

Grimal, Nicolas. *A History of Ancient Egypt.* Oxford: Blackwell, 1992.

Hallo, William W., and K. Lawson Younger Jr. *The Context of Scripture.* 3 vols. Leiden: Brill, 1997–2003.

Holladay, William L. *Jeremiah 1: A Commentary on the Book of the Prophet Jeremiah, Chapters 1–25.* Hermeneia. Philadelphia: Fortress, 1986.

_____. *Jeremiah 2: A Commentary on the Book of the Prophet Jeremiah, Chapters 26–52.* Hermeneia. Philadelphia: Fortress, 1989.

Hooker, Paul K. "Chronology of the OT." *NIDB* 1:636–42.

Janzen, J. Gerald. *Studies in the Text of Jeremiah.* HSM 6. Cambridge, MA: Harvard University Press, 1973.

Jobes, Karen H., and Moses Silva. *Invitation to the Septuagint.* Grand Rapids: Baker Academic, 2000.

Jones, Richard N., and Zbigniew T. Fiema. "Tahpanhes (Place)." *ABD* 6:308–9.

Katzenstein, H. J., and Douglas R. Edwards. "Tyre." *ABD* 6:686–92.

Kitchen, Kenneth A. "Egypt, History of: Chronology." *ABD* 2:321–31.

Klein, Ralph W. *1 Chronicles: A Commentary.* Hermeneia. Minneapolis: Fortress, 2006.

Knoppers, Gary N. *I Chronicles 1–9: A New Translation with Introduction and Commentary.* AB 12. New York: Doubleday, 2003.

Lane, William L. *Hebrews 1–8.* WBC 47A. Dallas: Word, 1991.

Lundbom, Jack R. *Jeremiah 1–20: A New Translation with Introduction and Commentary.* AB 21A. New York: Doubleday, 1999.

_____. *Jeremiah 21–36: A New Translation with Introduction and Commentary.* AB 21B. New York: Doubleday, 2004.

_____. *Jeremiah 37–52: A New Translation with Introduction and Commentary*. AB 21C. New York: Doubleday, 2004.

McKane, William. *A Critical and Exegetical Commentary on Jeremiah*. 2 vols. ICC. Edinburgh: T&T Clark, 1986, 1996.

Opperwall, Nola J. "Pashhur." *ISBE* 3:673–74.

Porten, Bezalel. "Elephantine Papyri." *ABD* 2:445–55.

_____. *The Elephantine Papyri in English: Three Millennia of Cross-Cultural Continuity and Change*. DMOA 22. Leiden: Brill, 1996.

Pritchard, James B. *Ancient Near Eastern Texts Relating to the Old Testament*. 3rd ed. Princeton, NJ: Princeton University Press, 1969.

Roberts, J. J. M. "Assyria and Babylonia." *NIDB* 1:312–35.

Rollston, Christopher A. "The Bullae of Baruch ben Neriah the Scribe and the Seal of Ma'adanah Daughter of the King: Epigraphic Forgeries of the 20th Century." *ErIsr* 32 (2016): 79–90.

_____. *Writing and Literacy in the World of Ancient Israel*. ABS 10. Atlanta: Society of Biblical Literature, 2010.

Sack, Ronald H. "Evil-Merodach (Person)." *ABD* 2:679.

_____. *Images of Nebuchadnezzar: The Emergence of a Legend*. 2nd ed. Selinsgrove, PA: Susquehanna University Press, 2004.

Shaw, Ian. *The Oxford History of Ancient Egypt*. Oxford: Oxford University Press, 2000.

Shaw, Ian, and Paul Nicholson. *The Dictionary of Ancient Egypt*. New York: Abrams, 1995.

Silverman, David P. *Ancient Egypt*. Oxford: Oxford University Press, 1997.

Smothers, Thomas G., Gerald Lynwood Keown, and Pamela J. Scalise. *Jeremiah 26–52*. WBC 27. Dallas: Word, 1995.

Soderlund, Sven. *The Greek Text of Jeremiah: A Revised Hypothesis*. JSOTSup 47. Sheffield: JSOT Press, 1985.

Steindorff, Georg, and Keith C. Seele. *When Egypt Ruled the East*. Chicago: University of Chicago Press, 1957.

van der Toorn, Karel. *Becoming Diaspora Jews: Behind the Story of Elephantine*. ABRL. New Haven, CT: Yale University Press, 2019.

Tov, Emanuel. *Textual Criticism of the Hebrew Bible*. 3rd ed. Minneapolis: Fortress, 2012.

Wildberger, Hans. *Isaiah 13–27*. Translated by Thomas H. Trapp. CC. Minneapolis: Fortress, 1997.

Wilson, R. R. *Prophecy and Society in Ancient Israel*. Philadelphia: Fortress, 1980.

Wiseman, D. J. "Babylon." *ISBE* 1:384–91.

_____. *Nebuchadrezzar and Babylon*. Schweich Lectures. Oxford: Oxford University Press, 1983.

Würthwein, Ernst. *The Text of the Old Testament*. Revised and expanded by Alexander A. Fischer. Translated by Erroll F. Rhodes. 3rd ed. Grand Rapids: Eerdmans, 2014.

OTHER KREGEL TITLES
BY DUANE GARRETT

KERUX COMMENTARIES

JEREMIAH AND LAMENTATIONS

A Commentary for Biblical Preaching and Teaching

DUANE GARRETT
CALVIN F. PEARSON

A COMMENTARY ON
EXODUS

DUANE A. GARRETT